Jürgen Habermas is one of the most important German philosophers and social theorists of the late twentieth and early twenty-first century. His work has been compared in scope with Max Weber's, and in philosophical breadth to that of Kant and Hegel.

In this much-needed introduction Kenneth Baynes engages with the full range of Habermas's philosophical work, addressing his early arguments concerning the emergence of the public sphere and his initial attempt to reconstruct a critical theory of society in *Knowledge and Human Interests*. He then examines one of Habermas's most influential works, *The Theory of Communicative Action*, including his controversial account of the rational interpretation of social action. Also covered is Habermas's work on discourse ethics, political and legal theory, as well as his views on the relation between democracy and constitutionalism, and arguments concerning human rights and cosmopolitanism.

The final chapter assesses Habermas's role as a polemical and prominent public intellectual and his criticism of postmodernism in *The Philosophical Discourse of Modernity*, in addition to his more recent writings on the relationship between religion and democracy.

Habermas is an invaluable guide to this key figure in contemporary philosophy, and suitable for anyone coming to his work for the first time.

Kenneth Baynes is Professor of Philosophy at Syracuse University, USA. He works primarily in social and political philosophy, with a special focus in critical theory and modern and contemporary German philosophy. He is a co-editor of *After Philosophy: End or Transformation?* and *Discourse and Democracy*, and the author of *The Normative Grounds of Social Criticism: Kant, Rawls and Habermas*.

Routledge Philosophers

Edited by Brian Leiter

University of Chicago

Routledge Philosophers is a major series of introductions to the great Western philosophers. Each book places a major philosopher or thinker in historical context, explains and assesses their key arguments, and considers their legacy. Additional features include a chronology of major dates and events, chapter summaries, annotated suggestions for further reading and a glossary of technical terms.

An ideal starting point for those new to philosophy, they are also essential reading for those interested in the subject at any level.

Available:

Hobbes
A. P. Martinich

Leibniz
Nicholas Jolley

Locke
E. J. Lowe

Hegel
Frederick Beiser

Rousseau
Nicholas Dent

Schopenhauer
Julian Young

Darwin
Tim Lewens

Rawls
Samuel Freeman

Spinoza
Michael Della Rocca

Merleau-Ponty
Taylor Carman

Russell
Gregory Landini

Wittgenstein
William Child

Heidegger
John Richardson

Adorno
Brian O'Connor

Husserl, second edition
David Woodruff Smith

Aristotle, second edition
Christopher Shields

Kant, second edition
Paul Guyer

Hume
Don Garrett

Dewey
Steven Fesmire

Freud, second edition
Jonathan Lear

Peirce
Albert Atkin

Forthcoming:

Plato
Constance Meinwald

Nietzsche
Maudemarie Clark

Mill
Daniel Jacobson

Einstein
Thomas Ryckman and Arthur Fine

Plotinus
Eyjólfur Emilsson

Berkeley
Lisa Downing and David Hilbert

Levinas
Michael Morgan

Cassirer
Samantha Matherne

Kierkegaard
Paul Muench

Anscombe
Candace Vogler

Marx
Jaime Edwards and Brian Leiter

Sartre
Kenneth Williford

Kenneth Baynes

Habermas

Routledge
Taylor & Francis Group

LONDON AND NEW YORK

First published 2016
by Routledge
2 Park Square, Milton Park, Abingdon, Oxon OX14 4RN

and by Routledge
711 Third Avenue, New York, NY 10017

Routledge is an imprint of the Taylor & Francis Group, an informa business

© 2016 Kenneth Baynes

The right of Kenneth Baynes to be identified as the author of this work
has been asserted by him in accordance with sections 77 and 78 of the
Copyright, Designs and Patents Act 1988.

British Library Cataloguing in Publication Data
A catalogue record for this book is available from the British Library

Library of Congress Cataloging in Publication Data
Baynes, Kenneth.
Habermas / by Kenneth Baynes. -- 1st [edition].
pages cm. -- (Routledge philosophers)
Includes bibliographical references and index.
1. Habermas, Jurgen. I. Title.
B3258.H324B365 2015
193--dc23
2015006412

ISBN 978-0-415-77324-9 (hbk)
ISBN 978-0-415-77325-6 (pbk)
ISBN 978-1-315-69642-3 (ebk)

Typeset in Joanna MT and Din
by Saxon Graphics Ltd, Derby

Printed and bound by CPI Group (UK) Ltd, Croydon, CR0 4YY

Contents

Acknowledgements

Generous support from the Humboldt Foundation and the Forschungskolleg Humanwissenschaften in Bad Homburg in 2010 greatly facilitated work on this book. I especially thank Rainer Forst for making my stay there possible. I have benefitted from conversations with many others about this work, but Amy Allen, Seyla Benhabib, Jim Bohman, Rainer Forst, Tom McCarthy, Glyn Morgan, Max Pensky, Bill Scheuerman and Lorenzo Simpson deserve special mention. Portions of the book incorporate previously published material in *The Cambridge Companion to Habermas* (1995) and *The Cambridge Companion to Critical Theory* (2004). I thank Cambridge University Press for permission to reprint it here.

Abbreviations

AS	*Autonomy and Solidarity: Interviews with Jürgen Habermas*. Edited by P. Dews. London: Verso, 1986.
BFN	*Between Facts and Norms*. Cambridge, MA: MIT Press, 1996.
BNR	*Between Naturalism and Religion*. Cambridge: Polity Press, 2008.
CES	*Communication and the Evolution of Society*. Boston: Beacon Press, 1979.
DW	*The Divided West*. Cambridge: Polity Press, 2006.
FK	"Faith and Knowledge" in *The Future of Human Nature*. Cambridge: Polity Press, 2003.
IO	*The Inclusion of the Other: Studies in Political Theory*. Cambridge: MIT Press, 1998.
IS	"Individuation through Socialization: Mead's Theory of Subjectivity," in *Postmetaphysical Thinking*, pp. 149–204.
JA	*Justification and Application: Remarks on Discourse Ethics*. Cambridge, MA: MIT Press, 1990
KHI	*Knowledge and Human Interests*. Boston: Beacon Press, 1971.
LC	*Legitimation Crisis*. Boston: Beacon Press, 1975.
LSS	*On the Logic of the Social Sciences*. Cambridge, MA: MIT Press, 1988.
MCCA	*Moral Consciousness and Communicative Action*. Cambridge, MA: MIT Press, 1990.
NC	*The New Conservatism*. Cambridge: MIT Press, 1989.

OPC	*On the Pragmatics of Communication.* Edited by M. Cooke. Cambridge, MA: MIT Press.
PDM	*The Philosophical Discourse of Modernity.* Cambridge, MA: MIT Press, 1985.
PNC	*The Post-National Constellation: Political Essays.* Cambridge, MA: MIT Press, 2001.
Postscript	"A Postscript to 'Knowledge and Human Interests'," *Philosophy of Social Science* 3 (1973): 157–189.
PPP	*Philosophical-Political Profiles.* Cambridge, MA: MIT Press, 1983.
PT	*Postmetaphysical Thinking.* Cambridge, MA: MIT Press, 1992.
QC	"Questions and Counterquestions" in *Habermas and Modernity.* Edited by R. Bernstein. Cambridge, MA: MIT Press, 1985.
R1	Reply in *Critical Debates.* Edited by J. Thompson. Cambridge, MA: MIT Press, 1982, pp. 219–284.
R2	Reply in *Communicative Action.* Edited by A. Honneth and H. Joas. Cambridge: Polity Press, 1991.
R3	Reply in *Habermas and Law.* Edited by M. Rosenfeld and A. Arato. Berkeley, CA: University of California Press, 1998.
R4	Reply in *Habermas and Rawls.* Edited by J. G. Finlayson and F. Freyenhagen. New York: Routledge, 2011.
R5	Reply in *Habermas and Religion.* Edited by C. Calhoun, E. Mendieta and J. Van Antwerpen. Cambridge: Polity Press, 2013.
STPS	*The Structural Transformation of the Public Sphere.* Cambridge, MA: MIT Press.
TCA 1 & 2	*The Theory of Communicative Action.* Boston: Beacon Press, 1985/1987.
TJ	*Truth and Justification.* Cambridge, MA: MIT Press, 2003.
TP	*Theory and Practice.* Boston: Beacon Press, 1973.
TRS	*Toward a Rational Society.* Boston: Beacon Press, 1970.
TT	*Time of Transitions.* Cambridge: Polity Press, 2006.

Chronology

1929   Born June 18, in Düsseldorf, Germany.

1944   Enrolls in Hitler Youth; sent to the Western Front in the final months before the end of the war where he serves as a field nurse.

1949–54   Studies at the universities in Göttingen, Zurich, and Bonn; completes his dissertation on Friedrich Schelling in Bonn under the direction of Erich Rothacker in 1954.

1953   Publishes Frankfurt newspaper editorial, "With Heidegger against Heidegger."

1955   Marries Ute Wesselhöft in July.

1956   Becomes a research assistant for Theodor Adorno at the Institute for Social Research in Frankfurt; son Tilman is born (the first of three children).

1959   Daughter Rebekka is born.

1961   Completes his *Habilitation* (or second dissertation), *The Structural Transformation of the Public Sphere* [English translation (ET), 1989], in Marburg under the direction of Wolfgang Abendroth; appointed Professor of Philosophy in Heidelberg.

1963   *Theory and Practice* [ET, 1971].

1964   Succeeds Max Horkheimer as Professor of Philosophy and Sociology at the Goethe University in Frankfurt.

1967   Daughter Judith is born; student protests for university reform and against the Vietnam War increase and Benno Ohnesorg is killed by police during a demonstration in Berlin.

1968   *Knowledge and Human Interests* [ET, 1971].
1969   *Student Protest and Reform in Higher Education*, a collection of essays on educational reform and the student movement; student occupation of rooms at the Institute in January led Adorno to telephone the police.
1970   Delivers the Gauss lectures at Princeton University—*On the Pragmatics of Social Interaction* [ET, 2001].
1971   Appointed co-director at Max Planck Institute, in Starnberg (near Münich); begins exchange with Niklas Luhmann on implications of a systems-theoretic approach to the study of society.
1973   *Legitimation Crisis* [ET, 1975].
1980   Visiting professor during second (winter) semester at the University of California, Berkeley; receives an honorary degree from the New School for Social Research in New York; awarded the Adorno Prize by the city of Frankfurt.
1981   *The Theory of Communicative Action* [ET, 1984/1987].
1982   Resigns his position in Starnberg and returns to Frankfurt as Professor of Philosophy and Sociology.
1983   *Moral Consciousness and Communicative Action* [ET, 1990].
1984   Delivers an address to the Spanish Parliament on the crisis of the welfare state.
1985   *The Philosophical Discourse on Modernity* [ET, 1987].
1986   Beginning of "historian's dispute" which continues into early 1990s; delivers the Tanner Lecture on "Law and Morality" at Harvard University.
1988   *Postmetaphysical Thinking* [ET, 1992].
1989   Fall of the Berlin Wall.
1990   German reunification.
1991   *Justification and Application* [ET, 1993].
1992   *Between Facts and Norms* [ET, 1996].
1994   Mandatory retirement from Goethe University, Frankfurt; begins a ten-year period as a visiting professor at Northwestern University, Evanston, IL.
1995   *A Berlin Republic: Writings on Germany* [ET, 1997]; receives the Karl Jaspers Prize in Heidelberg.
1996   *The Inclusion of the Other* [ET, 1998].

1998	*The Postnational Constellation* [ET, 2001]; participates in public debates on cloning and gene technology; conference in Freiburg, Switzerland on "*Knowledge and Human Interests* thirty years later".
1999	*Truth and Justification* [ET, 2003].
2000	Held joint seminar with Derrida in Frankfurt.
2001	*Times of Transition* [ET, 2006] and *The Future of Human Nature* [ET, 2003], which includes "Faith and Knowledge," a lecture given in Frankfurt shortly after 9/11 upon receiving the Peace Prize awarded by the German Booksellers Association.
2002	Lectures in Iran on topic of postsecularism.
2003	Publishes an editorial, co-signed by Derrida, protesting the US invasion of Iraq and calling for strengthened international law and a united Europe.
2004	Awarded the Kyoto Prize, Japan.
2005	*Between Naturalism and Religion* [ET, 2008].
2007	*The Dialectics of Secularization* [ET, 2006]—a dialogue between Habermas and Joseph Ratzinger (Pope Benedict XVI).
2008	*Europe: The Faltering Project* [ET, 2009].
2009	*Philosophical Texts*, a five-volume edition of his philosophical essays and central texts.
2010	*The Crisis of the European Union* [ET, 2012], which also includes the essay, "The Concept of Human Dignity and the Realistic Utopia of Human Rights"; received the Ulysses Medal in Dublin, Ireland.
2012	*Postmetaphysical Thinking II*; conference on "Habermas and Historical Materialism" in Wuppertal; awarded the Heinrich Heine Prize by the city of Wüppertal.
2013	*The Lure of Technocracy*, the twelfth volume of his "shorter political essays" [ET, 2015]; awarded the Erasmus Prize by the city of Amsterdam.

One

Life and works

Jürgen Habermas is arguably the most widely recognized and influential philosopher of the last half-century. He is often associated with the tradition of critical theory known as the "Frankfurt School"—which also included Max Horkheimer, Theodor Adorno, and Herbert Marcuse—but his philosophical contributions extend far beyond that origin in both their content and influence. His work reaches into a number of disciplines beyond philosophy—including sociology, legal and political theory, and cultural and media studies, and no other prominent philosopher has so actively entered into exchange and debate with others—from Adorno, Hans-Georg Gadamer, and Michel Foucault to Richard Rorty, Robert Brandom, and John Rawls (to mention only a few). His work also addresses some of the most pressing and difficult philosophical questions—from more abstract topics such as the nature and limits of human knowledge, the relation between agency and social structure, or the impact of modern science and technology on our mundane self-understanding to more immediately practical concerns about the relation between human rights and democracy, the value of toleration and multiculturalism, and the prospects for a "postnational" democracy. Finally, more than any other contemporary philosopher, Habermas has been a highly active public intellectual engaged in a wide range of political and social debates for more than sixty years.

The breadth and scope of his work—not to mention the vast amount—make the task of an introduction especially challenging. Many interesting aspects will have to be omitted or only mentioned briefly. A central aim of this book is to identify and develop in some detail the deeper philosophical perspective and commitments that unify his work, while at the same time giving greater attention to some of the topics on which Habermas has made significant contributions. Of course, even to claim that his work contains an underlying unity might seem controversial as his work has undergone substantial change over the years. Some of his earliest writings were inspired by his study of Heidegger in the early 1950s. These were soon overshadowed by a much longer period in which Marx (and the wider Hegelian–Marxist tradition of critical theory) engaged his thought. The publication of his magnum opus, The Theory of Communicative Action, marks another period in his career, one that might be described as more Weberian and in which his conception of social theory initially looks more "traditional" than "critical." Finally, some have discerned a more "liberal" and "Kantian" turn with the publication of Between Facts and Norms and works since then. Others have suggested that a similar shift from radicalism to liberalism can be found in his political views as well.[1]

Nonetheless, despite the changes in Habermas's philosophical positions—often directly in response to criticism of his earlier work—there is a remarkable and quite deep continuity to his work. For example, his relatively early engagement with both Heidegger and Marx importantly shaped his general understanding of philosophy and helps to explain his deep pragmatist convictions. More importantly, a career-long engagement with the work of Kant and Hegel has shaped his view that philosophy cannot be replaced by science even though it must remain in a more cooperative relationship with it. Habermas has recently described his position as a form of "Kantian pragmatism" (TJ, 8, 30; Aboulafia et al. 2002, 223). But this particular conception of philosophy can already be found in Knowledge and Human Interests where he refers to it as "transcendental pragmatism" and it informs his other work as well. In fact, the present study will make his Kantian pragmatism a guiding theme. Though, as we shall see, Habermas incorporates much from the Hegelian and Marxist critique of transcendental philosophy, he preserves a deep Kantian intuition in his belief that we cannot know reality an sich (or in-itself) and that knowledge is limited to the "human standpoint" (Longuenesse). At the same time a transcendental element is found in his belief that philosophy cannot be replaced by one or another of the empirical sciences and that one of its primary tasks involves a distinctive type of reflection on the "conditions of possibility" of our human practices and activities (including scientific activity) (BNR, 27; Hammer 2007).

Like Kant, Habermas maintains that there are a priori "world-disclosing" or "world-constituting" features of knowledge and action that cannot directly become the object of empirical inquiry precisely because they constitute conditions of possibility for such inquiry (TJ, 21). He shares this perspective with many other philosophers including, notably, Heidegger and Wittgenstein.[2] What importantly distinguishes his view from some others is his claim that transcendental (or world-disclosing) knowledge is not immune to criticism or revision as a result of "inner-worldly" learning (or knowledge acquired under those world-disclosing conditions) (TJ, 34; PDM, 319–320). In contrast to Kant then (for whom transcendental and empirical knowledge are sharply distinguished) the relation between world-disclosing knowledge and inner-worldly learning is more fluid—even if the former cannot become an explicit object of knowledge they can be altered or modified through cognitive achievements that take place in the world. For this reason one must also allow for the notion of an historical a priori (Foucault) or relative a priori (Putnam) as well—world-disclosing knowledge can and does change though not obviously at will. Finally, and here his pragmatist commitments are especially visible, Habermas insists on the priority of "knowing how" over "knowing that" or, in different words, on the priority of social practices (or the lifeworld) over any explicit (or theoretical) knowledge about those practices (PT, 43, 49). Robert Brandom refers to this as "fundamental pragmatism" and Habermas shares this view not only with Brandom, but Heidegger, Wittgenstein, Rorty and many others (Brandom 2011, 9).

The distinctive features of Habermas's Kantian pragmatism will thus have to be located in the more specific claims he makes about his version of this fundamental pragmatism. As we shall see in later chapters, these primarily have to do with the various idealizations that Habermas claims are "built into" our social practices: idealizations about an objective world, accountable agents, and demanding validity-claims (for example, about truth and moral rightness) (TJ, 87). These aspects of Habermas's Kantian pragmatism will be discussed in subsequent chapters, especially in Chapter 4 where I explore it in greater detail. At this point, I want to describe another longstanding and broadly Kantian dimension to his work by considering how his central concept of communicative action addresses a perennial topic in philosophy (I). The introduction will then conclude with a brief biographical sketch (II).

I. Communicative action and the "manifest image" of the person

A question that has been at the center of Habermas's thought throughout his career concerns the impact of the rise of modern science on our self-understanding as human beings. At one level, this is especially evident in his early essays where he criticized various attempts to apply the methods and insights of modern science and technology more or less directly within the domain of politics. In what was referred to at the time as the "technocracy thesis" the ambition was to replace the classical conception of politics with its orientation to a notion of the common good and a set of political virtues with a "science of politics" that offered a more somber assessment of human nature and human motivation.[3] Hobbes is an obvious inspiration here; but Joseph Schumpeter and the economic model of democracy are important later influences. It becomes a form of ideology when it is widely accepted as an acceptable way to conduct politics (TRS, chap. 6). Without advocating a simple retention of the classical model, Habermas nevertheless criticized the idea that modern science and technology could simply replace a notion of politics that still held to the idea of citizens deliberating collectively about their common good. The technocracy thesis—in the sense of (generally accepted) rule by a scientifically and technologically informed elite—would mean an end to democracy as it had been previously understood (see Specter 2010, 96). Many of his more occasional writings on politics and educational reform from this period also addressed this theme (see especially TRS; Moses 2007, 207f.).

But the rise of modern science, especially when understood to entail a naturalistic description of the world, also challenged human self-understanding at an even more profound level. In what the American philosopher Wilfrid Sellars described as a "clash" between the "scientific" and the "manifest" image of humans, a naturalistic world view threatens a conception of ourselves as centers of personal experience and agents who are capable of acting on the basis of their deliberative choices (Sellars 1963, 38). It also threatens our self-understanding as accountable or responsible actors. The claim that science is incompatible with this "folk psychological" understanding has many versions depending on the particular science under consideration (from behaviorism to evolutionary psychology to neurophysiology). But they all share the conviction that the "manifest image" or "folk-psychological conception" of the person must be radically revised if not eliminated altogether.

Philosophers have of course adopted a variety of positions on this question. Some have argued that the scientific image is basically correct and must be largely embraced. Others have denied that there is any genuine conflict or tension, either because a "naturalistic" interpretation of modern science can be rejected or because the two images refer to completely distinct subject matters (human agents qua rational or noumenal selves are not part of the phenomenal world). Finally, still others have argued that, though there is indeed a deep tension between these two images they can nonetheless be reconciled such that the "manifest image" can still be retained in some form. Habermas, along with many others, belongs within this last group. Although the naturalistic worldview may lead us to redescribe our self-understanding, it cannot completely replace the "manifest image." In the development of his own position, Habermas has been influenced by both Heidegger and Edmund Husserl, both of whom argued that in important ways the scientific image derives from and is fundamentally still dependent upon a prior "lifeworld" that presupposes the manifest image. It is thus not possible for the scientific image to displace the lifeworld with its manifest image without at the same time calling itself into question. This is in fact the core thesis of Husserl's last (unfinished) book, *The Crisis of European Science and Transcendental Phenomenology*.[4]

What is distinctive about Habermas's own argument for the priority of the everyday lifeworld (and so for the ineliminability of the manifest image) is the connection he makes between these ideas and the human capacity for ordinary or everyday linguistic communication. The capacity for rich and meaningful communication is the product of our species's evolutionary development, but it is at the same time what makes us distinct as human beings. As he stated it in his 1965 inaugural lecture in Frankfurt: "The human interest in autonomy and responsibility is not mere fancy for it can be apprehended *a priori*. What raises us out of nature is the only thing whose nature we can know: language. Through its structure autonomy and responsibility are posited for us" (KHI, 314). Though he later conceded that the claim was rather dramatically expressed, he continues to insist on its basic truth (Habermas 2000a). In KHI, which followed his inaugural lecture of the same title, Habermas argued that our capacity for linguistic communication imposes limits on a "naturalistic" description of the world since a scientific description of the world and science itself (as a form of rational inquiry) presupposes the ongoing inquiry of a scientific community (and its reliance on informal linguistic communication) (see Chapter 2). He makes a similar argument in his influential 1968 essay on Hegel's theory of mutual recognition (*Anerkennung*) where Habermas claims that Hegel also drew a basic distinction between "instrumental action" (including science and technology) and "communicative action" (which operates against the background of shared linguistic norms) and insisted that the latter could not be replaced by the former (and so by a thoroughgoing naturalism or naturalistic worldview) (TP, chap. 4).

By the early 1970s in his Gauss Lectures at Princeton University (Habermas 1998a)—and especially in his 1976 essay "What is Universal Pragmatics?" (in CES)—Habermas makes explicit the argumentative strategy that will henceforth frame his work. Drawing especially upon John Searle's *Speech Acts*, Habermas argues that core features of the manifest image of the person are built into the very structure of language use since illocutionary acts—speech acts such as asserting, promising, or requesting, etc.—presuppose that the addressee is "free" to respond to the claims raised in such acts on the basis of her own reasons. When, for example, I sincerely promise to meet someone at the café at noon I tacitly presuppose that she has the capacity to respond. She can acknowledge my promise and make her plans accordingly; but she can also (for any number of reasons) decline from undertaking the commitments that such an acknowledgment would bring about. She might equally question my ability to keep the promise (given my other obligations) or even my sincerity in making it. In any event, in making a promise (or in undertaking any number of other illocutionary acts) the speaker ascribes a normative status to the addressee and, in acknowledging the speech act offer, the addressee also locates herself (and the speaker) within a shared normative structure. It would contradict the very meaning or "illocutionary force" of such speech acts if the capacity of the addressee to respond on the basis of her own reasons were denied.[5] Though this might seem like a quite narrow foothold, it is crucial for Habermas in that the normative structure or status produced by illocutionary acts is importantly distinct from a naturalistic (or scientific) description of the world and cannot be replaced by it. Indeed, the latter presupposes such a normative competence for its own possibility for reflective inquiry and communication. For Habermas, it is this capacity for linguistic communication—for making use of the "rationally bonding/binding force" of illocutionary acts—that undergirds his defense of the manifest image (CES, 63).[6]

The concept of communicative action is unquestionably the most basic concept in Habermas's work. It is, however, a concept that has undergone revision as he struggled to give it shape and, though the basic idea is relatively straightforward, it does have some slightly different connotations in different contexts.[7] At one level, it is Habermas's preferred way to describe the manifest image: it refers to the folk-psychological understanding that humans can respond to and act on the basis of reasons or considered judgments and are not simply propelled by the strongest motive or desire. As importantly, however, the concept of communicative action captures Habermas's conviction that one's status as a person is in an important sense social or intersubjective. The individual capacity to act for reasons is rooted in the normative structure associated with our capacity for linguistic communication as I have just described it—that is, in the shared structure of illocutionary acts. One might say, then, in a manner intended to recall Hegel's master–slave dialectic, that my status as an individual accountable and responsible agent—that is, as "free"—is crucially dependent upon and coeval with my recognition of others as similarly situated (and vice-versa).

Of course, even this intersubjective or "recognitional" understanding is still extremely thin. It is the bare notion of a person or agent as someone who occupies the normative status of accepting or rejecting the claims raised in various types of speech acts. What gives the notion of communicative action more character or depth is Habermas's further claim that such action always occurs within the lifeworld where much more is assumed and taken for granted (TCA 2: 126). Communicative action generally presupposes "thick" contexts and takes place against a background of innumerable shared norms, expectations, and habits that are in play. In fact, it is often only when these shared norms and expectations begin to break down or are called into question that the "rational potential" built into illocutionary acts is more explicitly drawn upon—the demand, that is, to provide reasons for the claims becomes more explicit and depends less upon previously taken-for-granted background certainties. Nonetheless central to Habermas's basic thesis about communicative action is that even in our most mundane or everyday social interactions—as shot through as they also always are with various both unquestioned assumptions and forms of social power and domination—this "manifest image" of humans as accountable and responsible is present or, as he puts it, "counterfactually presupposed." Indeed, the manifest image can, however paradoxically, even be invoked to conceal forms of domination (by falsely ascribing levels of responsibility and/or consent when in fact it is absent at least in that context or in that form). I have in mind more or less straightforward cases of "blaming the victim"; but falsely ascribing responsibility with respect to some sequence of social interaction does not mean that social actors don't at the same time still possess a normative competence in virtue of more general (or more basic) structures of interaction (such as linguistic communication).

This is only a brief and preliminary sketch of Habermas's concept of communicative action. It is, to repeat, closely connected to his own construal of the "manifest image" of the person and his claim that, however real and deep the conflict with a scientific or naturalistic description of the world may be, the latter presupposes the former and so cannot completely displace it—at least not without so radically altering our understanding of ourselves that we cannot coherently (or rationally) imagine what living in that world would be like.[8] As I will suggest in Chapter 4, Habermas's position is at this point quite close to P. F. Strawson's claim in "Freedom and Resentment" that we cannot easily imagine a world in which the practice of praise and blame (and the reactive attitudes on which it is based) are absent (see Strawson 2003; and Habermas's remarks on Strawson in MCCA, 45f.). This is not surprising since, for both Strawson and Habermas, the "manifest image" (with its notion of accountable agency and the practice of praise and blame) is supported and sustained by a complex network of interpersonal relationships or structures of intersubjective recognition that in turn make it possible for us to describe that image as "rational."

As we will see in subsequent chapters, the concept of communicative action plays a central role in all of Habermas's later work. In *The Theory of Communicative Action* (1984/1987) he explicitly develops it in conjunction with the notion of the lifeworld in order to provide an alternative to the interpretation of occidental rationalization found in both Max Weber and in Horkheimer and Adorno's *Dialectic of Enlightenment* (1987). Modern "rational" societies need not, as a result of the continuous spread of instrumental reason, culminate in an "iron cage" (Weber) or in a "totally administered society" (Horkheimer and Adorno 1987). Rather, the process of social rationalization may so far have been extremely one-sided but it nonetheless contains possibilities for the development of more rational forms of social organization that make use of the resources of communicative action (Chapter 3). The analysis of communicative action is also at the basis of his own constructivist reading of a discourse ethics or, more accurately, discourse morality (Chapter 5) and it figures prominently in *Between Facts and Norms* (1996) and his account of deliberative politics, where the task is to see how a communicative power generated within the free associations of civil society (that is, within institutions of the lifeworld) can be channeled in ways to influence the formal decision-making processes and exercise a rationalizing influence on administrative power (Chapter 6 and 7). Finally, as Habermas argues in *The Philosophical Discourse of Modernity* (1987), many criticisms of occidental or "western reason" and its instrumentalizing effects are based on a failure to distinguish between the communicative reason connected with communicative action and communicative power and the instrumental and functionalist reason that has often been more visible in the organization of societies (Chapter 8).

II. A brief biographical sketch

Jürgen Habermas was born to Ernst and Grete Habermas in Düsseldorf on June 18, 1929, the second of three children. He was raised in the small town of Gummersbach, about twenty miles east of Cologne where his paternal grandfather had been the head of a small Lutheran seminary. His father, the director of the local Bureau of Trade and Industry, was a career civil servant and joined the National Socialist Party in the early 1930s. Habermas was enrolled in the Hitler Youth at the age of fourteen and at fifteen served as a field nurse for an anti-aircraft brigade in the last months of the war (AS, 74; Wiggershaus 2004, 11). In a later interview he remarked that "the political climate in our family home was probably not unusual for the time. It was marked by a bourgeois adaptation to a political situation with which one did not fully identify, but which one didn't seriously criticize either" (AS, 73). However two separate events from this period had a lasting impact on his subsequent development. First, he describes the tremendous shock he experienced upon learning of the Nazi atrocities and how confronting it became a "fundamental theme of his adult life" (BNR, 17): "Overnight, as it were, the society in which we had led what had seemed to be a halfway normal everyday life and the regime governing it were exposed as pathological and criminal" (BNR, 17). It would be difficult to overestimate how his efforts in "coming to terms with the past" have shaped Habermas's thought. Second, in a much later public lecture Habermas also suggests that his own physical disability—he was born with a cleft palate and had several operations as a child—and the challenges that created for his interaction with other youths may have made him more sensitive to feelings of vulnerability and exclusion (BNR, 13–15).

After completing Gymnasium, Habermas attended a number of universities, including Göttingen, Zürich, and Bonn, where he studied philosophy, history, literature, and psychology. He completed his doctoral thesis, under the direction of Erich Rothacker, in Bonn in 1954 on the German idealist philosopher Friedrich

Schelling. According to Habermas's own report, however, Martin Heidegger was the most important influence on his thought at this time and he later described himself as "a thoroughgoing Heideggerian for three to four years" (AS, 194; BNR, 19). During this period Habermas became active in left-wing politics and, in particular, was a pacifist and opposed to the rearmament of West Germany after the war (AS, 75; Müller-Doohm 2014, 85; Moses 2007, 114). He suggested in a later interview, however, that at this time there was very little connection between his philosophical studies and his political engagement (AS, 76).

Habermas began his career as a freelance journalist and wrote a wide variety of articles, several of which show the influence of Heidegger on his thinking at this time. A longer essay from this period—"The Dialectics of Rationalization" (1954)—anticipates many of the themes in his later work while employing Heideggerian terminology. Already in 1953, however, Habermas publicly criticized Heidegger in an article that caused a stir. The title, "With Heidegger against Heidegger," signals the philosopher's influence even as Habermas expresses his shock and dismay upon learning about the extent of Heidegger's relation to Nazism. What irritated Habermas—to put it mildly—was the fact that Heidegger would allow the publication of his 1935 lectures, which included a clear reference to the "greatness of the movement [National Socialism]," without feeling any need to comment on this fact (see Wolin 1991). The article appeared at a time when Habermas was apparently looking for a more satisfactory integration of his philosophical and political concerns. Habermas's disappointment in Heidegger may also have reflected his growing conviction, perhaps contrary to his initial hopes, that the latter's appeal to the history of Being made his philosophy unsuitable for Habermas's more democratic and egalitarian concerns (Habermas 1991, 196).

Habermas married Ute Wesselhöft (b. June 2, 1930) in 1955 and shortly thereafter they moved to Frankfurt. Through a colleague he met Theodor Adorno (who had read his essay on the dialectic of rationalization) and, in 1956, he was invited to become Adorno's assistant at the Institute for Social Research in Frankfurt (AS, 191). One of his initial projects was an empirical study on student attitudes toward politics and Habermas was responsible for writing the long introduction on the concept of political participation (Specter 2010, 32). He began work on his *Habilitation*—the second dissertation required for an appointment in a university—but because of opposition from Horkheimer who found his work too Marxist he could not submit the work in Frankfurt (Wiggershaus 1994, 555; Specter 2010, 32f.). In 1959 he left Frankfurt and moved to Marburg where he completed his thesis under Wolfgang Abendroth, one of the few Marxist political theorists in a German university at the time. *The Structural Transformation of the Public Sphere* (1962/1989) received a great deal of attention for a scholarly study and significantly influenced work in a number of disciplines.[9] In 1961 he joined the Philosophy Department in Heidelberg, where Hans-Georg Gadamer was a professor and had just recently published his magnum opus, *Truth and Method* (1960 [1989]). Habermas clearly learned much from his senior colleague and despite—or perhaps because of—their subsequent philosophical debate, each obviously held the other in high regard. In 1965 Habermas accepted the Chair in Philosophy and Sociology at the J. W. Goethe University in Frankfurt that had previously been held by Horkheimer. His inaugural address, "Knowledge and Human Interests," outlined the major themes pursued in greater detail in his book with the same title three years later (see Appendix to KHI).

Habermas's first academic appointment in Frankfurt (1965–71) coincided with a tumultuous period in the university and in Germany more generally. As in France and other countries, students engaged in protests to change economic and foreign policy (including the war in Southeast Asia) and to bring about reform of the university. Habermas sided with the students and was perceived by many as one of their intellectual leaders along with Herbert Marcuse and others associated with the Frankfurt School. The situation took a more dramatic turn in June 1967, however, after student protests in response to the killing of a protestor, Benno Ohnesorg, by the police in Berlin. Speaking at a gathering of student protestors in Hannover several days later Habermas warned the students about the dangers of naive "actionism" and described a romanticized view of revolutionary violence as "leftist fascism" (Müller-Doohm 2014, 192; Specter 2010, 114). Not surprisingly, the criticisms were not well received by the students and, despite Habermas's attempts to clarify his support for the demonstrations, the exchange produced a growing rift between Habermas and the students. In the midst of further protests the following year, students took over buildings at the University in Frankfurt, renaming it "Karl Marx University." Some students occupied classrooms at the Institute for Social Research and concerns were raised by some about the destruction of property. The police were called, apparently by Adorno, and several students were arrested (Müller-Doohm 2014, 211).[10]

After these events and Adorno's death in 1969, Habermas apparently began to consider alternatives to Frankfurt. At least his reasons for remaining were less strong. In 1971 he accepted an invitation to become one of the co-directors of the Max Planck Institute in Starnberg along with the physicist and philosopher Carl von Weisäcker. He remained in this position for a decade and was responsible for assembling a number of permanent research assistants and an even larger number of visiting scholars. During this time he produced his influential book *Legitimation Crisis*, conducted research on the "reconstruction of historical materialism and theories of social evolution" (in CES), and engaged in extensive research that eventually led to the publication of *The Theory of Communicative Action*. However, he was apparently never especially comfortable in his role as an administrator and later remarked that he regretted making the move to Starnberg (Wiggerhaus 2004, 112). In 1982 he returned to Frankfurt where he first offered seminars developing themes from his 1980 Adorno-Prize lecture, "Modernity: An Unfinished Project." These lectures were expanded and eventually published as *The Philosophical Discourse of Modernity* (1985/1987 [English trans.]). In (1992/1996) he published *Between Facts and Norms* which returned to some of the political themes he first broached in *The Structural Transformation of the Public Sphere* (1962/1989). He remained at the J.-W. Goethe University until he reached the age of mandatory retirement in 1994. Since his retirement Habermas has continued to lecture and publish at an astonishing rate. He was a permanent visiting professor for several years at Northwestern University in Chicago and has accepted invitations to lecture in cities all over the world.

A remarkable feature of Habermas's career is the extraordinary number of scholarly debates in which he has participated, some of which spilled over into discussions in the wider public and all of which had implications for his ongoing interest in the relation between the sciences and the manifest image of the person. In the early 1960s he participated in the "positivist dispute" in German sociology that had begun with an exchange between Adorno and Karl Popper, a prominent philosopher of science and advocate of "critical rationalism" (Adorno et al. 1976). One question in this discussion concerned the "value-neutrality" of the social sciences. But the dispute also raised again the issue of decisionism—that is, whether conflicts of value, including those relevant for basic social policy, are capable of rational resolution or whether they ultimately come down to matters of non-rational decision and what Max Weber called the unending battle of gods and demons. In the later 1960s Habermas wrote a review of Gadamer's *Truth and Method* (1960) in which he considered the implications of philosophical hermeneutics for the social sciences (in LSS). A wider exchange took place in which the issue was not the relevance of the "interpretive turn"—almost all acknowledged that—but rather what its limits were. Did it, for example, mean an end to a more "scientific" analysis of society and did it imply that the idea of a more radical rational critique of society was illusory? (see essays in Müller-Vollmer 1985). As we will see, though he is much indebted to hermeneutics or an interpretive approach in the social sciences, he argued—against Gadamer—that it has important limits.

In the 1970s Habermas took up a challenge from the other side, so to speak. The German sociologist Niklas Luhmann, a student of Talcott Parsons, proposed that society could be fruitfully analyzed through systems theory. On this conception, what is central for social reproduction is not the ability of social actors to coordinate their actions "rationally" (in the sense of collective argument and negotiated agreement) but the ability of society understood as an "autopoietic" (or self-producing) system to maintain its identity in response to changes in its environment (Luhmann 1995). Society is further interpreted as a system of systems—or economic, political, legal, educational "sub-systems"—each of which must also reproduce itself in response to its own environment. What Habermas argued—and Luhmann would not disagree—is that such an approach to society would radically call into question the manifest image noted above. On Habermas's view it would also have profound implications for the understanding of politics and law (see Cohen and Arato 1992, chap. 7; Holub 1991, and Moeller 2006 for more on this debate).

In the 1980s and 1990s Habermas was again at the center of two other significant debates within the academy. The first had to do with the interpretation of postmodernism, especially as that concept was taken up by other philosophers. This is the topic of *The Philosophical Discourse of Modernity* (1987) and will be discussed in the final chapter of this book. The second—the historians' debate—was an exchange that occurred as a result of Habermas's public intervention (in several newspaper editorials) concerning the question of the political identity of the Federal Republic and its public memory. Habermas detected a tendency among some historians to redescribe its National Socialist past in an attempt to "normalize" Germany and bring it into line with other Western liberal democracies. According to Habermas this was dangerous because part of Germany's attempt to rebuild itself as a democratic nation depended precisely on keeping alive the memory of its collective responsibility for National Socialism and the Holocaust (NC, 233). Other participants in the debate disagreed and argued that it was time to normalize Germany (see further Pensky 1989; Moses 2007, 236f; Müller 2000, 56f.)

As importantly, throughout his career Habermas has consistently displayed his sense of responsibility as a public intellectual. As in the case of the "historians' debate" he frequently publishes newspaper editorials and essays that appear in journals not limited to professional academics (Müller 2000). Often this has involved taking controversial positions that did not prevail—in his opposition to the stationing of Pershing missiles in Germany in the 1980s, in his calls to move more slowly on German reunification after the fall of the Berlin Wall, and (at least to date) in his most recent pleas for a European Union and a world constitution that would check the destructive excesses and massive inequalities of globalization. In some cases, his contributions have helped to increase an awareness of both the urgency and difficulty of promoting a robust and democratic political culture—as in his arguments about the right to asylum, the value of a constitutional patriotism against stronger forms of nationalism, and the need for secular societies to remain sensitive to the ways in which its policies might be unnecessarily exclusionary. In almost all cases, however, his interventions have helped to advance an understanding of the public sphere that he defends in his more academic writings.

Notes

1 Habermas, it should be noted, disputes this characterization. He states that his interest in legal theory stems from the 1950s and, "The idea of a liberal turn isn't correct in my view: I was a 'left-liberal, left of Social Democracy' in the '60s also" (Specter 2010, 209); Specter's excellent study lends support to Habermas's claim about his longstanding interest in legal theory.

2 The transcendental/empirical distinction is widespread in philosophy though it has been drawn in many ways: it is behind Heidegger's ontological/ontic distinction; it is also implicit in Rudolph Carnap's distinction between questions that are internal and those that are external to a linguistic framework (Carus 2007) and in Robert Brandom's distinction between "instituting" a conceptual norm and "applying" a conceptual norm (Brandom 2000a, 157). Habermas most often refers to the distinction in terms of a "world-disclosing" linguistic framework and "inner-worldly" or mundane learning (BNR, 26; PDM, 319–320; see Lafont 2000). Most forms of anti-realism or "internal realism" also assume this distinction and in one version it is the target of Davidson's influential critique of the scheme/content distinction (Davidson 1984).

3 See Specter 2010, 91f. for discussion; one variant of this broad thesis can be found in the debates in the US about "ungovernability"—the view that democratic demands on the state had become so great that society could not be administered in a "rational" manner.

4 Habermas explicitly makes this claim linking Sellar's manifest image to Husserl's understanding of the lifeworld in Habermas (2012a, 46); see also Moran (2012) and, for the connection between Husserl and Sellars, Hampe (2007).

5 It is important to note that this freedom is not the more familiar idea of negative liberty—the absence of interference—since it also carries with it an obligation for the addressee to provide reasons for her own response. As Habermas will later argue in BFN the traditional negative liberties should be seen as a release from this more basic notion of freedom (with its rationally binding obligation) (BFN, 120; Günther 1998).

6 For an extremely interesting and similar use of speech act theory for a defense of the manifest image and the "space of reason-giving," see Kukla and Lance (2009).

7 For example, as we will see in Chapter 3, Habermas does not limit the concept of communicative action to illocutionary acts (or even all linguistic action) but importantly extends the concept to include social action that relies upon or is "coordinated" on the basis of illocutionary acts (see TCA 1, 101).

8 See BNR, chap. 6, "Freedom and Determinism," for one of his few attempts to address this more specific "clash" between the scientific and the manifest image of the person; see also the essay by Habermas and responses from several critics on the topic of free will in Anderson (2007).

9 For an indication of this influence, see the collection edited by Craig Calhoun (1992). This work is discussed in Chapter 2.

10 Müller-Doohm reports that Adorno made the phone call (2014, 211); for further discussion of these events, see Holub 1991; Specter 2010; Habermas's essays on the student protests are contained in Habermas (1969).

Two
Habermas's initial attempts at a critical theory of society

I. Introduction

After joining the Institute for Social Research in Frankfurt in 1956, Habermas entered an extremely prolific period of research, even measured against his own later productivity. He published a number of essays in the history of modern political and social thought (most of which appeared in *Theory and Practice*); he conducted research on public opinion and student protest; along with Adorno, he participated in the "positivist dispute" against Karl Popper and other proponents of "critical rationalism"; and (in 1962) he completed his second dissertation (or *Habilitation*) on the history of the public sphere. At the same time, a leading concern for him during this period was the development of a plausible reading of the Hegelian-Marxist tradition of a critical social theory. How might a broadly Marxist project of radical social criticism—renewed in the early twentieth century in Georg Lukács's *History and Class Consciousness* (1923) and then in the early Frankfurt School—best be continued in the current situation? His preferred label for this project at this time was "a philosophy of history with practical intent" (or, less felicitously but more descriptively, "an empirically-falsifiable materialist philosophy of history with practical intent") (TP, 205, 212). At other times, he also refers to it as "a theory of society with practical intent" and sometimes simply as "critique" (TP, 195). As was the case for his predecessors, it took the form of a philosophy of history that had as its goal or *telos* the realization of human emancipation (Horkheimer 1972, 217). But, if such a project was to be credible within the context of current social science, it must rid itself of any dogmatic content (such as any assumptions about the inevitable development toward that goal within the "productive forces" [Marx]). Within a fairly short period of time (by the mid-1960s), however, Habermas seems to have had growing doubts about social criticism conceived as a philosophy of history and, in an effort to ground or justify this form of critique, he turned to the more explicitly epistemological project of *Knowledge and Human Interests*, which is his main work from this early period.[1]

II . A "philosophy of history with a practical intent"

One of the earliest and most interesting formulations of this initial project is "Between Philosophy and Science: Marxism as Critique" (1963, in TP). In this essay Habermas defends the continuing relevance of Marxism as critique against its perversions in orthodox Marxism—"Diamat" or the dialectical materialism of the Third (Communist) International—but also in contrast to various attempts to preserve some of Marx's insights into capitalist society either in the form of philosophy or as a more rigorous ("positivist") science. Marxism is not best understood either as a "first philosophy" or (perhaps more to the point) as an empirical science. Rather it should be read as "critique" or a "philosophy of history with practical intent" that proceeds through an analysis of the lived or experienced contradictions of social life—especially an analysis of the irrational character of the so-called rational social production of capitalism—in order to ascertain the "objective possibilities" for a more humane alternative.

In keeping with the earlier tradition of critical theory, in this period Habermas's idea of a "philosophy of history" is thus decidedly a version of Hegelian-Marxism that views society as a "totality" whose development and possibilities can be explained with reference to its own immanent (but not inevitable) dialectic.[2] Habermas disagrees with others who claim that Marx's dialectic presupposes Hegel's logic and absolute idealism (or the fundamental identity of thought and being) and, for that reason, often want to dismiss it. However, he does acknowledge that Marx is deeply indebted to the form of immanent critique found in the *Philosophy of Right* where Hegel attempts to show that a modern Sittlichkeit (ethical life) or the core institutions of modern society—a nuclear family, bourgeois market economy, and constitutional state—are the realization or embodiment of human freedom (TP, 217). For Marx, of course, modern (capitalist) society is very far from the embodiment of freedom and reason, but the developmental dynamic at work within it—the conflict between constantly expanding productive forces and their corresponding social relations—at least indicates (for those able to comprehend) how genuine human emancipation will eventually emerge from it. Habermas's intriguing gloss on Marxism as a "philosophy of history with practical intent" is found in his claim that with the emergence of these modern institutions and an increasingly interdependent world we can for the first time collectively look back on history "as if" it had a telos and thus now possess the ability to make history self-consciously. So, while the telos of history as human emancipation is by no means guaranteed or inevitable—nor, strictly speaking, was it previously really there—the possibility for its realization, however slight, could now be discerned:

> On the basis of industrial society and its technically mediated commerce, the interdependence of political events and the integration of social relations have progressed so far beyond what was even conceivable two centuries ago that within this overall complex of communication particular histories have coalesced in the history of one world. Yet at the same time, mankind has never before been confronted so sharply by the irony of a capacity to make its own history, yet still deprived of control over it, as is the case now that the means of self-assertion by force have developed to such a degree that their deployment for attaining specific political ends has become highly problematical. Thus the immanent presuppositions of the philosophy of history have not by any means become invalid; on the contrary, it is only today that they have become true.
>
> (TP, 250–251; see also PPP, 93)

What Habermas is evidently pursuing here (as well as in several other essays from this period) is the continuation of a form of Hegelian Marxism (in some ways still quite close to Lukács) in which the resources of social criticism are derived not from an abstract "ought"—recall Hegel's critique of both Kantian morality and natural law—but from the immanent logic or dynamic of capitalist society understood as a "totality" (TP, 205). To be sure, in this period Habermas does not endorse Marx's labor theory of value, and his own "materialist" reading of history is distinct from the economic or technological determinist reading often associated with Marx (TP, 277).[3] He nonetheless shares the broadly Marxist view that the existing form of society is defined by the dynamic relation between its productive forces (material resources, including labor and technology) and their social relations (or what Habermas calls the "institutional framework" of society). He also maintains that the resources for critique can be found not by appeal to ahistorical moral principles but by immanent criticism—that is, by exposing how the existing social reality fails to live up to the normative claims contained within it. Moreover, although Habermas's formulations also describe the social totality in terms of the dynamic between the means of material production (productive forces) and the prevailing "institutional framework" of society, the locus or cause for change is not primarily to be found within developments in the productive forces. Rather, in a more Hegelian vein, it also depends on a "struggle for recognition" or "critical-revolutionary activity" within the institutional framework of society itself (TP, 235f; KHI, 55). This more dynamic relation between "labor" and "interaction"—the title of another important essay from roughly the same time—marks an important feature of Habermas's own version of Hegelian Marxism or critical theory at this time (TP, chap. 4).

The Structural Transformation of the Public Sphere (1962/1989), Habermas's first book and his Habilitation (or second doctoral thesis required to obtain a university appointment), offers an illustration of what his idea of a "philosophy of history with practical intent" might look like when worked out in greater detail. The book is an informed critical study of the concept of the bourgeois public sphere and its historical development. It had a significant interdisciplinary impact and helped to establish Habermas's reputation as a young theorist of the radical left (Wiggershaus 1994, 561). Though in some ways it echoes central themes of Horkheimer and Adorno's

Dialectic of Enlightenment (1987), especially in its description of a culture industry that shapes citizens according to the demands of capitalism gone wild, it pays attention to empirical research in ways absent from their earlier work.

Habermas's central thesis is that the bourgeois public sphere, which arose in connection with the class struggles against absolutism, became an effective means for taming and rationalizing political power. In contrast to the "representational" public of feudalism in which political power was *displayed* before its subjects, the bourgeois public sphere is situated *between* the state and civil society (or market economy). It referred to any "space" where private citizens gathered to debate what was in their common good, and its more specifically political function was to serve as a check on the exercise of political power. As Habermas points out, this idea is also found in Kant's somewhat idiosyncratic understanding of "public reason" in "What is Enlightenment?" as the reasoning of citizens *not* in their official position as civil servants or functionaries of the state but in their "private" role as members of an "entire reading public" (Kant 1970, 55; STPS, 105; O'Neill 1989). Though of course always ideological in the sense that the legitimating rhetoric of public reason (like that of "natural rights") continued to work primarily in the interests of one social class, it was not "mere" ideology since, according to Habermas, it introduced a real means for the non-violent taming and legitimation of political power.

However, by the latter part of the nineteenth century, as Habermas tells the story, social conditions had again changed such that the prospects for such a critical public sphere were increasingly threatened. On the one hand, the re-emergence of private interests (corporations) more directly within the chambers of state power blurred the distinction between public and private and, on the other hand, state interventions into the economy made obsolete the bourgeois idea of an independent sphere of "independent" private property-owners. Habermas described this reintegration of state and civil society as a "refeudalization" of society which, together with rise of a mass media, also paved the way for the displacement of a "critical" by a "staged and manipulative" public (STPS, 232). Habermas concluded his study on an (at most) modestly optimistic note that this process might be reversed and suggested this could happen, under the changed conditions of the social welfare state, only if society as a whole were democratized—that is, only if a more radical social democracy was realized in contrast to a liberal welfare-state democracy. The possibility for the further transformation of welfare-state liberal democracy into a real democracy or democratic socialism through the realization of the egalitarian and democratic commitments of the liberal welfare state was nonetheless "immanent" within the existing social institutions (STPS, 232f.). Or, as he put it in another text from this period, the liberal state faced a "historical alternative": "That sooner or later the liberal *Rechtsstaat* (or constitutional state) fulfills its own intentions in a democratic and social *Rechtsstaat*, or reverts against its own inner essence, more or less openly, and assumes an authoritarian form" (Habermas et al. 1961, 42–43; see also TP, 233; TP, 117f.).[4]

By the mid-1960s, however, Habermas seems to have had growing doubts about this version of a "philosophy of history with practical intent." It is not entirely clear what motivated him to change course at this time, though it may have had to do with doubts that the specific form of immanent criticism he proposed would be sufficient. He suggests that "bourgeois consciousness has become cynical" in the sense that even exposing bourgeois society to its failure to live up to its own ideals might not be sufficient to persuade it of the need for change (CES, 97). He also seems to have concluded that in treating a critical theory as a "philosophy of history" it would be difficult to avoid a "totalizing" view of society which he was also beginning to question for other reasons. An extended remark he offers a bit later (in 1982) sheds some further light on the possible motivations for his change:

> One can learn from the course of critical theory why the foundation of the critique of ideology in a philosophy of history developed cracks. Assumptions about a dialectical relation between productive forces and productive relations are pseudo-normative statements about an objective teleology of history. For the critical theory of the 1930s this counted as the motor force behind the realization of a reason set forth in bourgeois ideals. This mixing of descriptive and normative contents was present in the basic concepts of historical materialism. It is

possible to avoid this confusion without surrendering the leading intention behind the theory, if we ascertain the rational content of anthropologically deep-seated structure in a transcendentally oriented analysis which is initially unhistorical. It is not so important whether one approaches this goal through the theory of knowledge or through the theory of language.

(R1, 253)

This passage is also of interest because it indicates the next two phases in Habermas's development and, in his remark, he seem to view both as viable and perhaps even complementary options. The first is the turn to epistemology where, in *Knowledge and Human Interests*, his strategy is twofold: to complete epistemology "by other means" (namely, social theory) but, at the same time, elaborate the epistemological categories in which such a critical social theory might be pursued. The other approach—*via* the theory of language— is a reference to *The Theory of Communicative Action*, which is the topic of the next chapter.

III. Knowledge and Human Interests

Knowledge and Human Interests (1968) is Habermas's first systematic attempt to reformulate the project of a critical social theory. It is an extremely ambitious work and, as he himself fairly quickly acknowledged, not entirely successful. Nonetheless it remains an important initial statement concerning his "transcendental pragmatism" (Postscript, 179)—or what he later calls "Kantian pragmatism"—and, despite some later changes and shifts in emphasis, his basic understanding of philosophy and its relation to the sciences remains the same. Most importantly, perhaps, is his claim that philosophy, as a form of reflection on human knowledge and practices, secures a unity between reason and freedom found in Kant and Kant's own understanding of philosophy as a critique of reason in a twofold sense: it is a critique of reason (against both rationalist metaphysics and a thorough-going empiricism or naturalism) but it is also a critique conducted by reason that must meet with a free and universal agreement among those who exercise it:

> Reason must subject itself to critique in all its undertakings, and
> cannot restrict the freedom of critique through any prohibition
> without damaging itself and drawing upon itself a
> disadvantageous suspicion. ... The very existence of reason
> depends upon this freedom, which has no dictatorial authority,
> but whose claim is never anything more than the agreement of
> free citizens, each of whom must be able to express his
> reservations, indeed even his veto, without holding back.
>   (Kant 1998, A738/B766)

Though Habermas is critical of Kant's transcendental idealism—
the attempt to ground and legitimate knowledge by reference to
the constitutive activity of a non-empirical (or noumenal) subject—
he nonetheless wants to renew the project of critical reflection that
Kant initiated but which after the death of Hegel was quickly (and
more or less quietly) lost. Roughly, this was a conception of
philosophy as engaged in an attempt to preserve the more or less
"manifest image" of the human being as a knowing and acting
agent against the rising "scientific image" but also against the
pretentions of a more ambitious understanding of philosophy as
metaphysics as well. Also important for Habermas's understanding
of philosophy at this time is the delicate way in which he seeks to
combine transcendental reflection (on the conditions of possibility
of knowing and acting) with a claim about the natural and social
evolution of those conditions. What we currently identify as
transcendental conditions of knowledge must nevertheless also be
regarded (in contrast to Kant and Hegel) as the contingent outcome
of a natural and social evolutionary process. Despite the later
changes in his thinking, Habermas continues to insist on this
precarious combination of Kant and Darwin (Postscript, 163; TJ,
22): There are "quasi-transcendental" conditions that frame or
structure our cognitive access to the world and yet these conditions
are at the same time a part of the world (and so can and do undergo
modification). As we will see, although this proposal is rife with
problems, it is a position that others have defended as well and one
that Habermas thinks should not be relinquished.[5]

Habermas's broad claim is that, with the decline of Hegelianism
almost immediately following Hegel's death in 1832, philosophy

and, in particular, the philosophy of science became dominated by various forms of naturalism and positivism that largely abandoned the Kantian project of a critique of reason.[6] Philosophy as epistemology (*Erkenntnistheorie*) in the Kantian sense was gradually replaced by philosophy as a theory of science (*Wissenschaftstheorie*) that generally deferred to the natural sciences (and especially physics) as the paradigmatic model of knowledge (KHI, 3, 67). As a result what Habermas calls "scientism"—treating science as the sole form of knowledge (PPP, 15)—and "positivism"—the "disavowal of reflection"—led to the denigration of other types of knowledge (including moral-practical knowledge)—consider, for example, the rise of emotivism early in the twentieth century. At the same time, according to this narrative, much of philosophy retreated from the more ambitious Kantian project of a critique of reason (again in both senses) and assumed the more modest task of clarifying the conditions for successful science. Of course, more traditional conceptions of philosophy also persisted, but these were largely overshadowed by philosophical approaches that were oriented to the natural sciences in the late nineteenth and early twentieth century. Moreover, as Habermas argues, even more critical projects—such as those found in the work of Marx and in Freud—also suffered from a scientistic and positivistic self-misunderstanding insofar as they were often presented as examples of a rigorous (naturalistic) science.

In view of this general understanding of the fate of philosophy, Habermas seeks a return to Kant's critical project—to "the forgotten experience of reflection" (KHI, vii)—though, to be sure, one that is now informed by Hegel and Marx as well: a critical (and chastened) philosophy continued by other means, namely, critical social theory. Habermas offers a succinct if somewhat enigmatic formulation of this project at the end of Part I of *Knowledge and Human Interests*:

> Philosophy is preserved in science as critique. A social theory that puts forth the claim to be a self-reflection of the history of the species cannot simply negate philosophy. Rather, the heritage of philosophy issues in the critique of ideology, a mode of thought that determines the method of scientific analysis itself. Outside of critique, however, philosophy retains no rights.
>
> (KHI, 63; see also Postscript, 164)[7]

As a form of reflective critique, philosophy engages with the sciences to clarify and ascertain their own appropriate methods of inquiry. On the one hand, philosophy is not identical with any science nor can it be replaced by science; on the other hand, neither does philosophy possess any special or privileged knowledge (as a "first philosophy," grounding metaphysics or strong form of transcendentalism). Rather, it can be preserved only as "critique" or as a critical and reflective inquiry into the conditions of possibility of knowledge.

As we shall see, Habermas remains remarkably consistent in his conception of philosophy, even if he vacillates slightly between a more Kantian and more Hegelian (or historicist) inflection to this understanding. Philosophy must relinquish any strong claim to be the final judge or arbiter over the sciences and, in an important sense, remains dependent on them and so is equally as fallible. At the same time, however, philosophy must not uncritically accept any interpretation or "self-understanding" the various sciences offer about the significance of their own achievements. Philosophy, perhaps more clearly than any individual science, also remains more directly connected to a general human "common sense" and the everyday practices in which it is rooted—what others have called the "manifest image"—and draws upon that common sense in its own efforts at "critique." Additionally, as Habermas later argues, philosophy historically (at least after Hegel) stands in a unique position to translate or interpret the significance of the sciences to the wider public culture. However, in either role—that of "stand-in" or "interpreter"—philosophy does not possess any privileged form of knowledge and remains indebted to a human common sense and mundane or "everyday" practice that present humans as competent and accountable actors.[8]

Both the structure of the argument in KHI and the problems to which it gives rise are instructive for the subsequent development of Habermas's thought. Part I, which offers a brief but highly engaging interpretation of Kant, Hegel, and Marx, presents in broad outline his version of a "materialist" epistemology or "critical theory of society." Parts II and III develop his claim that there are exactly three "anthropologically deep-seated" cognitive interests that form the conditions of possibility for all human knowledge (TP, 8). However, no one cognitive interest is any more entitled to the claim of offering genuine knowledge at the expense of another and (as we shall see) each in fact tends to complement and balance the other.

Habermas begins with a review of what he takes to be the forgotten strategy and achievements of Kant's critical project. Although Kant primarily undertook his critique of reason in order to defend the new science of his day against skeptical challenges, he also sought to establish the limits of human knowledge "in order to make room for faith" (Kant 1998, Bxxx) and criticized the excesses of a rationalist metaphysics that failed to respect those limits. A critique of reason would then importantly establish both the legitimacy of science and define its limits. The means for achieving this end is of course found in Kant's infamous "Copernican turn" in which the limits of knowledge are found not by looking more carefully at the world so to speak, but by a transcendental reflection on the nature of our cognitive faculties (see Guyer 2014, c. 2). This is the source of Kant's "transcendental idealism" in which he argued that scientific or empirical knowledge depended on two distinct roots: sensibility (in which something is given to us independent of our cognitive faculties) and understanding (or a conceptual framework provided by us) (Kant 1998, B29). By insisting that empirical knowledge required the contribution of each of these two radically distinct roots Kant believed he had found the means to respond to both the skepticism of the empiricists and the excessive claims to knowledge found in rationalist metaphysics. More generally, however, this defense of reason (and its limits) presupposed that there was a noumenal world beyond the reach of human knowledge—the world or nature *an sich*—as well as an equally inscrutable (transcendental) subject responsible for the spontaneous synthetic activity required for empirical knowledge. It is the status of these two central assumptions that became the center of debate in much of post-Kantian philosophy.

Few of Kant's immediate successors found his critical project successful even if they were attracted to the broad contours of his approach (e.g. his Copernican turn)—indeed, the question of how best to "complete" Kant's turn shaped much of the debate in German idealism. As Habermas notes, Hegel's *Phenomenology of Spirit* nicely captured one form of this dissatisfaction: Kant's critique was not sufficiently radical and remained dogmatic. This dogmatism was reflected not only in Kant's appeal to a nature *an sich* (or "in-itself") which, though it could not be known, nonetheless played an indispensable role in his critical philosophy but also in his unsatisfactory demonstration of the fundamental concepts (or categories) that the transcendental subject contributed to knowledge. The striking and innovative feature of Hegel's critique, according to Habermas, is to have replaced the transcendental subject (and its synthetic activity) with a historically situated and developmental account of a collective "we" (what Hegel calls shapes of consciousness or spirit) that would perform the same function—namely, to provide an account of the legitimacy of our epistemic claims. On this reading, the distinct "shapes of consciousness" (*Gestalten des Bewusstsein*) presented in the *Phenomenology* represent various attempts to provide a self-validating account or warrant of knowledge (see Pinkard 1994). The transition (or dialectical movement) from one shape of consciousness to the next—what Hegel calls the process of "determinate negation"—is driven by the inability of any one shape to give an account of its own object—that is, to explain how the object presented in that shape of consciousness is known by means of the conceptual resources also available within that shape. This transition comes to rest (assuming that it does) in a shape (or ensemble of shapes) that is able to provide a stable and self-sufficient account of knowledge. It would then also avoid the charge of dogmatism. More importantly, without invoking the transcendental subject and its synthetic activity, it would provide a justification for the authority of a given constellation of claims to knowledge.

Habermas is in general quite sympathetic to Hegel's project in the *Phenomenlogy* and its rejection of a sharp demarcation between transcendental conditions and empirical knowledge.[9] It seems to preserve the "experience of reflection" without the dogmatic assumptions of Kant's original efforts at critique. However, like others, he also argues that some deep ambiguities are contained in the project. First, Habermas questions whether the phenomenological (or dialectical) movement Hegel employs does not already presuppose absolute knowledge (that is, Hegel's claim concerning the fundamental identity of thought and being or his claim that we can have knowledge of the world *an sich* or as it really is). If it does, as Habermas suspects, then there is the further suspicion that, contrary to Hegel's own claims, the Phenomenology is not really presuppositionless (KHI, 20–22). Second, Hegel understood his project as a rejection of epistemology and an attempt to demonstrate knowledge through the phenomenological method instead. But, according to Habermas, this is the source of a further deep ambiguity: For Hegel, in contrast to Kant, method cannot precede science—this is reflected in Hegel's critique of the Kantian understanding of knowledge as an instrument or organon as well as in his quip that Kant wanted to learn how to swim without getting wet. But if absolute knowledge is what one achieves at the end of the Phenomenology, how is the latter any less a method? In fact, Habermas suggests, Hegel comes to regard the Phenomenology as a "ladder which we must throw away after climbing it to the standpoint of the Logic" (KHI, 23).[10]

Finally, with some important qualifications to be discussed below, Habermas is also drawn to the materialist critique of Hegel offered by Marx and others. In its original form, this is Marx's claim in The German Ideology that it is not "consciousness that determines life, but life [or material conditions] that determines consciousness" (Marx 1994, 112). Stated in terms of Marx's mature theory, this is the claim that the level of productive forces within a given society determines the other features of social life including the political and intellectual (geistige) ideas that legitimate it. However, even this claim must be formulated with care since there is considerable debate about how "productive forces" are finally to be understood and, as Habermas argues in the subsequent chapter, if Marx's own understanding of "labor"—as one element of the productive forces—is understood too narrowly his claims about determination become less plausible. This suggests that within the tradition of Western Marxism with which Habermas identifies, the materialist critique of Hegel has to proceed with caution: "Ideas" as well as material "interests" can play a role in defining the "social relations of production" and thus too in shaping the forms of knowledge and authority in a given social form. But this is a version of a "materialist" epistemology that in the end may not require such a radical departure from Hegel—at least not on some readings.[11]

Habermas's reading of Marx is equally instructive and controversial. As with his reading of Hegel, it reveals as much about

Habermas's proposal for continuing epistemology as "critique" or a critical theory as it does about Marx's own views. On the one hand, as just noted, Habermas is quite sympathetic to Marx's materialist critique of Hegel. This means, first, that he regards historical and social change as the consequence of intended and unintended human activity (rather than the product of a supra-human mind or *Geist*) but, second and more importantly for our purposes, it means that the (species-wide) conditions for the material reproduction of society play a formative role in shaping our cognitive access to the world. Science and technological knowledge don't offer "pure"— that is, "interest-free"—insight into what nature is really like *an sich* or in-itself, but rather reflect the human interest in predicting and controlling the natural environment. This is what Habermas seeks to capture with the rather awkward phrase "[cognitive] synthesis through social labor" (KHI, 34, 47). The idea suggests the fairly strong anti-realist (even instrumentalist) thesis that our cognitive capacities are shaped and informed by the way in which societies materially reproduce themselves—a thesis Marx identified with historical materialism and his view that changing modes of production determine shapes of consciousness. Though Habermas (like Marx) rejects the relativism sometimes associated with this thesis—and as found, for example, in some versions of the sociology of knowledge—and speaks of "deep-seated anthropological interests," he also argues that these interests have emerged over the long course of human evolution and thus are not (ahistorical) modes of cognition secured *via* the accomplishments of a transcendental subject (as in Kant).

Despite his appreciation for Marx's "materialist" epistemology, Habermas is nonetheless critical of the more or less "official" interpretation of it and prefers the "unofficial" version that he believes can be found in Marx's more occasional writings (KHI, 51f.). This critique is reflected in three important breaks with and/ or corrections to Marx. First, Habermas suggests that Marx often confuses his own materialist critique of Hegel with natural science itself, suggesting that science (in the form of historical materialism) might come to replace philosophy (KHI, 44). This "positivistic self-misunderstanding" in Marx betrays the deeper critical aspect of his project. Philosophy cannot simply be replaced by the natural sciences; rather, philosophy as radical self-reflective "critique" must be preserved, even as it relinquishes any claim to "absolute knowledge" or ultimate foundations.

Second, Habermas is critical of the more economistic or technological determinist readings of Marx, such as those inspired by his programmatic formulation in the Preface to *A Contribution to the Critique of Political Economy* and developed most forcefully by G. A. Cohen in *Karl Marx's Theory of History* (1978).[12] Rather, Habermas argues that Marx's central notion of a mode of production (with its distinction between productive forces and social relations) must be interpreted in a manner that is more dynamic or "dialectical" and does not locate the source of social change exclusively in expanding productive forces. What Habermas calls the "institutional framework" (his preferred term for "social relations of production") has a more prominent role than the technological deterministic readings allow. Not only expanding productive forces but also a "moral struggle" for recognition, in the sense of a struggle for emancipation from social domination, can make its own contribution to social change and is not centered only around class struggle (KHI, 55). As Habermas argues elsewhere at greater length, Marx's notion of the social relations of production—which he identified exclusively with the property relations of ownership and wage-labor in capitalism—must be understood more broadly to include other norms and institutions and may even display a developmental logic of its own (CES, chaps. 3 and 4).

Finally, and relatedly, Habermas argues that forms of power and domination are not limited to those associated with the institution of wage labor. Under late or advanced capitalism, domination can assume a more explicit political form. This means, in particular, that the "critique of ideology" will have to be modified and less dependent on Marx's theory of value. It also implies that we cannot assume that the continued expansion of productive forces will inevitably produce a more free or just or rational society (KHI, 61). As Habermas formulated it elsewhere:

> Even if technical control of physical and social conditions for preserving life and making it less burdensome had attained the level that Marx expected would characterize a communist state

of development, it does not follow that they would be linked automatically with social emancipation of the sort intended by the thinkers of the Enlightenment in the eighteenth century and the Young Hegelian in the nineteenth.

(TRS, 58)

Or, in an even more dramatic formulation that utilizes his own distinction between "labor" (productive forces) and "interaction" (social relations): "Liberation from hunger and misery does not necessarily converge with liberation from servitude and degradation, for there is no automatic developmental relation between labor and interaction" (TP, 169).

In the last two parts of *Knowledge and Human Interests* Habermas develops the central ideas of his conception of epistemology (or philosophy) as critique (or a critical social theory). This consists centrally in his claim that knowledge is not to be equated with a "pure" or "disinterested" description or account of how things "really are." Rather, different bodies of knowledge have developed around different logics of inquiry where each logic is guided by a distinct "cognitive interest": an interest in technical control, an interest in hermeneutic understanding or communication, and an interest in emancipation from power. The first two interests are described as "deep-seated anthropological" interests, by which Habermas means that they are not attitudes or "stances" that could easily be set aside (TP, 8). Rather, they are orientations that have emerged in the history of the species and are intimately connected to the requirements for social reproduction (KHI, 196). He thus also speaks of them as "transcendental frameworks" of purposive-rational action and communication that, although the products of a contingent evolutionary process, nonetheless play "world-constitutive" roles (KHI, 69; Postscript, 185; R1, 241f.). Briefly stated, under the first cognitive interest, the world appears as object for manipulative intervention and control (1). Under the second cognitive interest, objects appear as symbolically constituted objects of interpretation and mutual understanding (2). Finally, the third interest—an interest in emancipation—has a more "derivative" status, though one that is not for that reason less important (Postscript, 176). On the contrary, Habermas describes it as an "interest of reason" (in a Kantian sense) and he sees it at work in forms of knowledge aimed at overcoming conditions of oppression and domination (as, for example, in Marx's critique of ideology) (3).

(1) The first cognitive interest is developed in connection with a reading of Charles Peirce's pragmatism. On Habermas's view, Peirce's achievement was to focus not on the conditions of possibility for valid scientific *statements* but on the conditions of possibility for scientific *inquiry* itself. Such inquiry, Peirce argued, is simply a more reflective and organized continuation of the attempt to remove doubt when it arises in ordinary life. It is thus not best understood as an attempt to provide an accurate description of how the world is—that is, as an exercise in pure theory—but as an attempt to overcome obstacles or to solve problems that initially arise in the context of ordinary life. This suggests that science and technology are not "interest-free" but rather closely tied to a basic interest in solving problems that arise in human attempts to utilize nature and others for various practical ends. The ambition of a "pure" theory is at most a (somewhat misconceived) abstraction from this basic interest in "coping."

Further, Pierce regarded it as a basic assumption of such inquiry that scientific progress is possible—that is, that solutions to problems can (and will) be found in the long run. At one level, this assumption concerning progress is entailed by his early consensus theory of truth: truth is simply defined as that which will meet with the agreement of the community of scientific inquiry in the long run. Progress is therefore understood not as getting descriptions of the world that are closer to how things actually are, but as the convergence of inquirers in seeking solutions to the problems they encounter. Peirce also associated this non-realist conception of truth with a pragmatist understanding of meaning: the meaning of a statement—for example, that diamonds are hard—is exhausted by statements about what would happen under various experimental conditions (e.g. that various objects would not be able to scratch it, etc.). Finally, these claims about the nature of inquiry and truth also provided Peirce with a way of conceiving reality or the world: the world is the set of objects constituted by this practical interest in prediction and control. It is the totality of what is understood from this "instrumental" or "purposive rational" orientation and so there is no need to additionally postulate a world *an sich*.

Habermas does not question Peirce's broader anti-realist account. Rather, he sides with Peirce in challenging more realistic interpretations of scientific inquiry. What he does question is whether this first "world-constituting" orientation provides a sufficient basis for understanding the practice of scientific inquiry itself. In particular, in a critique of Peirce's pragmatic theory of meaning, Habermas suggests that the technical interest in manipulation and control that lies behind his account of meaning cannot explain the practice of the community of inquirers itself insofar as they do not simply attempt to shape the behavior of their colleagues but to persuade them through reasons and arguments (KHI, 139). If that is correct—if, that is, the practice of reason-giving and argumentation cannot itself be explained in connection with a basic technical interest in manipulation and control—then space is opened for introducing a second basic interest. Thus, despite Peirce's role in directing attention to the centrality of scientific inquiry and introducing a "consensus" theory of truth, Habermas concludes that ultimately Peirce too succumbs to a "positivistic misunderstanding" and interprets his own project as continuous with the natural sciences.[13]

(2) For a clarification of the second cognitive interest Habermas turns to theorists more directly engaged in debates in the cultural or human sciences (*Geisteswissenschaften*) and, in particular, to the work of Wilhelm Dilthey. The central claim Habermas seeks to establish is that the interpretation of (symbolic) meaning (whether linguistic or not) proceeds according to a different "logic" than that of the natural (and behavioral) sciences. Whereas the latter, as we've seen, center upon explanation (itself understood instrumentally in terms of prediction and control), the former are more directly connected with the skills involved with natural language learning and communication. Habermas's claim is that in this case the aim or goal is (mutual) understanding, whether it is the situation of actual dialogue (in which both parties aim at coming to understanding about something) or situations of "virtual" dialogue where it is a question of understanding a text, a cultural artifact, or social practice. In any of these situations, the aim is to reach agreement (or mutual understanding) about some aspect or feature of the world and this requires shared or common access to the meaning it has for the

author or for the participants involved. This presents challenges that are different from the natural sciences and involve centrally what has been called the "double hermeneutic"—that is, the need to develop an interpretation of an interpretation, or to seek to recover the meaning it had for the participants (see Giddens 1976). In this connection Habermas also refers to the important notion of the hermeneutic circle (discussed by Dilthey and later developed in particular by Hans-Georg Gadamer): All interpretation involves a back-and-forth movement between a projected understanding of the meaning of the "text" as a whole and a more specific interpretation of an isolated passage or sequence of action (Gadamer 1960 [1989], 170). The dialectic of part and whole—or fitting individual interpretations with more general anticipations—is, for these theorists, central to the process of communication as well. But, as we will see, for Habermas these concerns also figure prominently in the attempt to develop "rational interpretations" of meaningful action (see Chapter 3).

Habermas defends two strong claims in this context. First, interpretation cannot simply be replaced by an "objective" description or explanation offered from a third-person or observer's perspective. The attempt to do so risks losing sight of the object of inquiry altogether—symbolic meaning. Interpretation cannot be completely replaced by explanation. Second, and as importantly, the sorts of explanations developed in the natural sciences themselves presuppose interpretation since the community of scientific inquirers must engage in communication about the meaning of their own scientific research. Among other things, for Habermas this also means that attempts to introduce an artificial or constructed formal language to eliminate the ambiguities and confusions found in ordinary language cannot ultimately succeed. However useful for some more limited aims, ordinary language—as the medium for communication and interpretation and reproduction of symbolic meaning—cannot be entirely eliminated or replaced.[14]

(3) Habermas's attempt to identify the first two cognitive interests already gives rise to an important question: If the type of knowledge involved in clarifying these two interests is itself not a case of either technical control or hermeneutic understanding, how should it be understood? In response Habermas introduces a third

cognitive interest. In addition to the first two interests and forms of inquiry associated with them, humans also have the capacity to reflect on the processes of inquiry themselves. This is precisely the "forgotten experience of reflection" Habermas suggests was lost with the rise of positivism but that had been an important part of Kant's original project of a critique of reason. Our capacity for reflection on the processes of human inquiry thus points to a third cognitive interest that—following Kant—Habermas calls an "interest of reason" (KHI, 212).

In returning to this Kantian (and post-Kantian) insight, Habermas also invokes a rich (and almost certainly overtaxed) notion of self-reflection. On the one hand, self-reflection refers to the sort of transcendental inquiry into conditions of knowledge introduced by Kant and (in a modified form) this is also what Habermas appeals to in establishing claims about the "transcendental framework" associated with the first two cognitive interests. But, in this same tradition, self-reflection is also the process through which an agent becomes more explicitly aware of her capacity to act freely or autonomously. Further, for Kant and especially for those who attempted to "complete" his system after him, this second form of self-reflection is both a presupposition of and necessary condition for the first. As Habermas points out, Fichte's emphasis on the "primacy of practical reason" was intended to show that our capacity for reflection on the conditions of knowledge (the first sense of self-reflection) already presupposes or entails that we are free or autonomous (KHI, 205; Neuhouser 1990, 47). Habermas accordingly describes this third cognitive interest both as the capacity for reflection and as an interest in emancipation and autonomy. Moreover, this interest in emancipation is not incidental to reason or an indication of its corruption. Rather, reason is interested and the unity of freedom and reason is revealed in our capacity for self-reflection (now combining the two senses together).

What is novel and interesting about Habermas's interpretation of these early debates among Kant and his successors are not the connections he finds among the notions of self-reflection, reason, and freedom or the claim about the "primacy of practical reason." These are now more familiar points in the secondary literature, itself the result of criticisms of more narrowly "epistemological" readings of this tradition (see especially Neiman 1994, Beiser 1987, and Förster 2012). What is especially significant for the development of Habermas's own project is the way in which he links the three cognitive interests together. On the one hand, the interests of technical control and interpretive understanding are only "unambiguously comprehended" as cognitive interests "in connection with the emancipatory cognitive interest of rational reflection" (KHI, 198, 289). What Habermas apparently means by this is that these two interests—and also their "knowledge-constitutive" status—are only actually disclosed in the "self-reflective" insight afforded by the third interest. That is, we gain insight into these forms of inquiry through an exercise of the self-reflection associated with the third interest. Moreover, since the first two interests are established in this way, Habermas maintains that this also shows them to be not "mere" interests but rational interests. The "experience of reflection" associated with the third interest thus serves to legitimate the first two as sources of rational knowledge rather than arbitrary or particular preferences. The self-reflection identified with the third interest establishes a connection between reason and all three interests (KHI, 212).

The introduction of the third cognitive interest also gives rise to a challenge from another direction. Whereas the first two interests could plausibly claim at least some basis in well-established institutions and practices required for social reproduction, the interest in emancipation evidently lacks such a pedigree. More specifically, its origin is not found in necessary requirements for social reproduction but rather in the experiences of suffering and frustration that are responses to power and domination (which Habermas presumably does not think are necessary however ubiquitous they may be) (KHI, 310). It is also less clear what specific forms of knowledge might be developed in connection with this third interest and constitute a "critical science" or "critical theory." Habermas clearly does not have in mind simply transcendental inquiry of a Kantian sort. Rather his two examples are Marx's critique of ideology and Freud's model of analysis. What distinguishes these types of inquiry from the forms of knowledge associated with the first two interests is the fact that the hypotheses found in them are concerned specifically with the sources or causes of disturbances or distortions to ordinary interactions—that is, socially superfluous or unnecessary forms of power or domination—and the fact that they crucially involve hypothetical projections about what social actors could (or would) endorse under conditions free of such power or domination.

Habermas is aware of the more precarious status of this third interest. Its own "logic of inquiry" is not well-established (see also Geuss 1981, 88f.). He suggests that Freud's model of psychoanalysis, at least on its best metatheoretical interpretation—one freed, that is, from its own "scientistic" understanding—offers an important example. The idea of critique contained in that theory—and also at least some interpretations of Marx's notion of ideology-critique—involves the idea of "explanatory understanding" whose ultimate confirmation remains dependent on final acceptance by the subject-object (whether it is the patient or a social class) (KHI, 272; TP, 30–31). I won't pursue the details of this type of inquiry further here, since Habermas largely set aside this model in his later work. In fact, in his later work claims initially associated with this third interest (in emancipation) are largely subsumed under arguments about what is already implicit in language and communication and so are more immediately connected with the second cognitive interest. This elision of the distinction between the second and third cognitive interest can already be discerned in a passage from his inaugural address in Frankfurt in 1965: "The human interest in autonomy and responsibility is not mere fancy, for it can be apprehended *a priori*. What raises us out of nature is the only thing whose nature we can know: language. Through its structure, autonomy and responsibility are posited for us" (KHI, 314). That is, given their capacity for linguistic interaction or "communicative competence," social actors are also already implicitly aware of their status as free agents. In his subsequent writings Habermas relies more directly upon the idealizing suppositions of communicative action as a resource for critique and largely drops reference to a third cognitive interest.

IV. Conclusion: Challenges for epistemology as "critique"

Not surprisingly, many challenges and criticisms have been raised in connection with the ambitious project outlined in *Knowledge and Human*

Interests. Some of these center on Habermas's controversial interpretations of other theorists, while others focus on the more substantive claims of his own proposals. I will limit my attention here to three criticisms of the substantive claims since they are most relevant for his understanding of Kantian pragmatism.

(1) As mentioned above, Habermas combined two distinct notions of critique within his third cognitive interest: the idea of self-reflection found in the Kantian (and post-Kantian) tradition and the idea of self-reflection in Marxism and psychoanalysis with its connotations of emancipation from various forms of domination. However, as even sympathetic critics pointed out, this combination is problematic. The sort of self-reflection associated with the Kantian tradition is a critical reflection on the conditions of possible knowledge and one of its principal manifestations is various "transcendental arguments" whose aim or goal is to refute a skeptical challenge by showing that the position from which the challenge is made must already presuppose something that can be used to disarm the challenge. However, it is not at all obvious that this form of self-reflection has anything in common with the sort of self-reflection invoked in claims about a knowledge that will enable individuals to overcome hitherto unacknowledged forms of domination. This is the kind of self-knowledge, for example, that can lead an individual to free himself from the force that an unconscious desire might have over his behavior.

In a subsequent response to this criticism Habermas conceded that he had too quickly joined these two notions of self-reflection and proposed distinguishing more clearly between "reconstruction" and "critique" (Postscript, 182; R1). "Reconstruction" then refers to the type of transcendental (or "quasi-transcendental") inquiry of the first sort, while "critique" refers to the self-knowledge that would lead to emancipation. But if the two notions of reflection are sharply distinguished, problems for his idea of a critical social theory arise.

"Reconstruction" sounds much more like a fairly neutral (or "interest-free") theoretical enterprise (and Habermas basically treats it that way) and so would deny such inquiry its tie to an interest in emancipation (McCarthy 1978, 94f.). On the other hand, divorced from this more epistemological context, the second idea of reflection as critique of domination seems to lose its own claim to status as a distinct cognitive interest (rather than a practical task that one may or may not choose to care about or pursue). The idea of critique, in short, loses any epistemological grounding and with that too any claim about the "primacy of practical reason." In response to these criticisms, Habermas also seems to have accepted this division of labor and the consequences that follow from it, at least with respect to claims about the status of critique. But, in a later reply to a volume celebrating the thirtieth anniversary of *Knowledge and Human Interests* he still insists that the idea of a cognitive interest in emancipation could be defended even if by slightly different means (Habermas 2000a).

(2) One of the more distinctive features of Habermas's "transcendental pragmatism" in *Knowledge and Human Interests* is the way in which he proposes to combine transcendental inquiry and naturalism or, as he has also expressed it, join Kant and Darwin (PT, 45; BNR, 170). On the one hand, the cognitive interests and "transcendental framework" to which they give rise are the contingent outcome of the natural and social evolution of the species (KHI, 210–211, 287). On the other hand, in good Kantian fashion, the only nature and history we can know is that which is disclosed *via* those cognitive interests. This proposal, however, creates some distinct problems and challenges.

First, there is an epistemological worry. The attempt to combine transcendental knowledge and empirical knowledge—or claims about the conditions of possibility of "objective" or valid knowledge and claims about what is known under those conditions—suggests that the "transcendental framework" is itself an element within the world that can be known by the empirical sciences. Indeed, this seems to be exactly what Habermas claims (see Postscript, 165; KHI, 287). Initially, this might look like an improvement upon Kant since for him the transcendental conditions remained radically distinct from objects of empirical knowledge. But it is not easy to see how the transcendental framework that is constitutive for empirical or "inner-worldly" knowledge can at the same time be an inner-worldly object of that knowledge.

Second, the claim that the cognitive interests and transcendental framework are the products of our natural and social evolutionary history raises ontological problems as well (McCarthy 1978, 115f.). On the one hand, nature is said to be the source or origin of our cognitive interests and the framework to which they give rise:

> Since it is posited with the behavioral system of instrumental action, this framework cannot be conceived as the determination of a transcendental consciousness as such. Rather, it is dependent on the organic constitution of a species that is compelled to reproduce its life through purposive-rational action.
>
> (KHI, 133–134)

But at the same time, again in Kantian fashion, he claims that the only nature we can know is limited by those cognitive interests. This will require Habermas to make a distinction between a nature for us or that can be known and a nature *an sich* or in-itself. It also suggests that his attempt to ground and legitimate our cognitive faculties has an element of contingency or arbitrariness to it. At one level, these might not seem like especially surprising claims. But the distinction between a nature in itself and a nature for us presents a special challenge for a "transcendental pragmatism" that wants to distinguish itself both from epistemological realism, on the one hand, and more radical forms of relativism, on the other. It would also seem to present a challenge for Habermas's claim that it is the socio-cultural lifeworld that takes over the role Kant had assigned to the transcendental subject (or unity of apperception) (TJ, 19, 27; PT, 43). To distinguish that claim from, say, the more recent proposals of evolutionary psychology, it would seem that one would have to be able to distinguish more clearly between the contributions of nature and those of society. But if the transcendental conditions are the result of an unknowable nature *an sich* it is not clear how those disputes could be adjudicated.

Despite his acknowledgment of these important challenges, Habermas continues to endorse a form of transcendental pragmatism. He cites approvingly a passage from the physicist Carl von Weisäcker:

> Firstly, by being the act of a subject, every "objective" cognitive insight exists only as a result of certain 'subjective' conditions. Secondly, we must ask what we can know about the subject of

cognition when we consider that it lives in the world of objects, being one of its parts.

(Postscript, 163)

But while this passage clearly states his position, it does not obviously indicate how the challenges to it might be addressed. Nevertheless, Habermas's considered judgment seems to be that, despite the problems, this brand of "transcendental pragmatism" is still preferable to any of the alternatives on offer (R1, 242; AS, 152).

(3) Finally, criticisms have also been directed at the sharp division between the natural and human sciences implied by Habermas's distinction between the first two cognitive interests (Hesse 1982; Vogel 1996; Rouse 1991). On the one hand, he claimed that we could only know the natural world *via* our first technical interest in control. This thesis was, in part, intended to buttress a claim to the "objectivity" of scientific knowledge from more particular interests by grounding it in an "anthropologically deep-seated" interest. At the same time, however, he argued, as we saw in his treatment of Peirce, that the scientific community could not account for its own "logic of inquiry" by reference to this technical interest alone. As others have pointed out, this should lead to the conclusion that the natural sciences and human sciences cannot be so sharply separated: Scientific inquiry involves practices that are themselves founded on intersubjective meaning and open to contestation about their value and significance, as Habermas had argued earlier in his critique of Popper (Adorno 1976, 152f.). Thus, Habermas did not seem to draw all of the "post-Kuhnian" consequences that some of his own arguments anticipated.

Beginning in the early 1970s Habermas quite intentionally set aside these controversies and turned to a more direct engagement with substantive issues in social theory. Indeed, he specifically renounced a preference for an epistemological account or grounding in favor of a critical social theory that could be elucidated—but not grounded—in connection with a substantive account of social action. As he remarks in the 1982 Preface to *On the Logic of the Social Sciences* (1967 [1988]),

I was convinced for a time that the project of a critical social theory had to prove itself, in the first instance, from a methodological and epistemological standpoint. This was reflected in the fact that I held out the prospect of "grounding the social sciences in a theory of language" in the preface to the 1970 edition of this work. This is a prospect I no longer entertain. The theory of communicative action that I have since put forward is not a continuation of methodology by other means. It breaks with the primacy of epistemology and treats the presupposition of action oriented to mutual understanding independently of the transcendental preconditions of knowledge.

(LSS, xiv)

Nonetheless, when Habermas does eventually return to a discussion of epistemological issues in his writings in the 1990s it is not obvious that his position on these questions has significantly changed. However problematic, he still defends a "Kantian pragmatism" that seeks to combine Kant and Darwin (TJ, 22) and that insists on the interplay between transcendental (or world-disclosing) knowledge and inner-worldly learning (TJ, 34).

Further reading

McCarthy (1978) is still the best and most thorough treatment of Habermas's early development. Thompson and Held (1982) contains a very helpful collection of articles on KHI. See also Honneth (1991) for a general overview and the essays in Bernstein (1985). Outhwaite (2009) also offers a solid introduction to the early Habermas.

Notes

1 Geuss notes this same pivot in Habermas's work but (I think) mistakenly describes it as a shift from "contextualism" and immanent critique to transcendental critique (Geuss 1981, 64 n.25; see also AS, 8 and R1, 253).
2 In his very helpful introduction, Dews (1986) points out that Habermas refers to Merleau-Ponty's Marxism as expressing the same fallibilist idea of a philosophy of history as his own (AS, 9); for a discussion of the idea of totality within Western Marxism, see Jay (1984).
3 Roughly, Habermas argued that (1) more orthodox interpretations of the labor theory of value, including Marx's own, failed to consider how advances in science and technology, or what Habermas called "second-order productive

labor," altered the way in which value could be determined and that (2) changes in "late capitalism" blurred the possibility for any sharp distinction between the productive forces and the institutional framework in modern societies (see TP, 228f.; TRS, 104f.). For a detailed criticism of Habermas's interpretation of Marx, see Postone (1993).

4 Specter (2010) has a very good discussion of the importance of the Marxist/ social democratic legal theorist Abendroth on Habermas's thought at this time. His valuable book, which emphasizes the importance of legal debates on the early formation of Habermas's thinking, unfortunately misses his attempt to construct a "philosophy of history with practical intent" which, I am suggesting, is central in this period.

5 For some of the challenges see Gardner (2007); for another defense, which makes reference to Habermas's project, see Sacks (2000, 215f.).

6 Despite the marked contrast between the extremely vibrant period of philosophical activity from the publication of Kant's *Critique* to Hegel's death (1832) and what followed after the mid-century, Habermas's claim is overstated. It ignores, for example, the influence of Schopenhauer in this period. See Schnädelbach (1991) and Beiser (2014) for a more complete overview.

7 There are of course echoes in this passage of Adorno's famous quip in *Negative Dialectics* that philosophy "lives on because the moment to realize it was missed" (Adorno 1973, 3)—itself a reference to Marx's "Theses on Feuerbach" that philosophy only interprets the world when the point is to change the world. In both, it is a question of what form or status philosophy can retain after Marx's (not entirely successful) critique of Hegel.

8 See MCCA, chap. 1; in this sense Nielsen misses the point in his otherwise instructive discussion when he suggests (against Habermas) that philosophy offers no further perspective or insight than that of "any reflective all-purpose intellectual" (Nielsen 1994, 20). Habermas does not in fact think that there is any important difference between the philosopher and the reflective practitioner. Habermas's target is those who maintain that philosophy offers a privileged perspective uniquely different from that of the reflective citizen. Of course, training in one or another of the sciences brings particular and specialized insights but it does not afford a privileged insight which is not already available to competent actors engaged in social practices. This is also a Kantian theme; it also shows, I think, the proximity of Habermas to Rorty and other pragmatists, despite their disagreement about what sort of knowledge actors possess; for a recent and quite comparable description of the role of philosophy, see Kitcher (2011, 254).

9 In general Habermas has a very ambivalent attitude toward Hegel's project: he appreciates the critique of a strong transcendental/empirical distinction, but he is highly suspicious of the "reinstatement" of philosophy in the form of absolute idealism—see also his later essay in TJ, chap. 4: "From Kant to Hegel and back again."

10 The relation of the *Phenomenology* to Hegel's "system" and *Science of Logic* is a controversial topic in the secondary literature; for a helpful survey and view different from Habermas's own, see Pippin (1993); see also Fulda (2011).

11 This remark is meant only as a gesture toward the extensive debate on how to understand the relation between Hegel and Marx. For less "idealistic" readings of Hegel than this gloss suggests, see Pinkard (1994) and Honneth (2014).

12 For a critique of Cohen that complements Habermas's own "unofficial" reading of Marx, see Miller (1984, chap. 5) and Lukes (1983).

13 Habermas offers a more sympathetic reading of Peirce in PT, chap. 5.

14 This was the early project of Rudolph Carnap and other members of the Vienna Circle whom Habermas also criticized earlier in the "positivist disputes": see Adorno (1976).

Three
The Theory of Communicative Action
Habermas's model of a critical social science

I. Introduction

In his magnum opus, *The Theory of Communicative Action* (hereafter, TCA), Habermas introduces a new outline and foundation for a critical theory of society (TCA 1: xxxix). In contrast to *Knowledge and Human Interests* (as well as the early Horkheimer of *Critical Theory*), he no longer insists that a critical theory must begin with an epistemological justification of its basic conceptual framework. Rather, it can proceed directly on the basis of substantive claims about social action and, in this respect, will also be more in keeping with the approach of classical sociology (especially Max Weber). The merits of the theory will then have to be assessed by the insights it provides rather than by its epistemological grounding.[1] Further, though TCA is still presented as a form of immanent criticism (in that it exposes limits and possibilities available to a society given the processes of rationalization or "reason" at work within it), it no longer proceeds on the basis of juxtaposing the ideals of bourgeois society (e.g. freedom and equality) to actual practices since "bourgeois consciousness has [in the meantime] become cynical" (CES, 97). Neo-liberals (and others) can too easily either dismiss those ideals or reinterpret them according to their own ends. For this reason a deeper framework for social analysis and critique must be developed even while (in keeping with his more modest or "sobered" view of philosophy as "critique") Habermas still resists the project of "ultimate grounding" (see Chapter 8). The general aim is to show how the critical theorist has tools for rational critique precisely because those rational criteria are deep features of the object domain itself: there is, in other words, a "reason in history" (or society) that is available for the purposes of normative criticism.[2] Finally, as he indicates in the last section, TCA should provide at least a broad outline of the potential for a more rational society, even while it resists a direct or immediate link between "theory" and "practice" in the sense of concrete proposals for action (see TJ, chap. 7).

Habermas now hopes to achieve these goals primarily through a re-reading of classical social theory. Max Weber plays a prominent role, but so too do other major figures such as Marx, Emile Durkheim, and Talcott Parsons. Stated in very broad terms, the aim of the first volume is to present (through a re-reading of Weber) a notion of social reason or rationality that is tied to the basic dispositions or competences of social actors as they must understand themselves. The purpose of the second volume is then to integrate that view of social rationality into a broader "two-level" conception of society as "lifeworld" and "system" so that current social pathologies can be appropriately diagnosed. Actors experience the modern world as a "loss of meaning and freedom" (Weber), but the diagnosis of the causes of that experience requires a theoretical perspective that is able to reach beyond the intuitive know-how of those actors. As was the case for Marx, Habermas still tends to see societal rationalization (as well as its pathologies) as triggered by developments in material reproduction or the economy, but in contrast to Marx he does not restrict rationality to developments in technology and the instrumental control of nature and the pathologies produced by such growth are no longer manifest only in class-conflicts (TCA 2: 350; Honneth 2009, chap. 2). Also in keeping with Weber's approach, TCA begins with a set of (1) metatheoretical, (2) methodological, and (3) substantive claims.

(1) Like Weber who began by introducing a distinction between formal and substantive (or value) rationality and a parallel distinction between instrumental (or "means-ends") action and a more traditional notion of "objective" or "value-based" action, Habermas begins with a set of metatheoretical reflections that also yields a typology of action. His basic distinction is between "consent-oriented" (or communicative) and "success-oriented" (or purposive-rational) actions. Within the latter class he distinguishes further between

strategic and instrumental action. Instrumental actions are goal-oriented interventions in the physical world. They can be appraised from the standpoint of efficiency and described as the following of technical rules. Strategic action, by contrast, is action that aims at influencing others for the purpose of achieving some end. It too can be appraised in terms of its efficiency and described with the tools of game theory and theories of rational choice. Many instrumental actions can also be strategic, and some forms of strategic action may be instrumental. Communicative action, however, constitutes an independent and distinct type of social action. The goal or *telos* of communicative action is not expressed in an attempt to influence others, but in the attempt to reach an agreement or mutual understanding (*Verständigung*) with one or more actors about something in the world (TCA 1: 86). Thus, while all action is goal-oriented in a broad sense, in the case of communicative action any further ends the agent may have are subordinated to the goal of achieving a mutually shared definition of the agent's life-worldly situation through a cooperative process of interpretation. It is this latter notion of communicative action based on a (traditionally secured or discursively achieved) consensual agreement that lies at the core of his theory. In acting communicatively, individuals more or less naively accept as valid the various claims raised with their utterance or action and mutually suppose that each is prepared to provide reasons for them should the validity of those claims be questioned. In a slightly more technical (and controversial) sense, and one tied more specifically to modern structures of rationality, Habermas also holds that individuals who act communicatively at least tacitly aim at reaching understanding about something in the world by relating their interpretations to three general types of validity claims that are constitutive for three basic types of speech acts: a claim to truth raised in constative speech acts, a claim to normative rightness raised in regulative speech acts, and a claim to authenticity or truthfulness raised in expressive speech acts (TCA 1, 319f.). Since Habermas also argues that any speech act potentially involves all three claims, his point here is best understood to mean that one validity claim *predominates* in each type of speech act. Similarly, since actions are often "overdetermined" with respect to their meaning, Habermas's claim is best read as holding that an actor can sincerely and consciously prioritize only one general motivation—e.g. communicative or strategic—at any one time (R2, 291n.63).

(2) At a *methodological* level, this analysis of social action underscores the need for an interpretive or *Verstehende* approach in the social sciences. The requirement of *Verstehen* arises because the objects that the social sciences study—actions and their products—are embedded in "complexes of meaning" (*Sinnzusammenhänge*) that can be understood by the social inquirer only as he or she relates them to his or her own pre-theoretical knowledge as a member of the lifeworld. This, in turn, gives rise to the "disquieting thesis" that the interpretation of action cannot be separated from the interpreter's taking a position on the validity of the claims explicitly or implicitly connected with the action (TCA 1, 107). The process of identifying the reasons for an action unavoidably draws one into the process of assessment in which the inquirer must adopt the perspective of a (at least virtual) participant. Understanding the reasons for action requires taking a position on the validity of those reasons according to our own lights, and that means (at least initially) setting aside an external or "third person" perspective in favor or an internal or "second person" perspective in which both actor and interpreter belong to the same "universe of discourse." It is in this way that Habermas is able to connect the notion of social rationality more generally with his specific claim that reason is (most fundamentally) a dispositional property of agents to challenge and negotiate the claims to validity raised in their speech and action. To speak of a "reason in history" is thus, in the final instance, to make a claim about the rational capacities of speaking and acting subjects or, to use slightly different terms, it is to make a claim about the normative statuses the social actors—as well as their interpreters—must mutually ascribe to one another.[3]

However, despite this emphasis on social (or communicative) rationality with its ties to criticizable validity claims, Habermas does not think that society should be viewed as a sort of large-scale debating club. Actors' interpretations are generally taken for granted and form part of an implicit background of knowledge and practices that constitute what he calls (following Edmund Husserl and Alfred Schutz) the "lifeworld." Though this background is therefore in some sense common or shared, it is not always (or even for the most part) the product of a discursively achieved agreement. It may also be the result of a more traditionally secured agreement (as when norms are more or less passively accepted) or the result of a disturbance to the communicative structure in which one or more actors are coerced. Further, social integration can in large measure also be achieved when the task of coordinating action is shifted to mechanisms that do not depend directly on the intentions of actors (consider, for example, Smith's "invisible hand" of the market). In those cases what Habermas calls "systems integration" refers to the way that a society (or one of its subsystems) can be stabilized not through the consensual agreement of social actors but through the outcomes or consequences of their decisions (see Lockwood 1992; Mouzelis 1991). Habermas's introduction of a "two-level" concept of society—along with his distinction between society as lifeworld and society as system—is done in order to secure access methodologically to this dominant feature of modern societies (see below).

Already in *On the Logic of the Social Sciences* (1967) Habermas described his approach as "a hermeneutically enlightened and historically oriented functionalism" that combined interpretive and causal (or functional) approaches (LSS, 187). In this sense Habermas again reflects a classical approach within the social sciences (including Marxism and critical theory) against both reductionist approaches (including various forms of naturalism and systems theory) and more radical hermeneutic and/or postmodern approaches that are generally less sanguine about the place of nomological (causal or functional) explanations in the social sciences. As Weber also maintained, the social sciences make use of both "rational interpretations" of actors' subjective meanings or intentions that can be worked up into broader generalizations *and* causal explanations that acquire their explanatory power by locating those generalizations in a wider theoretical framework (such as, for example, systems theory). As we saw in the last chapter, a hybrid form of explanatory understanding was an important aspect of a critical theory in which the theorist hypothesized both a goal or end-state and a causal explanation for the failure to attain it (see also LSS, 187).

Although the prominence of this hybrid form of explanatory understanding recedes significantly in Habermas's later writings, the more general strategy of combining action theoretic and functional (or systems-theoretic) components remains and it is an important feature of *The Theory of Communicative Action*. As he puts it,

> My guiding idea is that, on the one hand, the dynamics of development are steered by [systemic] imperatives issuing from problems of self-maintenance, that is, problems of materially reproducing the lifeworld; but that, on the other hand, this societal development draws upon structural possibilities and is subject to structural limitations that, with the rationalization of the lifeworld, undergo systematic change in dependence upon corresponding learning processes.
>
> (TCA 2, 148)

Despite the different vocabulary, this idea can easily be translated back into the language of his earlier project, developments in the "productive forces" may be an initiating cause of social disturbances or "crises," but the "productive relations" (or what Habermas also called the "institutional framework") of society has its own developmental logic that imposes its own possibilities and constraints for resolving those crises.

(3) Finally, beyond these metatheoretical and methodological concerns, *The Theory of Communicative Action* presents an interpretation of modern society as the outcome of a process of rationalization and societal differentiation. Rationalization, like Weber, refers most generally to the extension of calculation, methodical treatment and systematic ordering to ever more aspects of social life (e.g. science, law, business, and even religion and the arts). Societal differentiation involves two related processes: first, the (functional) separation of the economic and political subsystems from society as a whole and, second, within the complex of institutions devoted to symbolic reproduction (or what he calls the lifeworld), the differentiation among those institutions devoted, respectively, to the tasks of the transmission of knowledge and interpretive patterns (*culture*), social integration ("*society*" in the narrower sense of normative orders), and individual socialization (*personality*). Finally, within *culture* one can also trace a differentiation among the three value spheres of science and technology, law and morality, and art and aesthetic criticism, as each becomes independent from the others and develops

its own internal standards of critique and evaluation. This interpretation of modern society as a process of rationalization is, of course, not new. However, in contrast to the classical theorists who generally viewed it as primarily threatening social life—Weber's "iron cage," Marx's thesis of reification, or Durkheim's analysis of *anomie*—Habermas emphasizes the potential for emancipation also made available. Social pathologies are not the inevitable consequence of rationalization *per se* but result rather from a lopsided process in which the market and administrative state invade the lifeworld, displacing modes of integration based on communicative reason with their own form of functional rationality. Habermas describes this process in dramatic terms as the "colonization of the lifeworld." An important task of a critical theory is to describe this process of colonization and indicate the ways in which various social movements can be construed as responses to it. In what follows I will first outline in some detail Habermas's notion of the rational explanation of action and its place in the broadly interpretive (or hermeneutic) approach in the social sciences (II); I will then consider its relation to his central idea of the sociocultural lifeworld (III). In the final section I discuss Habermas's idea of a reconstructive science and his introduction of a two-level concept of society, that is, one that makes use of both action-theoretic and systems-theoretic perspectives in order to illuminate what he describes as the "colonization of the lifeworld" and the prospects for a more rational social order (IV).

II. The rational explanation of action and interpretive social science

Despite his critical remarks about the limits of hermeneutics within the social sciences, Habermas defends a broadly interpretive approach since, according to him, the primary field of inquiry or object domain is the "symbolically pre-structured reality"—the socio-cultural lifeworld—which is constituted by the meaningful behavior (or action) of its members (and which, in turn, constitutes them) (TCA 2, 145; PDM, 342). Such an approach gives rise to the problem of *Verstehen* (or interpretive understanding) since the interpreter must not only learn the rules and practices of the community of inquirers

to which she belongs, but must also become familiar with the rules
and practices that define the particular lifeworld (or segment of it)
that she is interpreting. Following Peter Winch, Anthony Giddens
refers to this interpretive requirement as the "double hermeneutic"
(Giddens 1976; see Taylor 1985, 111; Celikates 2006, 27); according
to Habermas, it provides the principal basis for the methodical
distinction between the natural and social sciences.

> The problem of *Verstehen* is of methodological importance in the
> humanities and social sciences primarily because the scientist
> cannot gain access to a symbolically prestructured reality
> through *observation* alone, and because *understanding meaning*
> [*Sinnverstehen*] cannot be methodically brought under control in
> the same way as can observation in the course of experimentation.
> The social scientist basically has no other access to the lifeworld
> than the social-scientific layman does. He must already belong
> in a certain way to the lifeworld whose elements he wishes to
> describe. In order to describe them, he must understand them;
> in order to understand them, he must be able in principle to
> participate in their production; and participation presupposes
> that one belongs.
>
> (TCA 1, 108)

The requirement of *Verstehen* thus arises because the objects that the
social sciences study are "complexes of meaning" (*Sinnzusammenhänge*)
that actors produce through their "interpretive accomplishments"
(and on which they in turn rely for those accomplishments) and
because the inquirer can only understand these meaning-complexes
by systematically relating them to his or her own pretheoretical
knowledge as a member of his own lifeworld (TCA 1, 110, 132–133).
Without such an interpretation of the meaning that social agents
connect with their action, the objects of social-scientific inquiry cannot
even come into view.[4]

Habermas further contends that a recognition of the fuller
implications of an interpretive approach yields "methodologically
shocking consequences" (TCA 1, 111). In particular, it gives rise to
the "disquieting thesis" that the interpretation of action cannot be
separated from the interpreter's taking a position on the validity of

the claims explicitly or implicitly connected with the action (TCA 1, 107). The interpretation of action (as well as its products) requires making clear the reasons that actors would give for their action (or could possibly give within their social and historical setting); but,

> [o]ne can understand reasons only to the extent that one understand why they are or are not sound, or why in a given case a decision as to whether reasons are good or bad is not (yet) possible. An interpreter cannot, therefore, interpret expressions connected through criticizable validity claims with a potential of reasons (and thus represent knowledge) without taking a position on them.
>
> (TCA 1, 116)

The interpretation of action unavoidably draws the inquirer into the process of identifying the agent's reasons for the action, but reasons can appear as reasons (as opposed to local causal determinants) only to the extent that one adopts the performative attitude of a communicative participant.[5] Understanding the reasons for action requires taking a position on the validity or warrantedness of those reasons according to our own lights, and that means (at least initially) setting aside an external or "third-person" perspective in favor of an internal or "first-person" perspective in which both actor and interpreter belong to the same "universe of discourse."

> Now the interesting point is that reasons are of a special nature. They can always be expanded into arguments which we then understand only when we *recapitulate* (*nachvollziehen*) them in the light of some standards of rationality. This "recapitulation" requires a reconstructive activity in which we bring into play our own standards of rationality, at least intuitively. From the perspective of the participant, however, one's own rationality standards must always claim general validity; this claim to general validity can be restricted only subsequently, from the perspective of a third person. In short, the interpretive reconstruction of reasons makes it necessary for us to place "their" standards in relation to "ours," so that in the case of a

contradiction we either revise our preconceptions or relativize "their" standards of rationality against "ours."

(QC, 204)

It would seem that this strong formulation of the implications of an interpretive approach would preclude the possibility of acquiring any objective knowledge in the social sciences or of developing a general social theory. Yet Habermas criticizes hermeneutic approaches like Hans-Georg Gadamer's precisely for having abandoned such aims for social science and he poses his own project in terms of the following question: "How can the objectivity of understanding be reconciled with the performative attitude of one who participates in a process of reaching understanding?" (TCA 1, 112).[6] At the same time, however, Habermas also rejects the solution offered by Schutz (and adopted by some ethnomethodologists), whereby the objectivity of interpretation is assured by the requirement that the social inquirer adopt a "theoretical attitude" detached from the practical interests of the everyday actor (TCA 1, 122; see also Schutz 1962, 63 and Pollner 1987).

Habermas's own alternative is to claim that the conditions for the objectivity of interpretation (and even the formation of law-like generalizations) can already be found within the "general structures of the processes of reaching understanding" that the interpreter shares with the actors in the object domain (TCA 1, 123). At times, Habermas's position seems like a case of wanting to have his cake and eat it too, as when he is obliged to distinguish between the objective knowledge available from within a performative attitude (or the participant's perspective) from an "objectivating" (third-person) knowledge and argue that the performative attitude adopted by the social inquirer makes possible objective interpretations— "subject to the withdrawal, as it were, of his qualities as an actor" (TCA 1, 114, 116).[7] But the intent of his position seems fairly clear: On the one hand, consistent with the pragmatism I outlined in Chapter 1, Habermas resists the idea that there is a neutral or disinterested point of view available to the "pure" theorist (Alfred Schutz and, before him, Husserl). On the other hand, acknowledging this situation does not mean that the inquirer must relinquish any claim to objective understanding—in the sense that some interpretations may make better sense of the larger social situation than others—or relinquish all forms of "reflective self-control." Rather, the criteria for such evaluations—so Habermas claims—can be derived from standards of rationality that are contained within the most general structures of communication and "it is this potential for critique built into communicative action itself that the social scientist, by entering into the contexts of everyday action as a virtual participant, can systematically exploit and bring into play outside these contexts and against their particularity" (TCA 1, 121). This position permits Habermas to make the further claim that, without relinquishing the priority of the participants' perspective, the inquirer can also propose *either* a reconstruction of criteria of rationality that are commonly shared by the inquirer and those in the object-domain *or*—and more ambitiously—a reconstruction of how competing criteria of rationality might be connected (by the inquirer) *via* plausible claims about social evolution and developmental logics. I will return to this last claim in the discussion of Habermas's notion of reconstructive science below after some further remarks on his general interpretive approach.

Without disputing the "methodologically shocking consequences" of his approach or denying some of the paradoxes to which it leads, I want to suggest that Habermas's "methodological dualism" and defense of an interpretive approach are nonetheless more plausible than some of his critics have supposed (Rouse 1991; Okrent 1984). As a first step in defending this claim, I suggest that Habermas's model of the "rational interpretation" of action can be seen as roughly analogous to the type of action explanation offered by Donald Davidson. Like Habermas, Davidson argues that the explanation of action is a normative (or evaluative) enterprise and so requires that the interpreter make use of the same standards of rationality she would employ in providing an account of her own action. However, Davidson's interpretive strategy is limited by its adherence to an overly restricted model of rationality and, contrary to his own claims, is thus unable adequately to take into account the social (or intersubjective) dimension of rationality. This may be due in turn to a strong form of naturalism or physicalism, not shared by Habermas, that motivates Davidson's (quasi-reductionist) program of radical interpretation.[8]

According to Davidson, an interpreter has explained an action when she has identified the combination of the agent's beliefs and desires (or "pro-attitudes")—or "real reason"—that caused or produced that action (Davidson 1980). Such an explanation of the action will typically include a principle of the following form:

> If A wants PHI and believes x-ing is a way to bring about PHI and that there is no better way to bring about PHI, and A has no overriding want, and knows how to x, and is able to x, then A x's.
>
> (Davidson 1980, 77)

Such explanations are distinguished from (and irreducible to) explanations in the natural sciences since they are both intentional in structure and normative in character. Action explanations are intentional because propositional attitudes (beliefs and pro-attitudes) are included as part of the *explanans*. They are normative not only in the sense that such explanations apply norms or standards to the phenomenon to be explained but (more importantly) in the sense that the interpreter cannot avoid invoking her own norms of rational action in the process of identifying the agent's reasons for the action.

> The point is ... that in explaining action we are identifying the phenomena to be explained, and the phenomena that do the explaining, as directly answering to our own norms; reason explanations make others intelligible to us only to the extent that we can recognize something like our own reasoning powers at work.
>
> (Davidson 2004, 47)[9]

The most fundamental of these norms for Davidson is a norm of rationality: the interpreter assumes that the agent is both attitudinally and behaviorally rational. That is, the interpreter assumes that the beliefs that form part of the agent's reason for the action are reasonable and consistent with other beliefs the agent holds (attitudinal rationality) and the action is treated as a reasonable consequence of beliefs and desires held by the agent (behavioral rationality). Davidson argues that this norm of rationality requires that the interpreter employ a "principle of charity" in interpreting an agent's beliefs and desires (Davidson 1980, xvii). Unless the interpreter initially assumes that a large number of the beliefs an agent holds true are, in fact, true (by the interpreter's lights), it will not be possible to interpret a particular belief (the one that produced the action in question) as reasonable and the aim of rational explanation will be thwarted. Understood in a weak sense, the principle of charity entails that, if a combination of beliefs and desires attributed to the agent are to be identified as the reason for an action, then those beliefs and desires must also be intelligible to us.[10] They cannot appear as reasons if they do not cohere with a wider set of beliefs and desires attributed to the agent and that seem intelligible to us, but this wider set of beliefs would be unintelligible to us if, by our own lights, we judged them to be largely false.

So formulated, Davidson's model of a reason explanation is similar to Max Weber's own model of "rational interpretation." According to Weber, a "rational interpretation of an action need not remain limited to the 'subjective' point of view of the actor" (Weber 1981, 188; Weber 1968, 5–6). Rather, once the interpreter has ideal-typically reconstructed the intentions (i.e. beliefs and pro-attitudes) of the actor, it is possible to assess from the interpreter's standpoint whether the beliefs were rational in light of other beliefs held by the actor, whether the means chosen were the most efficient for realizing the intended goal, and whether the means produced consequences other than those intended. In summarizing Weber's view (which thus far coincides with his own position), Habermas writes,

> In advancing what Weber calls rational interpretation, the interpreter himself takes a position on the claim with which purposive-rational actions appear; he relinquishes the attitude of a third person for the performative attitude of a participant who is examining a problematic validity claim and, if need be, criticizing it. Rational interpretations are undertaken in a performative attitude, since the interpreter presupposes a basis for judgment that is shared by all parties, including the actors.
>
> (TCA 1, 103)

If this comparison with Weber is apt, then Davidson's model of action explanation, like Habermas's, also assumes a connection between meaning and validity, at least with respect to claims about the truth of beliefs and the efficacy of action. Interpretation can proceed only if we attribute our standards of rationality to the agent whose action we are interpreting; but, in attributing our standards of rationality to the agent, we cannot avoid evaluating the rationality of their beliefs and actions in light of those shared standards. At the same time, however, Habermas's model of interpretive social science requires modifying Davidson's project in at least three respects.

First, the formulation of the method of rational interpretation in the preceding paragraph is obviously too strong as it stands. In developing such interpretations, we do not simply attribute our standards of rationality to actors in the object domain. That would be to commit the most extreme form of the "ethnocentric fallacy." Rather, as we have seen, what is necessary is that the explication of the agent's reasons for acting be placed in relation to "our" standards of rationality within the framework of one, hypothetically reconstructed "universe of discourse."[11]

Second, Habermas argues that "rational interpretations" in Weber's sense need not be limited to judgments about the truth of the agent's belief or the efficacy of his action in obtaining the desired goal. It is also possible to develop rational interpretations concerning the appropriateness of the beliefs and actions with respect to existing social norms and concerning the sincerity of the agent's intentions. In these cases, it is not a claim to truth which is being judged by the inquirer, but a claim to normative rightness or sincerity (or authenticity), respectively. Just as in the case of a rational interpretation of the truth of a belief or efficacy of an action, however, rational interpretations in these two further cases require that the interpreter make use of her own norms of rationality in assessing the agent's action, and thus that the interpreter move beyond the standpoint of the "subjective" rationality of the actor to a judgment about the objective (i.e. intersubjectively warranted) rationality of the action.

Habermas clarifies this expanded schema of rational interpretations in connection with his own theory of communicative action. This means that actions can be assessed not only with respect to their efficacy, but in connection with a wider range of validity claims. As noted above, in acting communicatively, individuals more or less naively accept as valid the various claims raised with their utterance or actions, and mutually suppose that they each stand ready to provide reasons for them should the validity of these claims be questioned. This intimate connection between validity, reasons, and action further underscores—in addition to its linguistically structured character—why (communicative) action must initially be approached from the internal perspective of the participant. Communicative action is connected to domains of validity which can only be understood "from the inside" or, to invoke an idiom from a related context, from "within the space of reasons," that is, by those who as (virtual) participants are able to give and assess the reasons for an action. As noted above, in a slightly more technical sense, Habermas states that individuals who act communicatively self-reflectively aim at reaching understanding about something in the world by relating their interpretations to three general types of validity claims connected with three basic types of speech acts: a claim to truth raised in constative speech acts, a claim to normative rightness raised in regulative speech acts, and a claim to authenticity raised in expressive speech acts (TCA 1, 319f.; see also Cooke 1994).

Rational interpretations of normatively regulated and dramaturgical (or self-expressive) action, like the interpretations of purposive action, thus make use of standards of validity that are already operative in the general structures of communicative action. Habermas speaks of these standards as "suppositions of commonality" which the interpreter shares with the social actor (TCA 1, 104). He also refers to this interpretive process as one in which the interpreter "equips" the actors with the same formal world concepts of an objective, social, and subjective world as those employed by the interpreter (TCA 1, 118–119). This schema of concepts provides a "reference system" or "categorical scaffolding" to which the interpreter can appeal in developing rational interpretations and advancing "thicker" or more culturally saturated descriptions. If, for example, the interpretation involves reference to a culture other than the interpreters, it might be possible to make an action intelligible only by observing a failure to make use of such differentiated world concepts (TCA 1, 63f.).

Finally, such a modification of Davidson's model of action explanation would also require that the interpreter attend more closely to social institutions, rules and practices—in short, again, "thick" descriptions—than Davidson seems to think is necessary. For the rational explanation of an action, it is not sufficient merely to cite the agent's beliefs and desires that produced the action. It is also necessary to locate those beliefs and desires within the context of specific social institutions and practices if they are to be recognized as reasons. Alasdair MacIntyre vividly illustrates this point with the following anecdote:

> I am being shown by my fellow-scientists the first and so far the only specimen of a new hybrid fruit developed because of its possible ease of cultivation and food-value for peoples in some particularly barren and starvation-prone part of the world. I snatch them from the hands of the scientist who is preparing to analyze them and gobble them down. When asked, 'why on earth did you do that?' I reply 'I just felt hungry. I like fruit.' It is important to notice that this answer renders my behavior more rather than less unintelligible than it was before. For in the context of this kind of scientific practice eating something just because one felt hungry is not an intelligible way of behaving. The practice imposes norms which constrain and limit expression of immediate desire in the institutionalized social settings informed by the practice.
>
> (MacIntyre 1986, 73)

Citing the relevant belief and pro-attitude "rationalizes" the action only if it presents a good or at least plausible reason within the context of specific social norms and practices. Although Davidson states that "rationality is a social trait, only communicators have it," he does not seem sufficiently to appreciate that what counts as rational might depend crucially on the social contexts of action. Although an interpreter needs to be familiar with the social contexts of action to determine whether an action is rational, the conception of rationality Davidson connects with an action is not one that allows for the "sociality of reason" or for a social history of reason in a stronger sense.[12]

This point about the sociality of reason can be more clearly seen by contrasting Davidson's notion of a "pro-attitude" to Taylor's notion of the "desirability characterization" of an action. Davidson introduces this neologism to cover, not only the desires and wants of an agent, but also "a great variety of moral views, aesthetic principles, economic prejudices, social conventions, and public and private goals and values in so far as these can be interpreted as attitude of an agent directed toward actions of a certain kind" (Davidson 1980, 4). The fact that a pro-attitude is asked to perform such "yeoman service" (Davidson) suggests, however, that these different stances toward an action are, in the last analysis, not particularly relevant for an assessment of its rationality. What is crucial is simply that the agent's belief be accompanied by some desire (or pro-attitude). For Taylor (and Habermas), by contrast, making an action intelligible (and thus assessing its rationality) requires being able to apply the "desirability characterizations" that are constitutive for the agent and his world:

> I come to understand someone when I understand his emotions, his aspirations, what he finds admirable and contemptible, in himself and others, what he yearns for, what he loathes, etc. Being able to formulate this understanding is being able to apply correctly the desirability characterizations which he applies in the way that he applies them. ... My claim is that the explicit formulation of what I understand when I understand you requires my grasping the desirability characterizations that you self-clairvoyantly use, or else those which you would use if you had arrived at a more reflective formulation of your loves, hates, aspirations, admirabilia, etc.
>
> (Taylor 1981, 192)

Desirability characterizations, according to Taylor, are not simply desires or preferences that the agent simply happens to have; rather, they "are portrayals (or imply portrayals) of how things are with us" and thus they entail claims about what the (social) world is like (Taylor 1981, 200). We can understand others only when we are able to make clear the ontological and evaluative commitments implicit in the agent's desirability characterizations, but this requires becoming familiar with the social rules and practices in which those characterizations operate.

Of course, the claim that reason explanations require familiarity with the social context of action should not be pushed to the point of insisting that it is social convention rather than the agent's intention that rationalizes the action. The claim is rather that it is only possible to identify the agent's intention (in this case his possible reason for the action) by reference to the social (and linguistic) conventions in connection with which intentions of that kind are standardly displayed. Nor should the claim about the relevance of social practices and institutions be taken to imply that the agent is always conscious of the conventions that render his action intelligible. In many cases, the institutionalized social setting that makes the action intelligible is one provided by "whatever the established routines are which in a particular group constitute the structure of the normal day" (MacIntyre 1986, 66). These routines are for the most part performed habitually and thus, though they render action intelligible, they are not among the reasons for which an agent acts (if, indeed, the agent in that situation can be said to be acting for a reason at all).

In sum, the above sketch is meant to show that reference to social practices and institutions will be incorporated into the account the agent would provide, were he asked to give the reasons for his action. That is, an understanding of these practices and institutions form a large part of the cultural stock of knowledge to which the agent has access and which he at least implicitly draws upon as a result of having been educated or socialized into them. The claim that rational interpretations of action can only be developed by locating the action within the context of specific social institutions and practices inevitably raises the specter of relativism. Winch's *Idea of a Social Science* has often been so interpreted, and MacIntyre and Taylor have sought hard to distinguish their own interpretive models from that position. The charge of relativism is complex and can take many forms—not all of which are problematic. However, the claim that common suppositions of rationality are a condition of possibility for offering rational interpretations at all—if it can be upheld—would seem to provide Habermas with even more resources to respond to objectionable forms.[13]

III. Rational action and the concept of the lifeworld

Habermas describes the lifeworld as "the culturally transmitted and linguistically organized stock of interpretive patterns" which forms the symbolic core of a society and introduces it as a correlate to the concept of communicative action:

> Subjects acting communicatively always come to an understanding in the horizon of a lifeworld. Their lifeworld is formed from more or less diffuse, always unproblematic, background convictions. This lifeworld background serves as a source of situation definitions that are presupposed by participants as unproblematic.
>
> (TCA 1, 70)

Habermas's treatment of the lifeworld is greatly indebted to the phenomenological analysis of Alfred Schutz and Thomas Luckmann which emphasizes its fundamentally implicit or taken-for-granted character, its holistic structure, and the fact that it does not stand at the conscious disposition of actors but remains in the background as a pre-interpreted horizon (Schutz and Luckmann 1973; TCA 2, 131ff.). So understood, the lifeworld forms a "vast and incalculable web of presuppositions" against which particular actions and utterances acquire their meaning. Furthermore, in stressing its holistic character, he suggests that the lifeworld cannot in its entirety become problematic or a topic of debate; at most, it can fall apart (TCA 2, 130). Rather, it is only specific themes or aspects of an action situation that are open to problematization.

However, in contrast to most phenomenological accounts which remain more or less focused on the idea of the transmission of knowledge or "culture," Habermas broadens the concept of the lifeworld to include forms of "solidarity" (or normative social orders) and individual identity and motivations (or "personality") as well. More specifically, he describes the basic symbolic structures of the lifeworld in connection with the general institutional components of societies singled out by Talcott Parsons (e.g. culture, society [in the narrower sense of a normative order] and personality):

> I call culture the store of knowledge from which those engaged in communicative action draw interpretations susceptible of consensus as they come to an understanding about something in the world. I call society (in the narrower sense of a component

of the lifeworld) the legitimate orders from which those engaged in communicative action gather a solidarity, based on belonging to groups, as they enter into interpersonal relationships with one another. Personality serves as a term of art for acquired competences that render a subject capable of speech and action and hence able to participate in processes of mutual understanding in a given context and to maintain his own identity in the shifting contexts of interaction.

(TCA 2, 138; PDM, 343)

Social actors make use of the lifeworld as a resource that provides cultural knowledge, legitimate orders, and acquired competences; at the same time, the symbolic reproduction of the lifeworld depends on the interpretive accomplishments of its members across these institutional domains. Although an adequate description of an agent's reason for an action might ultimately need to refer to the components of the lifeworld in which the action takes place, if the agent is not simply to be viewed as a "cultural dope" the essential role of this "interpretive accomplishment" cannot be neglected. It must be possible to see the reasons as the agent's own and thus to regard her as an accountable person. This is why the concept of the lifeworld is introduced as a necessary correlate of the notion of communicative action (along with the supposition of an accountable agent contained in the latter).

By correlating the concept of the lifeworld with the concept of communicative action in this way Habermas is able to highlight an important distinction that is only implicit in phenomenological analyses. On the one hand, as a *resource* that is drawn upon in communicative action, the lifeworld serves as the background. On the other hand, as a *topic* about which communicative actors seek to reach agreement, segments of the lifeworld are selectively thematized as problems (TCA 1, 82). In communicative action social actors draw upon the resources of the lifeworld "from behind," but they also make use of the reference system of formal world concepts (and their related validity claims) in their efforts to reach agreement about some element or feature within the world. Habermas also distinguishes these two dimensions of the lifeworld in connection with a spatial metaphor:

While the segment of the lifeworld relevant to the situation encounters the actor as a problem which he has to solve as something standing as it were in front of him, he is supported in the rear by the background of his lifeworld. Coping with situations is a circular process in which the actor is two things at the same time: the initiator of actions that can be attributed to him and the product of traditions in which he stands as well as of group solidarities to which he belongs and processes of socialization and learning to which he is subjected.

(Habermas 1985, 167; TCA 2, 135)

However, he also warns that this description of a circular process should be accepted with caution: actors are not products of the lifeworld in a way that renders them passive nor should the lifeworld be regarded as a self-perpetuating process—a macro-subject—that has a life of its own. Rather, it is individuals (and groups) who reproduce the lifeworld through their communicative action and the lifeworld is "saddled upon" the interpretive accomplishments of its members (TCA 2, 145; PT, 43; CES, 121). Or, to express the same point in somewhat different terminology, reference to the sociality of the agent (and her reasons)—a "product" of the lifeworld—must not be at the expense of her status as a rational and accountable agent, but rather must be seen as a central condition or feature of that agency. Thus, the model of social agency Habermas proposes offers a way to avoid the extremes of treating agents as "cultural dopes" who passively reproduce their lifeworld, on the one hand, and as individual utility-maximizers who despite their situation always act (insofar as they are rational) to maximize their own self-interest, on the other. Neither of these extremes captures adequately the idea that actors are both deeply embedded in their lifeworld and accountable agents who reproduce it *via* communicative action (PT, 43; Grannoveter 1985).

This brief summary of the general structures of the lifeworld also enables us to see more clearly what Habermas means by the "rationalization of the lifeworld." What is central to this notion is not, as for Weber, solely the expansion of formal or instrumental reason to more and more dimensions of social life. Rather, it refers to an opening up of the processes of symbolic reproduction (or, curtly expressed, the renewal of meaning and motivations) within the various structural components of the lifeworld—culture, society, and personality—to consensual agreement among its members in light of criticizable validity claims. He describes this rationalization in connection with three related processes: (1) the structural differentiation of its basic components (culture, society, and personality); (2) the separation of form (or process) and content; and (3) the increasing reflexivity (and "risk-filled" character) of symbolic reproduction (TCA 2, 145–146):

Structural components / Reproduction processes	Culture	Society	Personality
Cultural reproduction	Culture	Legitimations	Socialization patterns / Educational goals
Social integration	Obligations	Legitimately ordered interpersonal relations	Social memberships
Socialization	Interpretive accomplishments	Motivations for actions that conform to norms	Interactive capabilities ("personal identity")

Figure 3.1 Contribution of reproduction processes to maintaining the structural components of the lifeworld

(1) The *structural differentiation* between culture and society consists in "the gradual uncoupling of the institutional system from [e.g. strong religious or traditional] worldviews"; between society and personality, in "the extension of the scope of contingency for establishing interpersonal relationships"; and between culture and personality, in "the fact that the renewal of traditions depends more and more on individuals' readiness to criticize and their ability to innovate" (TCA 2, 146). In the wake of such societal differentiation, the components of the lifeworld become less concretely homogeneous and "interpenetrate" (Parsons) one another in more general and abstract ways (see Münch 1987, 35f.).

(2) A *separation of form and content* accompanies this differentiation of the structural components of the lifeworld as each relies upon processes and procedures specified independent of their content or outcome (TCA 2, 146). This means that the symbolic reproduction of society through the interpretive accomplishments of its members increasingly depends upon highly abstract cultural norms and values, formal principles and institutionalized procedures of social order, and decentered forms of intellectual, social, and moral cognition. It also means that it is possible to criticize and revise these interpretive accomplishments in light of norms, principles, and individual competences that are realized within these differentiated institutional complexes. (As we will see in Chapter 5, in modern societies law plays a crucial role in facilitating this.)

(3) Finally, the processes of symbolic reproduction—cultural transmission, social integration, and socialization—associated with each of the structural components of the lifeworld become *increasingly reflexive* and are in many cases also given over to treatment by professionals. This occurs not only, as Weber observed, in connection with the transmission of culture (in the differentiated spheres of science and technology, law and morality, and art and art criticism), but also with respect to the renewal of social solidarity (through democratic forms of collective political will formation and decision-making) and the socialization of individuals (with the development of formal systems of education and the pedagogical sciences) (TCA 2, 147).

According to Habermas, the rationalization of the lifeworld along these lines proceeds only to the extent that symbolic reproduction comes to rely more upon the interpretive accomplishments of participants who are able to reciprocally raise and redeem the validity claims inherent in their communicative practices and less upon a pre-existing "normatively secured" agreement. For this reason, while such differentiation "signals a release of the rationality potential inherent in communicative action" (TCA 2, 146), it also brings about a situation in which symbolic reproduction is increasingly fragile and risk-filled (TCA 1, 340; PDM, 350).

To summarize the argument of this section, a model of interpretive social science that is concerned with constructing rational interpretations in Weber's sense and that takes seriously the social dimensions of rationality cannot rest content with an interpretation of the beliefs and desires of an individual agent. It must, in addition, develop those interpretations in connection with the social practices and institutions in which the action occurs and, finally, clarify them in connection with the rational potential contained within the general structures of the particular socio-cultural lifeworld in question. Habermas also hopes to meet the charge of relativism (or strong contextualism) that is inevitably brought against such interpretive approaches by developing those interpretations in connection with principles and criteria derived from an internal reconstruction of the development of individual and collective learning processes—what he refers to as the "rationalization of the lifeworld."

IV. Rational reconstruction, the two-level concept of society, and the "colonization of the lifeworld"

As noted at the beginning of this chapter, Habermas's model of interpretive social science forms only one part of his attempt to outline a critical social theory, even if it is a central part. In order for them to be made more serviceable for the purposes of social criticism, rational interpretations as we've outlined them thus far need to be (1) supplemented with insights from what he calls "reconstructive science" and (2) combined with a two-level concept of society that also makes uses of systems theory (especially as it is found in the work of Parsons and Luhmann). In this final section, I will indicate briefly the main features of these two further components of a critical social theory and note some of the criticisms and reservations that have been raised against them.

(1) In connection with the idea of rational interpretations, Habermas has introduced the more or less novel category of "reconstructive science" (which, however, has earlier roots in the writings of both Rudolph Carnap and Imre Lakatos).[14] Although distinct from the "objectivating" or nomological sciences, he claims that reconstructive sciences can also generate "some sort of objective knowledge" that might provide for a "critical stance" on individual conduct and social institutions.[15] Habermas mentions several examples for such a science, but the cases he has most in mind are formal pragmatics (or speech act theory) and theories of meaning, theories of rationality and argumentation, and moral theory and theories of action. What these areas of inquiry share, when practiced at their best, is the attempt to make explicit the intuitive know-how that speakers and actors possess and that makes possible the successful exercise of the relevant competence or ability. For this reason, in each case the theorist must herself initially adopt a performative attitude and take up the internal perspective of the participant since these forms of inquiry assume that the actor/speaker is intuitively able to produce and identify valid expressions and performances.

Nevertheless, the goal of reconstruction is to provide a kind of theoretical explication of this intuitive knowledge: "Insofar as we succeed in analyzing very general conditions of validity, rational reconstructions can claim to identify universals and thus to produce a type of *theoretical* knowledge capable of competing with other such knowledge" (MCCA, 32). Moreover, such reconstructions are not limited to individual competences but can also treat "the collective knowledge of traditions" (TCA 2, 399). Their object then becomes "collective learning processes," and the theorist aims at reconstructing "the emergence and the internal history of those modern complexes of knowledge that have been differentiated out, each under a different single aspect of validity—truth, normative rightness, or authenticity" (TCA 2, 398). Habermas presumably again has in mind the Lakatosian notion of rationally reconstructing the internal history and "progress" of scientific disciplines and this idea informs his own approach to reconstructing the developmental logics of collective learning processes (Lakatos 1981; Habermas 1979a; and Owen 2002 for discussion).

Further, since they deal with validity claims accessible (at least initially) only in connection with the performative attitude of the participant, reconstructive sciences involve a claim to universality that preserves a "transcendental flavor" and stands in need of philosophical argument and clarification. That is, they attempt to describe the pre-theoretical knowledge of rule systems for different performances in such a way that a possible alternative description is shown to be derivative or "to utilize portions of the very hypothesis it seeks to supplant" (MCCA, xx). As with other cases of modest transcendental arguments, they try to show conditions of possibility for the practice in question for which no alternative can be found (Korner 1967). At the same time, however, they renounce the search for "ultimate foundations" characteristic of strong forms of transcendental argument, since the claims possess a hypothetical status and can be submitted to forms of indirect testing in connection with empirical theory.[16]

Finally, when they are developed in connection with rational interpretation, reconstructions of individual competences acquire a critical dimension and can help to identify distorted or deformed cases of belief and action (e.g. instances of fallacious arguments, inadequate explanations, infelicitous speech acts, inappropriate evaluations, and the like). At the level of collective learning processes, such reconstructions can be used to identify what Habermas calls more generally "processes of unlearning": "Processes of unlearning can be gotten at through a critique of deformations that are rooted in the selective exploitation of a potential for rationality and mutual understanding that was once available but is now buried over" (TCA 2, 400). In both cases, however the idea is that such deformations can only be identified by means of a theoretical reconstruction of the goals or end states of highly abstract learning processes that are embodied in the structures of the lifeworld and expressed in the exercise of individual competences (see also Eder 1999). The reconstructions enable the social inquirer to discern "systematic distortions to communication" and one-sided or unbalanced processes of social rationalization—phenomena often previously referred to in the tradition of Western Marxism as forms of social reification (Honneth 2008, 55).

(2) The aim of a critical theory of society is not limited only to that of identifying processes of unlearning or other disturbances to the communicative infrastructure of the lifeworld *via* a reconstructive

science. It also seeks to uncover the possible roots or causes of such distortions and disturbances. However, since the claim now is that these disturbances operate by definition "behind the backs" of social participants, this further aim in social critique requires the introduction of a theoretical or "observer-perspective." In order to capture this further perspective, Habermas introduces a "two-level" concept whereby society can be analytically viewed from either of two perspectives. Although society as a whole is (defined as) one object—"the *systemically-stabilized* complexes of action of *socially-integrated* groups" (TCA 2, 152; R2, 252)—it can fruitfully be viewed *either* from the standpoint of an interpretive social science that entails a participant's perspective ("society as lifeworld") *or* from the standpoint of systems theory that employs a third-person or observer's perspective ("society as system"). In the first approach, the "rational interpretations" of the social participants are foregrounded; whereas in the second it is the hypothesized causal (or functional) interconnections among action-consequences that are foregrounded. In a further (and more controversial) step, Habermas also speaks of two different "social orders" which are themselves distinguished according to which mode of integration predominates in each: The "social integration" of an order is achieved primarily through the agreement of actors—whether that agreement is normatively secured or communicatively achieved—and so makes reference to actors intentions; "systems integration," by contrast, is achieved primarily through a coordination of the consequences of their choices (see Heath 2011). Or, as Habermas summarizes it elsewhere,

> Social integration is to be measured in terms of criteria of internal stabilization and the preservation of ego and group identities that depend on what actors attribute to themselves. System integration can be assessed in terms of criteria of external stabilization and the preservation of the boundaries of a system vis-à-vis its environment.
>
> (R2, 252)

This second approach allows the theorist to describe a form of integration (and so type of social order) that is achieved without any direct reference to the rational interpretations (or self-understandings) of the actors themselves. Consider, as a simple example, how traffic flow can be efficiently regulated without any knowledge of the travel plans of drivers. Markets, as Adam Smith famously pointed out, can also be usefully viewed from the perspective of systems integration—and, if he is correct, must be viewed from that perspective if their specific beneficial features are to be visible. More controversially, Habermas (following Parsons and Niklas Luhmann) extends this type of societal integration (or action-coordination) to the political system as well: The behavior of the political system or "state apparatus" (and so too, though to a lesser extent, that of individuals within it) can be fruitfully described as responses to its environment in accordance with the functional demands required for its own stabilization and maintenance.

   With these tools in hand Habermas is then able to give a creative re-reading of Weber and Marx by locating disturbances to communication in a lopsided process of social rationalization spurred on by capital accumulation (TCA 1, 342–343). The process of societal rationalization that led to the differentiation of the structural components of the lifeworld described above (culture, society, and personality) also produced conditions for the relative autonomy of the subsystems of the economy and political administration vis-á-vis the traditional normative constraints of the lifeworld (TCA 2, 153f.). These two social subsystems or "orders" come to depend for their integration less upon the mutually shared interpretations of social actors and more upon the functional interconnections of the consequences of action via a high generalized media of exchange (or what Habermas calls, following Parsons, "money" and "power") (TCA 2, 173, 183). A central claim for Habermas is that this "uncoupling" of "system" and "lifeworld" has multiple and ambivalent consequences. On the one hand, it relieves large segments of society from more immediate dependence upon the demanding requirements of the interpretive accomplishments and normative expectations of citizens. But at the same time the subsystems produce effects that can also endanger the institutions of the lifeworld (on which they ultimately depend). According to Habermas this second order process of decoupling does not necessarily or inevitably produce social crises and pathologies within the lifeworld (TCA 2, 318, 330). Rather, the individual and collective pathologies associated with modernity—e.g. what Weber described as the loss of freedom and meaning—occur only when "mediatization" disturbs or displaces the communicative infrastructure of the lifeworld, that is, only when aspects of social life that necessarily depend on symbolic reproduction are displaced and/or when symbolic reproduction becomes subordinated to the systemic imperatives of material reproduction (TCA 2, 305, 330). In a vivid metaphor meant to recall Marx's own notion of commodity fetishism and the process of "real abstraction," Habermas refers to such systemically induced disturbances as the "colonization of the lifeworld" (TCA 2, 322, 332f.). The process that Marx had described as reification—the substitution of exchange-value for use-value (or "dead labor" for "living labor")—is recast at a more abstract level. It nonetheless remains true for Habermas that disturbances to the lifeworld are largely induced by uncontrolled expansion in the realm of material reproduction. Or, in other words, reification still has roots in the processes of capitalist production even if it is no longer immediately discernible (or even best described) in terms of class conflict (TCA 2, 350; see also LC, 93–94).[17]

Numerous criticisms have been made of Habermas's introduction of a two-level concept of society and his use of systems theory. One objection is that Habermas turns an analytic distinction into a real social distinction and as a result divides society into distinct domains integrated *via* different mechanisms. At one level, this is a fair description of his position and the question would then turn to whether it yields any explanatory benefits. Does it enable the theorist to explain phenomena in an illuminating way that would not otherwise be possible? A slightly stronger version of this criticism is that, with his distinction between society as lifeworld and system, Habermas tends to assume that the economy and political subsystems operate solely in terms of systems integration while the lifeworld is integrated solely on the basis of consensual norms (McCarthy 1991; Joas 1991; Baxter 1987, 2011). This leads in turn to the additional charge that he tends to regard the lifeworld as power-free; while the susbsystems of the economy and the state rely exclusively on strategic action.[18]

In a response Habermas has slightly modified his claim and attempted to clarify his position. On the one hand, he conceded that his description of the subsystems as "norm free" was misleading: they remain "embedded" (Polanyi) or "anchored" (Habermas) in the normative expectations of the lifeworld and would not operate successfully without such ties (R2, 257). Further, the operation of institutions in these subsystems continues to draw upon and make use of the normative expectations of actors. Habermas's claim is rather that "in the final instance" it is the requirements of system maintenance that prevail and thus are relevant for causally explaining their behavior.[19] On the other hand, there is some confusion around what his distinction implies: while the lifeworld is "socially" and not "systemically" integrated this does not mean that there are no other forms of power and domination that operate within it. "The lifeworld by no means offers an innocent image of 'power free spheres of communication'" (R2, 254). Rather, the claim about systemically induced disturbances to communication—that is, the colonization thesis—is meant to identify only one specific form of power and need not deny that other types of domination (including some of those analyzed by Foucault) are also present in the lifeworld. The claim need only be that these types of power are already accessible via a more interpretive approach (see Iser and Strecker 2010, 189). At the same time, the claim that the economy and state are largely systemically integrated does not mean that actors in these subsystems relate only on the basis of strategic action. This is to confuse types of individual action with types of social order and integration—something that Habermas's own substitution of "functionalist reason" (in TCA 2) for "instrumental reason" (in Weber and earlier critical theory) was intended to avoid (TCA 2, 306).

Finally, some have questioned whether his use of systems theory compromises the potential for more radical social criticism (McCarthy 1991; Scheuerman 2002, 2013). The criticism holds that Habermas now so fully embraces Luhmann's claims concerning societal differentiation and the independence of subsystems—perhaps in response to his earlier Hegelian-Marxist holism—that he is forced to abandon the hope of a more radical democratization of both the economy and the bureaucratic state. A revised critical theory on his view can be at most "defensive" and attempt to "contain" (but not conquer) these subsystems that operate according to their own logic (R2, 261; see also NC, 63). Although his views about the extent and scope of democratization clearly seem to have undergone change since STPS, Habermas insists it is not because he has given up on the project of radical democracy (R2, 260; AS, 112f.). Rather, he claims that his changes are primarily at the level of broad strategies—for example, perhaps guaranteed minimum income rather than worker self-management—rather than a change of mind about the deep conflict between democracy and capitalism (see Habermas 1990a).

Thus, despite some of the difficulties and challenges confronting it, Habermas has continued to maintain that the two-level concept of society—one that combines both interpretive social science and functionalist or systems-theoretic perspective—remains important for his model of a critical social theory. On the one hand, working solely from within the internal perspectives of the participant—and thus treating action and their products as tied to the domain of reasons—the social inquirer is unable to perceive systemic causes of distortions to the structures of communication as such.

> A *verstehende* sociology that allows society to be wholly absorbed into the lifeworld ties itself to the perspective of self-interpretation of the culture under investigation; this internal perspective screens out everything that inconspicuously affects a sociocultural lifeworld from the outside.
>
> (TCA 2, 150)

In particular, the inquirer will be unable to perceive phenomena such as mediatization since "the mediatization of the lifeworld takes effect on and with the structures of the lifeworld; it is not one of those processes that are available as themes within the lifeworld, and thus it cannot be read off from the intuitive knowledge of members" (TCA 2, 186).

On the other hand, systemic disturbances to the communicative infrastructure of the lifeworld cannot be identified exclusively from an external or observer's perspective since, as we have seen, the structures of the lifeworld (and the forms of collective learning processes connected to them) are only accessible through a reconstructive analysis that begins with the member's intuitive knowledge (TCA 2, 151). This emphasis on the need to begin with an interpretive approach also reveals the limits of a theoretical approach—such as Luhmann's systems theory—that relies exclusively on an external perspective (see also McCarthy 1991, 122). If communicative disturbances *and* their systemic causes are to be identified, the critical theorist must be able to work simultaneously with an internal (participant's) and external (observer's) perspective—that is, with an analytic perspective on society as lifeworld and system. At the same time, the extent to which the lifeworld is actually given over to systemic imperative *via* the media of money and power—that is, the extent to which it has been colonized—is, however, an empirical question and not one that can be determined by the conceptual features of theory alone.

So conceived, the project of a critical social theory certainly implies a more modest conception of the relation between theory and practice than that found in traditional Marxism or even earlier critical theory. On the one hand, theory is both more fallible and stands in a more indirect relation to social practice. This is especially evident in Habermas's idea of a reconstructive science which would seem to be in a poor position to provide any direct guidance for practical social change. On the other hand, this conception of critical theory remains even more dependent on specific social movements and demands for change arising from within the lifeworld—that is, on the responses of those who experience the effects of an uneven process of social rationalization. Although historical processes might be illuminated with the aid of a broadly developmental logic, history does not have a predetermined *telos*. Whether or not a more balanced process of societal rationalization will be realized in the future depends on the types of social conflict (and proposals for their resolution) that arise on the boundaries between "system" and "lifeworld." As Habermas suggests in the final section of *The Theory of Communicative Action*, the critical theorist can offer some broad insight into what is more or less progressive within new social movements and forms of social protest—though even here it is difficult to see from this height what constructive proposals might be offered in connection with the specific demands of, say, the "Occupy Wall Street" movement or new modes of surveillance by an expanding security state. On Habermas's view, the realization of a more "rational society"—e.g. a more communicatively balanced and rationalized lifeworld—ultimately depends upon the collective learning and practice of the social actors themselves and only minimally (if at all) upon the insights of the critical theorist. The theorist can offer a diagnosis of social trends and disturbances, but whether these are confirmed or not must finally be decided by the social actors within the object domain (see Celikates 2006).

Further reading

White (1989) and Outhwaite (2009) both offer a good introduction to Habermas's theory of social action. Fultner (2011) and Günther (1998) offer good guides to his notion of communicative action. Taylor (1985) is an important statement of interpretive social science and many essays in Hiley et al. (1991) are devoted to that topic. Honneth and Joas (1991) is a valuable collection of essays on TCA. McCarthy's critique of the two-level concept in that volume offers a clear discussion; so too does Heath (2011). Further discussion of the value of systems theory for Habermas's project can be found in Mouzelis (1991), Peters (1993), and Baxter (2011).

Notes

1 It is not that Habermas thinks such an epistemological grounding is not possible; rather he seems to think that, with the decline of positivism in the social sciences, it is no longer necessary. See his remarks in the Preface to LSS, xiv. In an essay reflecting on KHI thirty years later Habermas claims he would still defend the idea of three cognitive interests though in a slightly different manner (Habermas 2000a, 20); for my purposes this strengthens the claim about a Kantian pragmatism that underlies his work.

2 Honneth captures this point nicely (Honneth 2009, 50). Finlayson (2013) also correctly identifies Habermas's strategy in what he calls a "sideways-on" theory and rightly notes that Habermas does not seek to ground social criticism in a substantive or even procedural moral theory. For reasons not fully clear to me, however, he seems to think that Habermas has not satisfactorily completed the task of "justifying the normative grounds of a social theory" (528). By contrast, I think this pretty much exhausts what Habermas thinks can be done to justify a critical theory; see also Iser (2008). For the view that there remains more justificatory work to be done, see also Schnädelbach (1991) and Stahl (2013).

3 This last description is intended to invoke the work of Robert Brandom whose analysis of rationality in connection with the normative statuses social actors mutually ascribe to one another has much in common with Habermas's

account. For further discussion see the exchange between Habermas and Brandom (Brandom 2000); Baynes 2004; and Honneth (2009, chap. 3).

4 Charles Taylor also defends this version of the *Verstehen* thesis in Taylor (1985) and Taylor (1981).

5 This is not to deny that reasons can (also) be causes, but only to insist that the participant's perspective is required to first identify a reason as such. In this respect, despite my comparison below, Habermas differs importantly from Davidson, since, for Davidson, reasons *qua* reasons cannot be causes—see Stoutland (1980, 2011).

6 For Habermas's remarks on the limits of philosophical hermeneutics and a criticism of its dismissal of general social theory see his review of Gadamer's *Truth and Method*, in LSS, 166–170; and TCA 2, 148.

7 See also his distinction between "objectivating attitude1" (observer) and "objectivating attitude2" (performer) and his remarks on the importance of recognizing a "hierarchy of attitudes" in Habermas (1985a, 109).

8 I refer to it as "quasi-reductionist" since, though he is a non-reductive physicalist, Davidson requires that his radical interpreter must be able to provide an "extensionalist" interpretation that does not presuppose any semantic terms—see Ellis (2011), Ramberg (1989) and Ramberg's contrast between Gadamer and Davidson in Ramberg (2003).

9 Davidson (2004, 47); Davidson's view on the normative character of rational explanations is helpfully discussed in Root (1986).

10 This "weak" sense of the principle of charity is close to what has been called a "principle of humanity" in contrast to a "strong" reading that would require attributing true beliefs to the agent even when it would seem more reasonable to regard them as in error; Davidson subsequently endorsed the "weak" interpretation, see his comments cited in Lukes (1982, 264, n.6).

11 On this point, Habermas's model is thus closer to Taylor's notion of the "language of perspicuous contrast," and Gadamer's notion of the "fusion of horizons," though, in contrast to both, Habermas is more confident about the identification of cross-culturally shared criteria of rationality that can, in turn, be defended by weak transcendental arguments; see also John McDowell's comparison of Gadamer and Davidson which contrasts an "I-We" sociality of the former to the "I-Thou" sociality of the latter (McDowell 2002). Habermas is probably also closer to the "I-We" sociality but with some important qualifications (see below). Relevant here too is whether one considers practices or individual capacities to be explanatorily most basic.

12 This question of the sociality of reason is closely connected with the account one offers of norms and normativity. Habermas, in contrast to Davidson, would endorse a "practice-based" account as part of his pragmatism. For a very informative discussion of this question, see Rouse (2007) and Risjord (2013). It is also relevant for the question of "I-Thou" or "I-We" sociality raised by McDowell (2002) (see note 11 above).

13 Habermas resists some forms of relativism or what he calls "strong contextualism" (which he attributes to Rorty) but at another point describes

his own position as a "consistent contextualism" (TJ, 8). He clearly thinks that acknowledging the social character of rational interpretations does not prevent the theorist (or social inquirer) from making any cross-cultural comparative judgments—in fact, his "disquieting thesis" is that they cannot avoid doing so. For a sensible treatment of relativism in the context of social inquiry that expresses an attitude similar to Habermas's, see Moody-Adams (1997).

14 Though the term seems to have originated from Carnap, Habermas's use of it is quite different and, in fact, is closer to what Carnap later called "explication," which aimed at clarifying the concepts of ordinary language rather than replacing them (the aim of reconstruction for Carnap). For an interesting and informative discussion, see Carus (2007); for Lakatos, see Lakatos (1981).

15 MCCA, 32; for Habermas's other remarks on reconstructive science, see R1, 229f; and QC, 205; and, for more recent discussions, Peters (1993) and Gaus (2013).

16 See MCCA, 54. As I understand his position the lifeworld that "constitutes" our access to the world (and so imposes transcendental limits) is at the same time the product of our natural and socio-cultural evolution (and so part of the world). This is the paradoxical status Habermas has accepted since KHI. Further because the transcendental (or "world-disclosing") structures are part of the world, "inner-worldly learning" can have an impact on those structures. It is Heidegger's denial of the interactive dimension that Habermas takes issue with and not (I think) the claim that the transcendental or *a priori* features are historical and/or pragmatic (see TJ, 32). Finally, the task of the philosopher or reconstructive theorist is to render explicit the know-how in virtue of which achievements are possible; but his reconstructive knowledge—though it aims at identifying the "constitutive features"—is itself fallible and not the privilege of a special sort of philosophical insight.

17 For this reason I think Heath in his otherwise very helpful discussion too quickly dismisses one of Habermas's guiding questions at this point—why are there still disturbances and social conflicts in the social-welfare state (Heath 2011, 90). For a related discussion, see Honneth and Hartman (2014).

18 Honneth (1991, 298); Fraser 1989; Allen 2008, 98; there is some support for this position in the text where Habermas refers to the subsystems as "norm free" (TCA 2, 307; see also 150 and 185); Baxter 2011 raises more general worries about the connection between system and lifeworld in TCA.

19 R2, 257. This clarification is not a revision of his position in TCA as there are passages there that make this point; see, for example, TCA 2, 311 and the discussion in Jütten (2013, 590).

Four
Habermas's "Kantian pragmatism"

I. Introduction

It was noted in the Introduction that since the late 1990s Habermas has described his philosophical position as a form of Kantian pragmatism. He suggests that the approaches of Hilary Putnam (in some phases) and Robert Brandom can also be characterized in this way and other contemporary philosophers might be cited as well—for example, Michael Friedman and Philip Kitcher. In Habermas's case, the description is proposed to highlight the strong idealizing presuppositions he associates with the concept of communicative action developed in *The Theory of Communicative Action*. Since this understanding of philosophy also figures prominently in his later writings, it will be useful to outline its central features and note some similarities and differences with other related views.

In fact Habermas's entire philosophical career can instructively be read as a succession of attempts to appropriate the achievements of Kant's critical philosophy without taking on board some of its more controversial assumptions (such as transcendental idealism with its world-constituting subject). *Knowledge and Human Interests* (1968), in some ways Habermas's least Kantian work, opens with an appreciation of Kant's enterprise:

> The critique of knowledge was still conceived in reference to a system of cognitive faculties that included practical reason and reflective judgment as naturally as critique itself, that is a

theoretical reason that can dialectically ascertain not only its limits but also its own Idea.

(KHI, 3)

Similarly, Habermas's later conception of philosophy as a "reconstructive science" that aims to make explicit the pre-theoretical know-how of speaking and acting subjects—expressed most clearly in the project of a formal or universal pragmatics—shares many features with other roughly contemporary attempts to deploy transcendental (or "quasi-transcendental") arguments without the trappings of transcendental idealism (MCCA, chaps. 1 and 2). Finally, perhaps most obviously, the project of discourse morality, first outlined in the early 1980s, is explicitly conceived as a defense of a Kantian conception of morality within the context of his theory of communicative action (MCCA, chap. 3).

It is therefore not surprising that Habermas would describe his own position as a form of Kantian pragmatism.[1] At one point, in a somewhat free-spirited reading of Kant, he suggests that the various idealizing presuppositions implicit in the idea of communicative action are analogous to Kant's "ideas" of reason (in the "Transcendental Dialectic" of the *Critique of Pure Reason*): Kant's ideas of a single world, the soul, and the "unconditioned" (or God), then, correspond to the presuppositions, in Habermas's work, of a common world, an accountable subject, and context-transcending validity claims (TJ, 87). This embrace of Kant is nonetheless striking since elsewhere he strongly criticizes Kant for his reliance upon the philosophy of the subject and, in particular, the "spontaneity of a subjectivity that is world-constituting yet itself without a world" (PT, 142). This tension at least raises the question of how far one can follow Kant without also taking onboard his philosophy of the subject (or consciousness). An examination of Habermas's brand of Kantian pragmatism—and especially its relation to his central idea of communicative action—will also make it possible to see some of the similarities and differences with others who preserve an important connection with Kant's project (e.g. Brandom, Putnam, Korsgaard).

It will be useful to begin with a sketch, in very broad strokes, of a reading of Kant with which Habermas would be largely sympathetic. First, Kant's critique of reason is arguably not foundationalist but coherentist or "constructivist" (O'Neill 1992). That is, Kant did not attempt to ground the nature and limits of our cognitive powers (reason) through a form of deductive argument that appeals to certain self-evident axioms or principles. Rather, he sought to vindicate the broadly human capacity for reason (theoretical and practical) against "empiricism" (that is, broadly naturalist accounts that would inevitably lead to skepticism) and "dogmatism" (that is, metaphysical accounts that allowed a much greater scope for knowledge than Kant believed was warranted) (Neiman 1994). His project can be called "constructivist" in that it seeks to establish the basic principles and "ideas" that reason is more or less obliged to acknowledge in its efforts to reflect critically on its own exercise. It thus neither assumes the skeptical (Humean) position that we lack a capacity for (anything other than instrumental) reason nor does it appeal to something beyond our capacity for reason in order to justify its claims. Moreover, Kant's critique of reason concedes a certain primacy to practical over theoretical reason. In the Preface to the second *Critique* Kant states that freedom is the "keystone" for the entire edifice of reason (Kant 1956, 3). It is our capacity for freedom or, in his words, to "set ends"—that is, to think and act on the basis of considerations (or reasons) that one can reflectively endorse— that is central to Kant's account of human reason as a whole. Though at times he describes this capacity as an original "spontaneity" and suggests it discloses our membership in a noumenal world, his crucial claim is that freedom, and hence reason, are irreducibly normative concepts. An adequate account of our capacity for reason cannot be given exclusively in terms of the natural sciences—in fact, the latter presuppose the exercise of reason normatively understood— but neither must this capacity be construed as entailing any more metaphysically obscure notions than our capacity to be "reasons-responsive." Rather, what Kant must show is that a (normative) account of agency (and hence reasoning generally) assumes a "logical space of reasons" (Sellars 1963) that, however such agency may supervene on features of the natural world, cannot be reduced to it (Sellars 1963; Meerbote 1984). A central feature of this normative (and ultimately "compatibilist") reading of Kant depends on an interpretation of his claim that, in acting freely, an agent must "incorporate" his desire into the maxim of his action or, as it has also been more recently expressed, the agent must treat the desire as a reason for action (Bratman 1999). Finally, Kant's somewhat later doctrine of the "fact of reason," as others have shown, need not be construed as a desperate attempt to keep the critical enterprise from collapse. Rather, it again shows the roots of Kant's critique in a conception of practical agency and in the exercise of common human understanding (Neiman 1994; Rawls 1999a).

Habermas's own Kantian pragmatism exhibits a great deal in common with this reading of Kant's critical project. It accepts that philosophy assumes a task of critical reflection that is not identical with theoretical or scientific inquiry. It also accords a primacy to practical reason (or practical agency). One of the distinctive contributions of the theory of communicative action is to provide a framework for a conception of agency that helps make that conception more intelligible. More specifically, on Habermas's model, the normativity associated with agency—in the idea of being guided by a norm or acting for a reason—does not derive from a radically voluntarist notion of the capacity of an agent to give a law to itself or "set ends." Rather, for Habermas, reflecting a more Hegelian view, this basic idea of agency as normative arises in connection with social practices of reciprocal recognition, where individuals mutually ascribe the status of reason-giver to one another (see Honneth 2014, 42f.). Thus, in contrast to some interpretations, it is not the individual agent's reflection on his own capacity for thought or end-setting that, so to speak, transports him into the logical space of reasons (Korsgaard 1996). Rather, to put it somewhat sharply, the social practice of reason-giving presupposes (in order for that practice to be intelligible as one involving reasons rather than causes) that agents possess not only a (defeasible) first-personal authority but also the (equally defeasible) capacity to set ends. In Habermas's related terminology, it presupposes an authority or capacity to take a yes/no position with respect to the claims raised in their utterances and actions (BFN, 119). Our agency is rooted in and fundamentally (or "constitutively") depends upon a social practice of mutual recognition (PT, 183–184).

This brief sketch of Habermas's understanding of communicative action also highlights its parallels in some respects with Robert Brandom's normative pragmatics (Brandom 1994).[2] The idea common to both projects is, again, that rational agency is fundamentally a normative status dependent on social practices and the attitudes displayed by individuals in the context of those practices: The capacity for incorporation, "reflective endorsement," or treating as a reason is a function of practices in which actors already find themselves (but which it is also practically impossible for them to imagine doing without). Brandom summarizes this view nicely in a commentary on Rorty: "Pragmatism about norms ... is the thought that any normative matter of epistemic authority or privilege [and one could add, of practical authority or agency— KB] is ultimately intelligible only in terms of social practices that involve implicitly recognizing or acknowledging such authority" (Brandom 2000a, 159). The further differences between Habermas and both Brandom and Rorty will have to do with how strongly one emphasizes the idealizations concerning the authority built into these social practices.

II. Communicative action and the deliberative stance

As was noted in the Introduction, the concept of communicative action is the central concept in Habermas's work. In addition to providing a novel way to characterize the "manifest image" it captures his guiding conviction that social actors are not only or even fundamentally "utility maximizers" who relate to one another instrumentally or strategically. In his account, social actors fundamentally relate to each other as mutually accountable agents engaged in a common project of interpreting (and coping) with a world and striving to reach a shared understanding of it. Of course, like the assumption that we are fundamentally utility maximizers, the assumptions about communicative action are also idealizations. Crucial for Habermas's argument, however, is that these idealizations are not simply regulative ideals but are also constitutive for social practices. For example, the assumption that we are "reason-givers" and accountable agents—that is, agents who are able to give reasons for action and demand them from others—plays an indispensable role in the practices required for social reproduction. Thus, despite the coercion, manipulation, and forms of domination that are a pervasive feature of social life, socialization and social reproduction would not be successful if these basic (and idealizing) assumptions were not made. It is for this reason that Habermas resists attempts to treat all types of action as strategic action and finds it problematic to say that agency is constituted (exclusively) through relations of power (Foucault 1980, 98).

As we saw in the last chapter the concept of communicative action as a normative understanding of agency is also relevant for social theory. According to Habermas, communicative action constitutes a distinct and important type of social action. The goal or "telos" of communicative action is not expressed or realized in an attempt to influence others, but in the attempt to reach an agreement or mutual understanding (*Verständigung*) with one or more actors about something in the world. In acting communicatively, individuals more or less naively accept as valid the various claims raised with their utterance or action and mutually suppose that each is prepared to provide reasons for them should the validity of those claims be questioned. In a slightly more technical (and controversial) sense, and one tied more directly to specifically modern structures of rationality, Habermas also holds that individuals who act communicatively self-reflectively aim at reaching understanding about something in the world by relating their interpretations to three general types of validity claims that are constitutive for three basic types of speech acts: a claim to truth raised in constative speech acts, a claim to normative rightness raised in regulative speech acts, and a claim to truthfulness raised in expressive speech acts (TCA 1, 319–320). The central and crucial claim is not that actors always act communicatively, or that a clear line can always be drawn between when individuals are acting communicatively and when they are acting strategically, but rather that in order to interpret behavior as meaningful or rational action, we must, at least as an initial default position, assume that individuals act under these idealizing presuppositions. Unless we make such assumptions about social actors, we won't be able to view their behavior as intelligible or meaningful at all.[3]

What is easily overlooked in this account of communicative action is that it amounts, essentially, to a claim about normative statuses that are ascribed to actors in the context of certain social practices—and, specifically, practices that involve the exchange of reasons. Utterances or speech acts can count as an exchange of reasons—and actions can count as actions done for reasons—only if they can be viewed as issuing from agents who occupy a normative status. Similarly, agents can be seen as occupying a normative status only in virtue of attitudes that others adopt toward them and which they adopt toward others— that is, in virtue of a reciprocal or mutual recognition. Thus, to be accountable agents who act for reasons—or to borrow Sellars's phrase, to be located in the "logical space of reasons," assumes a social practice in which actors recognize one another as occupying that normative status. The validity claims identified by Habermas (together with the idea of agents as accountable) are, in effect, constitutive rules for the practice of reason-giving—rules that the interpreter must assume in order to interpret action as rational, but also, rules that the agents must be assumed to be acting under insofar as they view themselves as rational agents—that is, as capable of giving and responding to reasons.

Some have suggested that communicative action with its idealizing suppositions is a mere fiction or at least not an assumption that must be made in order to view social actors as rational. How might one respond? Clearly, this does not seem to be a question that can simply be settled empirically. In fact, one of the distinctive features of Habermas's philosophical position is the way in which his Kantian pragmatism is used to support his account of communicative action. The broad thesis, to repeat, is that acting under the idealizing assumptions of communicative action is a condition of possibility for being a rational agent—or to borrow related terminology by Jonathan Lear, to be "minded" at all (Lear 1998, 253). This claim does not mean that every action performed actually fulfills such idealizing presuppositions. Rather, it means that to understand individuals as capable of acting for reasons at all, they must generally be supposed to be acting under these assumptions. Or, to use a different expression, it must be assumed that individuals (including those engaged in offering interpretations) can adopt a "communicative" or "deliberative stance." In fact, to be an accountable and reason-giving agent consists in being viewed from the deliberative stance—though, as we shall see, this stance is not something that we can easily imagine setting aside.

How might such an argument for communicative action (or agents as co-deliberators) be developed? One strategy, suggested by

Davidson, Dennett, and others, is to identify the assumptions that are required for rational interpretations, and see how far these lead. On this view, to be "minded" is, first, to be a subject to whom intentional states (beliefs, desires, and other proattitudes) are ascribed. However, as holists like Davidson and Dennett have argued, to be "minded" requires more than the ascription of individual beliefs and other intentional states. It is also necessary that these intentional states (and the agent's actions) stand in relation to one another in accordance with various norms or principles (e.g. a norm of rationality or a norm of continence). It also assumes a principle of "first-personal authority": To view an individual as rational requires that she be at least implicitly aware of the beliefs and desires that rationalize or guide her action and that she has a (perhaps defeasible) authority to state what they are. Thus, to be minded is to be viewed from the perspective or stance defined by these interpretive norms and principles. But is being an intentional agent (minded) something that exists only in the "eye of the beholder" (or interpreter)? And does this stance also include the idealizing suppositions of communicative action?

In the case of what Dennett calls "simple" intentionality, we ascribe beliefs and desires to another agent and interpret it under certain norms of rationality. My dog nudges her food dish with her nose because she wants her dinner and believes this will get my attention. Sometimes, however, we ascribe more complex forms of intentionality to other intentional systems as well: we attribute to them not only rationality, but the capacity to view others as intentional systems—this is what Brandom calls the "discursive-scorekeeping stance" (Brandom 1994, 628). It is also possible to view other intentional systems as not only capable of ascribing (simple) intentionality to others, but also as capable of acting from (and viewing others as capable of acting from) considerations for which they assume responsibility or with which they otherwise identify. This stance involves seeing systems as importantly active and not merely passive with respect to their desires. They are able to ask whether they have reason to act upon their desires, where this question is settled not solely by appeal to further desires, but by reference to norms and principles that are in a relevant sense their own (Korsgaard 1996, 99). Finally, from the perspective of the deliberative stance, agents or complex intentional systems are viewed (and view themselves) as capable of acting on the basis of considerations for which they are prepared to give reasons or to justify to other co-deliberators (see also Pettit and Smith).

Still, the suggestion thus far is only that the deliberative stance is required if we want to develop rational interpretations of a certain sort (ones which view agents as co-deliberators). Can an argument be provided to show that the deliberative stance is required for any rational interpretations at all? And can an argument be provided to support the claim that the deliberative stance is not simply in the eye of the beholder, or that, if it is, why it is not contingently so—that is, why we are nonetheless required to take it up? Two responses to this challenge have been made and both can be found in Habermas's writings. The first has a more transcendental character; while the second appeals to the centrality of the deliberative stance to our social practices.

One way in which the claim that we "must" adopt the deliberative stance (toward ourselves and others) might be defended is by way of a transcendental argument. The claim would be that the idealizations that together make up the "deliberative stance" are presupposed by—"conditions of possibility for"—agency (or practical rationality) even in the more minimal sense of the capacity to act on the basis of beliefs and desires. The transcendental argument begins with the claim that even in standard ("folk psychological") cases of agency more is presupposed than Dennett's account of simple intentional systems. Ascriptions of agency involve not only the assumption that the agent's conduct can be predicted *via* beliefs and desires attributed to him, but also that the agent is appropriately sensitive or responsive to reasons—this further assumption is central to the view that an agent acts not only in accordance with a rule or norm, but from a rule or norm or that it is guided by a rule (Burge 1998, 262). Sensitivity to reason, in turn, requires a conception of the agent as "active" and not merely passive with respect to her desires. Further, the notion of an agent as "active" and not merely passive entails something like the capacity for critical reflection and/or "reflective endorsement": the ability to step back from a potentially motivating desire and ask whether one endorses it or wants to treat is as a reason for action (Korsgaard 1996, 49f.).

Finally, the capacity for reflective endorsement, I shall argue below, is best understood in connection with what I will call the "sociality of reason"—roughly the claim that reflective endorsement is not a solitary endeavor but requires social practices of justification that include other reason-givers or "co-deliberators." An agent can identify with or reflectively endorse a desire only if she sees herself as someone who is accountable to others and others in the community treat her as accountable. To be a reason-giver (or to be an accountable agent) presupposes a social practice that itself involves mutual or reciprocal recognition among actors (PT, 183; compare also Westlund 2009).

A second approach takes the form, not of a transcendental argument about the conditions of agency, but a claim about what, given certain social practices, it is extremely difficult (or even impossible) to imagine doing without. It parallels an argument that can be found in P. F. Strawson's influential essay, "Freedom and Resentment" (2003), and also bears a strong resemblance to Kant's doctrine of the "fact of reason." According to standard interpretations of this doctrine, Kant abandons the attempt to provide a transcendental argument for freedom. In the second *Critique* he instead treats it as a "fact" which can't be independently justified. Arguments about freedom (and morality) finally come to rest on this fact, which is known by "conscience" or "common human understanding" (Rawls 1999a, 519). Thus, rather than an independent (transcendental) argument for freedom, the doctrine of the "fact of reason" helps us to better understand (and to resist naturalist or skeptical objections to) what, from a practical point of view, is already familiar to ordinary human reason.

Habermas employs both of these strategies at various points in his writings. For example, the transcendental argument offers the best way to understand his claims in *The Theory of Communicative Action* that strategic action is parasitic upon communicative action (TCA 1, 292). It can also be found in his response to Richard Rorty's contextualist "ethnocentrism" and his critique of Dieter Henrich (Habermas 2000; PT, 23f.). At the same time the more "modest" argument, which appeals to what is (nearly) unimaginable from a practical point of view, is most clearly seen in his remark that we are all "children of modernity"—that is, the products of historical and thus contingent traditions which are, nonetheless, practically inescapable for us. As Habermas has expressed it in a quite sweeping formulation:

> Communicative reason, too, treats almost everything as contingent, even the conditions for the emergence of its own linguistic medium. But for everything that claims validity within linguistically structured forms of life, the structures of possible mutual understanding in language constitute something that cannot be gotten around.
>
> (PT, 139–140)

In fact, the two approaches need not be regarded as mutually exclusive: It might be, that is, that while skepticism or a "bald naturalism" (McDowell 2002) with respect to human behavior is theoretically possible, viewing others (and ourselves) as "minded" is so deeply embedded in a wide range of practices that abandoning it is simply not a practical alternative for us. If this is so, then the idealizing presuppositions of communicative action will be relatively secure and the transcendental argument from the conditions of agency helps us to see why (BNR, 27).

III. Rational interpretations, normativity, and the second-person perspective—Habermas and Brandom

The account sketched thus far closely aligns Habermas's theory of communicative action with the idea of rational interpretations found in the work of Davidson and Dennett. Like them, it asks what must be supposed in order for such interpretations to be possible. It goes beyond those accounts in the suggestion that in developing interpretations we must also adopt a deliberative stance: We must view others as also moving within a "logical space of reasons" and as acting under the idealizing suppositions of communicative action, including the idea of actors as accountable and as reason-givers.

However, it might be objected that this description of Habermas's project is too limited. Habermas is not interested only in the (otherwise legitimate) question of how rational interpretations are possible, but in the more ambitious goal of developing the normative foundations for a critical theory of society. This objection is certainly correct about Habermas's aim. But the argument about what is required for rational interpretations might also be just one step toward that more ambitious goal (see Chapter 3). Still, by way of conclusion, it might be helpful to point out some other differences between Habermas's approach and other attempts to clarify the conditions for rational interpretations. Pointing out these differences will also show how Habermas remains close to the Kantian conception of reason outlined earlier. Central to these differences is both the "primacy of practical reason" and the ineliminability of the participant's or second-person perspective.

First, on the view most closely associated with Davidson and Dennett the point of developing rational interpretations could be described as primarily theoretical. Its aim is to make reasonably accurate predictions about how others will behave and thereby explain their action. This aim is certainly important. However, Habermas's interest in rational interpretations—and reason generally—is not primarily a theoretical one in this sense. His aim is practical in that he sees reason as not primarily connected with successful prediction of behavior. Reasoning can also be practical in two related senses: It is about providing justifications to others and it involves deliberation about ends—that is, deliberation about who we want to be and what we ought to do. Thus, our interest in taking up the deliberative stance toward others (as well as toward ourselves) is not solely for purposes of prediction and explanation. In viewing others from the deliberative stance—viewing them as complex intentional systems—we see them (like ourselves) as actors concerned with providing justifications and interested in these sorts of practical questions. Of course, Habermas also argues that viewing social actors from the perspective of the deliberative stance, or viewing them under the idealizing assumptions of communicative action, is necessary to explain social reproduction. But this is a claim from the theoretical perspective of a sociologist that is subsequent to and dependent upon a prior argument about the ineliminability of the participant's perspective and the deliberative stance (TCA 2, 148).

Second, and perhaps more importantly, Habermas's account of communicative action has important consequences for an analysis of the grounds or source of normativity—one that is again best understood as "constructivist" or Kantian. According to Habermas, to adopt the deliberative stance is to view the conduct of others (like ourselves) as norm-guided. Norms, on this view, are embedded in practices and practices are constituted by the relevant attitudes or commitments of social actors. In viewing others from the deliberative stance, we treat them as guided by and accountable to the norms contained in their practices. In other words, in viewing them from the "deliberative stance" (as complex discursive scorekeepers) we not only see their practices as normative, but see those practices themselves are sustained and reproduced by the actors in those practices. Social actors are both subject to the norms of those practices and reproduce them through their "interpretive accomplishments.", (see Chapter Three, p. 54). This view of relation between actors and practices is again at the core of his notion of communicative action.

However, and this once again goes to the root of Habermas's approach, this means interpreters must view themselves as at least "virtual participants" in the practices that are considered from the deliberative stance (TCA 1, 103). That is, the interpreter must see the social actors as reason-givers whose reasons must convince her and (again at least virtually) as entitled to reasons for her interpretations in response. This entails that, on Habermas's view, adopting the deliberative stance is ineliminably second-personal and that this second-person or participant's perspective is important for his account of normativity since the norms are instituted through the (participants') attitudes—both those of the interpreter and those of the (interpreted) actors.

The question of whether normativity requires a second-person or participant's perspective—that is, attitudes involving certain specifically interpersonal expectations—emerges explicitly in a recent exchange between Habermas and Brandom (TJ, chap. 3; Brandom 2000b). The exchange is particularly significant given the apparently deep agreement between their respective projects. Like Habermas, Brandom also locates the source of normativity in the attitudes adopted by actors in the context of social practices:

> Now it is a fundamental claim of *Making It Explicit* that normative facts of the sort appealed to in making explicit defining features of discursive practice—those pertaining to commitments and entitlements—should be understood as socially instituted. That

is, apart from our scorekeeping attitudes of attributing and acknowledging such deontic statuses, there are no such statuses, and hence no corresponding normative facts about them.

(Brandom 2000b, 365)

Nonetheless, in his review of Brandom's book Habermas suggests that Brandom's account falls back into a type of individualism and hence fails to do justice to the role of the second person. More specifically, he claims that "on closer examination [of his account], it becomes evident that the act of attributing, which is of fundamental importance for discursive practice, is not really carried out by a second person [or "virtual participant"—KB]" (TJ, 162). Rather, on Brandom's account, the attitudes that institute normativity— fundamentally, taking or treating another as a discursive scorekeeper, or treating another as undertaking a commitment—either bottom out in dispositions to sanction by others in the community or in factual assertions about those practices by a third person or non-participating observer (TJ, 162).

In his reply, Brandom accepts this characterization of his account and suggests that it reflects an important motivation: namely, to explain the normativity intrinsic to intentionality (e.g. he "ought" to go because he promised) without already presupposing it or, as he has elsewhere expressed it, its aim is "to make intentional soup out of non-intentional bones" (Brandom 2000b, 364). The weakness of Habermas's account of communicative action, according to Brandom, is that it presupposes the normativity intrinsic to intentionality rather than explaining it. In acting communicatively, actors are "committed" to make good their claims and they "expect" others to provide reasons for the claims they make. On Brandom's view, these second-person attitudes presuppose both intentionality and normativity and so are not able to offer an explanation of it.

At least two questions can be raised in connection with this exchange. Does the account of the second-person attitudes central to communicative action presuppose an "original" intentionality? And, is it possible to explain (intentional) normativity from a conceptually prior (non-intentional) normativity that Brandom identifies with the third-person attitudes of treating as scorekeepers (assuming here that treating as a scorekeeper is just to attribute a more complex set of entitlements and commitments to the actors being interpreted)? Distinguishing these two questions also exposes a different motivation behind the two projects: Habermas is not primarily interested in explaining how "intentional soup can be made from non-intentional bones." He is rather concerned to show how the (normative) resources for coordinating social action can be derived from the pragmatic suppositions of "mutual understanding" or communicative action. (And, if the argument I have sketched here is sound, in showing—in a roughly Kantian fashion—how the idealizing suppositions of communicative action must be presupposed insofar as we treat others as "acting for reasons" at all.)

It is, of course, also true that in opposing the "philosophy of the subject" Habermas is interested in developing an account of action (and meaning) that does not treat a particular model of intentionality—the intrinsic directedness of private mental states—as a fundamental starting point for developing an account of normativity. Rather, it begins with the intersubjective recognition (*via* a practice of mutual ascription) of ego and alter as "reason-givers." But this social practice—in which ego and alter are, so to speak, "co-posited"—does not bottom out in brute dispositions to sanction. That is, it may be that Brandom is correct that the "second-person" attitude identified by Habermas does assume (rather than explain) intentionality (and its distinctive normativity).

On the other hand, one might also ask whether Brandom's own account of ascribing normative status to others is convincingly able to avoid the second-person perspective described by Habermas. Brandom describes the perspective as one in which the interpreter attributes (but does not acknowledge) a range of commitments and entitlements to another (Brandom 2000b, 367). But is it possible for an interpreter to attribute a commitment to another without himself having some grasp of what it would mean for that person to undertake it—that is, what would be rational for that person to do by our own lights? If not then this description of the "third-person" perspective as one of attributing but not acknowledging a commitment would not seem to represent a genuine alternative to Habermas's notion of a virtual participant. In treating another as a discursive scorekeeper, one treats her as a "reason-giver" who is (at least virtually) within the same logical space of reasons as the interpreter, that is, subject to the same sorts of commitments that one would oneself acknowledge (and not only attribute to another). Brandom might reply that whether the third-person interpreter is himself a discursive scorekeeper who acknowledges (as well as attributes) scorekeeping attitudes is itself a question that can only be answered from the perspective of yet another, higher-order scorekeeper who attributes the relevant attitudes to the lower-order interpreter. But this would seem to open up an unsatisfying regress of attributions.

To conclude this section, I have argued that Habermas's interest in developing rational interpretations—or rational explanations—is not an exclusively (or even primarily) theoretical task. To the extent that we must view the subjects of our interpretations as co-deliberators and as engaged in deliberation about ends as well as means, the interest in rational interpretations is also practical in this sense. Second, the account of rational interpretations—and the claim that it involves idealizing suppositions—is relevant for the larger question of the origin or source of normativity. Habermas, like Brandom, locates normativity in the attitudes (we suppose) actors take up toward one another—there is no normativity apart for the statuses instituted via these attitudes. However, with Habermas and against Brandom, these attitudes are importantly (and irreducibly) second-personal in the sense that to adopt the deliberative stance is to treat them as "co-participants" in the "space of reasons." In adopting the deliberative stance, we view others as at least virtual participants in the exchange of reasons that must convince us as well. Finally, so construed, the deliberative stance (and Habermas's account of communicative action, generally) can be seen as a "pragmatic" rendering of Kant's claim that in so far as we view ourselves as capable of acting for reasons at all we must view ourselves as acting under the idea of freedom.

I have given extended attention to Habermas's Kantian pragmatism and its relation to communicative action since both are central to his work. As we saw in Chapter 2, in KHI Habermas described his own position as "transcendental pragmatism." In TCA, the core idea of communicative action with its idealizing presuppositions is offered as an alternative to "epistemology as the *via regia*" (AS, 152): that is, the fruitfulness of this approach in social theory need not depend upon a convincing prior epistemological grounding. As we will see in the next chapters, the concept of communicative action plays a central role in the development of his "discourse morality" (Chapter 5) and in his political writings—and especially in BFN—it is presupposed in his argument that a convincing normative political theory must do justice to both the public and private autonomy of citizens (Chapter 6). The claim that communicative action is a fundamental concept, or that we can't avoid rational interpretations that make strong idealizing assumptions about the capacities of social actors, is thus basic to Habermas's work as a whole.

Notes

1 Several recent commentators have also explored Habermas's Kantian pragmatism. See Bernstein 2010; Flynn 2014; Levine 2010.
2 Although Brandom's *Making it Explicit* (1994) and other writings are important for clarifying Habermas's position, it should not be assumed that the influence has only been in one direction in framing the basic idea of rational action as normative and hence social. Brandom's early 1979 essay "Freedom and Constraint by Norms" makes reference to Habermas's *Knowledge and Human Interests*.
3 For this reason I believe that Habermas's approach to rational (meaningful) action can be characterized as a type of "constitutive interpretationism" (see Child 1994, 48f.; Ellis 2011).

Five
Locating discourse morality

Morality is made for man, not man for morality.

(W. Frankena, *Ethics*, 1973, 116)

Since moralities are tailored to suit the fragility of human beings individuated
through socialization, they must solve two tasks at once. The must emphasize the
inviolability of the individual by postulating equal respect for the dignity of each
individual. But they must also protect the web of intersubjective relations of mutual
recognition by which these individuals survive as members of a community.

(MCCA, 200)

Habermas's conception of a communicative or discourse ethics—
or, more accurately, discourse *morality*—has emerged only gradually
over the course of his career and did not receive sustained attention
until the early 1980s after the publication of *The Theory of Communicative
Action*. This may surprise some readers who first became acquainted
with Habermas through his moral writings or his later engagement
with Rawls, but it is worth pointing out in order not to overemphasize
the position of morality and moral theory within his larger project
of social criticism.[1] For Habermas moral norms emerged in
connection with and often out of religious traditions and as such are
one type of social norm among others, even if the binding or
obligatory force now associated with them is unique.

In his earlier writings Habermas conceived of morality in ways
similar to other Hegelian Marxists. Morality is one element of the
wider "institutional framework" of society—his more abstract label
for what Marx called the "social relations of production"—and

develops along with other social institutions in connection with expanding productive forces. At times it can play a critical role in society but as often it serves a primarily legitimating role. However, in contrast to more orthodox Marxist views which tend to dismiss morality as largely determined by "material" forces, Habermas reads Marx's dialectic (between the productive forces of society and their social relations) as a "dialectic of the moral life" in which the original "crime"—"disproportional appropriation of the social product" (KHI, 57)—can only be "avenged" or compensated with the development of an institutional framework in which the harm done has been recognized and the injured party restored to the social community (KHI, 57; Honneth 1991, 271; Bernstein 1995). In Habermas's suggestive reading of the early Marx (and the early Hegel) this requires the realization of an institutional framework based on communication free from domination (KHI, 53, and TP, chap. 4: "Labor and [moral] interaction"). On this understanding, morality most fundamentally concerns the relations among members of a society especially as the demands made upon those relations increase as more conventional and religious norms lose their binding authority. As others have noted, and as Habermas described it in TCA, this is also a deeply "Durkheimian" understanding of morality: "the normatively integrated fabric of social relations is moral *in and of itself*, as Durkheim has shown" (MCCA, 164; Heath 2014). What this means, for Habermas, is that morality is most fundamentally not about abstract moral principles or "natural laws," but about a class of social norms connected to the legitimacy of a social order and responsible for the integration of individuals as "singular" or "unique" into that social order (IS, 153).

In *Legitimation Crisis* (1973b) Habermas offers some further remarks consistent with this earlier description insofar as a developmental history of morality can be traced (from the natural law tradition through a general welfarism to a formalistic or "principled" ethics) as it emerges over against but in close connection with modern positive law and the political state (LC, 95f.). He also refers for the first time to an "ethics of speech" (*Sprachethik*) and acknowledges his indebtedness to the work of his career-long friend and colleague Karl-Otto Apel. As he describes it at this time, such an ethics would make it possible for members of a society to assess social norms in connection with a "counterfactually projected reconstruction" based on the question:

> How would the members of a social system, at a given stage in the development of productive forces, have collectively and bindingly interpreted their needs (and which norms would they have accepted as justified) if they could and would have decided on organization of social intercourse through discursive will-formation, with adequate knowledge of the limiting conditions and functional imperatives of their society?
>
> (LC, 113)

So conceived, an "ethics of speech" would play a primarily critical and "advocacy" role in order to expose interests that were not generalizable or to identify suppressed but generalizable interests. Given that such "counterfactual projections" are hypothetical, Habermas argued they would also have to be subsequently confirmed by those affected in actual discourses. Nonetheless, and despite that rather significant caveat, this "ethics of speech" was presented as an alternative to the popular "decisionism" of Weber and others insofar as it claimed that practical questions were in principle open to rational resolution. They must in the last analysis be settled with reference to "no force except that of the better argument" (LC, 108).

It is important to keep this earlier understanding of morality in mind when considering Habermas's subsequent discussion. Morality is continuous with other social norms and primarily serves the dual roles of social integration and legitimation. As importantly, however, many questions about this proposal remain: Why is this "discourse" model preferable to competing proposals for a secular or rational morality? Why assume that a consensus or convergence on generalizable interests would be forthcoming even hypothetically? Doesn't this idea of rational consensus present the (misleading) image of a utopianism that will inevitably make a hostage of the "second best"—or, how should the relation between ideal and non-ideal theorizing be conceived?

Habermas did not attempt to address these and other questions further until a decade later with the publication of his 1983 essay, "Discourse Ethics: Notes on a Program of Philosophical Justification" (in MCCA). The essay remains his most systematic attempt to outline the first-order normative theory that he claims can be developed from his theory of communicative action. Although there are some changes from his earlier views—there is clearly a more Kantian tone in his later work—the differences have sometimes been overstated and it would indeed be quite troubling if later developments were to deprive discourse morality of "almost everything that was interesting in the initial formulation."[2] In fact, Habermas continues to regard moral norms as a special class of social norms—namely, those that are intended to highlight the inviolability of the individual and to protect "the web of intersubjective relations of mutual recognition by which these individuals survive as members of a community" (MCCA, 200). Insofar as modern societies are less able to rely upon traditional (and historically religious) norms to achieve these goals, they become more dependent on the fragile and risk-filled resource of communicative action itself: "The liberated subjects, no longer bound and directed by traditional roles, have to create binding obligations by dint of their own communicative efforts" (PNC, 155; also TCA 1, 340; see also Chapter 3, p. 66–67). Thus the emergence of a (detranscendentalized) Kantian element in discourse morality is not a sign that Habermas has abandoned a more Durkheimian understanding of morality, but an indication that in modern societies marked by a high degree of pluralism moral norms will inevitably become more abstract and formal in character—a trend that Habermas had already indicated in his discussion of Durkheim in *The Theory of Communicative Action* (TCA 2, 50). Other developments in his understanding of discourse morality are also more or less a result of his further reflections on the complex relation between morality and positive law (again in a pluralist society) and on the complex interlocking and overlapping of different types of practical discourses in modern complex societies (see below).

I. The core idea of a discourse morality

In its most elaborated form discourse morality is defined in connection with a demanding principle of universalizability. Habermas's "Principle U" states that a norm is valid (or morally justified) if and only if "all affected can accept the consequences and the side effects its *general* observance can be anticipated to have for the satisfaction of *everyone's* interests (and these consequences are preferred to those of known alternative possibilities for regulation)" (MCCA, 65; IO, 42). This means that a controversial or contested moral norm can only retain its *prima facie* status (or should only be first granted status as a moral norm) to the extent that it would be agreed to by all affected in a discourse in which the aim is to determine whether the norm satisfies the conditions specified in Principle U. Discourse morality is thus, like Kant's moral theory, "constructivist" since the moral validity or correctness of a norm depends on whether the norm in question either actually is—or could reasonably be regarded as—the outcome of a deliberative procedure that incorporates all the relevant requirements of correct reasoning—namely, the conditions specified in Principle U.

Discourse morality shares several other features with other broadly Kantian moral theories. It is a formalistic ethic in the sense that it does not presuppose any substantive moral content (beyond a very general idea of practical reason) but rather specifies a formal procedure which any norm must satisfy if it is to be morally acceptable. It is also a cognitivist ethic, not in the sense that it supposes an independent order of moral facts, but in its insistence that there exists a sufficient analogy between moral discourse and scientific discourse that makes it possible to speak, for example, of progress in learning or of a comparable notion of "good reason" or argument in both. Finally, discourse morality is a deontological moral theory in two senses. It assumes the priority of the right over the good. The basic moral principle must be specified in a way that does not presuppose a specific conception of the good life since that would violate the liberal commitment to a plurality of conceptions of the good. In a further sense the distinction between deontological and teleological theories is closely related to Kant's distinction between categorical and hypothetical imperatives, a distinction strongly contested in contemporary analytic moral philosophy. Habermas sides with those who argue that morality consists of categorical imperatives—this is the special obligatory force associated with moral norms mentioned above—but he also agrees with critics that Kant's own attempt to derive such imperatives from a minimal notion of practical rationality (or agency) was not successful. For Habermas the strong obligatory character of moral norms initially derived from their connection to religion. Given that discourse morality is a secular morality, however, he now seeks to locate the oughtness or obligatory character of moral norms in terms of their relation to communicative action: Valid norms are morally binding because of their intimate connection with the rationally binding force contained in illocutionary speech acts—that is, in the "yes/no position-taking" of social actors in communicative action (MCCA, 109; see C.1 below).

However, Habermas's discourse morality also differs from Kant's moral theory in some important respects. It breaks with Kant's two-world metaphysics (noumenal/phenomenal) and rejects his exclusively monological interpretation of the categorical imperative in favor of an intersubjective or communicative version of the principle of universalizability. Of course, Kant's categorical imperative—especially in its "Kingdom of Ends" formulation—already has an intersubjective dimension to it. However, it is only because of his two-world metaphysics that Kant was able to equate what *one* person can consistently and rationally will with what *everyone* could consistently and rationally agree to. Only because interests, desires, and inclinations are set over against reason and purged from the Kingdom of Ends can Kant assume a harmony between the individual and the collective rational will. In discourse morality, by contrast, such simulated thought experiments should ideally be replaced by practical discourses. Even though any actual discourse will always be limited by constraints of space and time and will thus fall short of their ideal, virtual dialogues carried out by a few on behalf of others are not an adequate substitute. What this means in effect is that there will be very few norms that can be identified as the outcome of a moral discourse. At most, perhaps, basic moral norms will come to resemble a core set of basic human rights.

In a series of essays since "Discourse Ethics" Habermas has responded to various criticisms of his idea of a discourse morality and sought to show how it might be realized or institutionalized. He now distinguishes between various types of practical discourses—moral, ethical, and pragmatic—and insists on a fairly sharp demarcation between moral questions (or questions of right or justice) and ethical questions (questions of an individual or collective good). He argues that a discourse morality that focuses on individual interests need not be at the expense of forms of social solidarity (JA; see Pensky 2008). And he has proposed an important distinction (within moral discourses) between "discourses of justification" and "discourses of application." This distinction is crucial if the idea of a moral discourse about a norm is to have any traction: In discourses of justification, the foreseeable contexts of a norm's application are held fixed and the question of its acceptability for satisfying interests made central; in discourses of application, by contrast, the interpretation of the norm is held fixed and its consequences in different contexts of application is made central (Günther 1993). This discussion, in turn, has led to further attempts to specify how different types of practical discourses might be interconnected. Finally, in *Between Facts and Norms*, Habermas seeks to clarify the complex relation between moral norms and legal norms within the context of a pluralist and democratic society (see Chapter 5). The remainder of this chapter will focus primarily on the basic idea of a discourse morality and attempts to construe it as a form of moral constructivism. Some of the other topics will be taken up in later chapters.

II. Discourse morality and moral constructivism

A. What is moral constructivism, and why?

Moral rightness, according to Habermas, is "constructed" not discovered. "Ideally warranted assertability"—or agreement about norms reached under ideal discursive conditions—"exhausts" the idea of normative rightness (TJ, 258; OPC, 381n.55). Nonetheless, against various forms of moral skepticism and decisionism, Habermas insists that moral judgments can be objective and that moral rightness is "analogous" to truth insofar as both types of claims must meet demanding standards of rational validity. It is just this combination of claiming a form of objectivity and yet not being "independent" of our (ideal) practices that distinguishes moral constructivism from other normative theories. It is also what leaves it open to criticism.

Cristina Lafont, along with other sympathetic readers of Habermas, has directly addressed this topic (Lafont 2003, 2004). According to

Lafont, moral constructivisms, including Habermas's, are poised in a very "unstable position" between realism and anti-realism. On her view, the only convincing recourse is a move in the direction of greater realism: unless there are something like real "generalizable interests" that exist prior to and independent of the deliberative procedure that identifies them, constructivism will fail to capture a central feature of the "phenomenology" of ordinary moral judgments, namely, our belief that moral judgments are objective. "But," she continues, "as long as we can reasonably presuppose that there is an overlap of basic interests among all human beings our judgments about the justice [viz, morality] of norms *can already be objectively valid*: If a norm protects those interests for everyone it is just, if it does not, it is unjust" (Lafont 2004, 34; italics in original). If Lafont is correct, then moral constructivism would fail to constitute a unique contribution to moral theory distinct from moral realism. At most it would offer a kind of heuristic device for discovering antecedent objective moral norms, rather than a deliberative procedure that defines or specifies the conditions a moral norm must satisfy (see Lafont 2003, 177; Finlayson 2000, 329).

In a similar vein, other critics have suggested that the basic moral principle of Habermas's discourse morality (especially one centered on Principle U) is either trivial and "empty" or circular (see Benhabib and Dallmayr 1990; McMahon 2000). The claim is roughly that the proposed deliberative procedure—that is, the rule of argument provided by Principle U—contributes little if anything as a moral principle (or first-order decision procedure) or as a clarification of what moral rightness consists in. Proceduralism (or constructivism) does little (if any) of the real work in moral deliberation and judgment and cannot provide an explanation of the "rightness" of our moral norms and practices (Pettit 2000 and 2006).

These criticisms, if correct, would undermine the constructivist character of discourse morality: namely, that practical discourses (or deliberative procedures) are not just heuristic aids but, on the contrary, "constitute" or establish the status of a norm as a moral norm (TJ, 258). Of course, that is precisely the critics' point. Constructivism stands or falls with the claim that morality is conceptually linked to the idea of reasonable agreement or, more generally, the idea of an ideal deliberative procedure. Candidate norms are justified as valid moral norms if and only if (and "because") they are or would be the outcome of an ideal deliberative procedure.[3]

Given the challenges facing such an interpretation of discourse morality, it might be helpful to pause and consider what motivates the development of a constructivist account. Why bother, if there aren't some compelling reasons? Some of these motivations might also be more appealing than others and different motivations might help us to distinguish among the competing constructivist accounts on offer.

One motivation for developing a constructivist account of morality might be to locate (moral) normativity in an otherwise naturalistic view of the world. This, to be sure, is an ambitious aim: it takes seriously the claim, popularized by Mackie, that moral properties fit uncomfortably in the world as described by the sciences and, as a result, seeks to ground normativity in another way, without however resorting to suspect forms of non-naturalism (Mackie 1977, 38). It also motivates the attempt to account for the "objectivity" of our moral judgments without recourse to strong metaphysical claims about (non-natural) properties. Certainly, this is one way of viewing Kant's critical project as a whole and it's continuation among some of his successors. Habermas shares some of this motivation as well, given, as we have seen, his strong defense of interpretive social science and insistence that the symbolically structured lifeworld is *sui generis* and not to be confused with the world of stance-independent facts known *via* the natural sciences.

A second but equally ambitious motivation for constructivism is found in those accounts which seek to ground or justify a basic moral principle in non-moral considerations alone. David Gauthier, who describes his own position as Hobbesian constructivism, expresses this motivation as follows: "Morality can be generated as a rational constraint from the non-moral premises of rational choice" (Gauthier 1987, 5). But it is worth pointing out that other forms of constructivism explicitly reject this motivation: John Rawls, Tim Scanlon, and (at least in writings since "Discourse Ethics") Habermas all belong to this latter group.

Finally, a slightly less ambitious but still quite important motivation for constructivism can be found in those accounts that attempt to capture a thin or minimal set of moral ideals directly in a deliberative procedure such that, if the procedures are then correctly executed, the outcome will be one that also preserves the initial ideals. Kant's categorical imperative can be seen as such an attempt to capture the idea of freedom as autonomy or "self-legislation"; Rawls's Original Position is an attempt to mirror in a determinate procedure what he calls the "two fundamental moral powers of the person" (or the "reasonable" and the "rational"); and, finally, Habermas claims that his Principle U expresses the basic moral ideal of mutual respect or reciprocal recognition. Thus, while all three reject the idea that morality can be derived from non-moral principles of rationality, they all hope to capture in a procedure certain basic, abstract, but widely shared normative ideals.

I believe this is a primary motivation for Habermas's moral constructivism. If so, it represents an attempt to locate discourse morality, so to speak, between more radical contextualism, on the one hand, and various forms of moral realism on the other. So understood, constructivism also attempts to defend a broadly cognitivist morality against various skeptical criticisms, but does so not by locating it in an order of reason independent of social practices and institutions. Rather, it attempts to construct (or reconstruct) it in connection with processes of mutual or reciprocal recognition—forms of communicative action—that are immanent within and constitutive for those social practices.[4] In the following I will consider this understanding of moral constructivism by further clarifying some of its core features through a comparison with Scanlon. I will then take up some other features of Habermas's own constructivst view of discourse morality and some further criticisms that have been raised against it.

B. A comparison: Scanlon's contractualism

Tim Scanlon has proposed an account of "moral contractualism" that is also a form of moral constructivism. According to his theory, "an act is wrong if its performance under the circumstances would be disallowed by any set of principles for the general regulation of behavior that no one could reasonably reject as a basis for informed, unforced general agreement" (Scanlon 1998, 153). Or, more conveniently for our own purposes, moral wrongness is specified in connection with the idea of reasonable rejectability: an act is wrong if it would be prohibited by principles that no one could reasonably reject. Many commentators have noted some of the similarities and differences between Scanlon's contractualism and Habermas's discourse morality (Kelly 2000; McMahon 2000, 2011; Heath 2014).

However getting clear on just what the real points of convergence and difference are is not an easy task. For example, Habermas has suggested that his view is dialogical while Scanlon's is not; and Scanlon seems to have accepted this contrast (as did I in an earlier work—Baynes 1992). Similarly, Habermas has claimed that discourse morality depends importantly on real or actual discourses taking place, whereas Scanlon claims his idea of reasonable rejectablity is solely a hypothetical test. Yet, there is reason to think that both of these contrasts are mistaken or at least overdrawn. For example, although Scanlon does claim that his view is monological, he also states that individual judgments must be "reasonable" (Scanlon 1998, 168–169). In response, one might ask whether a judgment could be reasonable if (either intentionally or through mere negligence) it fails to take the perspective of others into consideration (Chambers). On the other hand, Habermas's claim that discourses must be actual and not merely hypothetical has met with a great deal of skepticism even by his most sympathetic critics (see for example Rehg 2011, 127). How could moral rightness depend on any actual agreement, given the strong likelihood that any actual agreement will fail to meet the conditions specified in Principle U?

Though there is no doubt that more could be said on either side concerning both of these points (see below), this should be enough to suggest that a closer examination is required to identify the real points of agreement and disagreement. These initial observations, however, raise important and difficult questions for both discourse morality and Scanlon's contractualism: Does the notion of a discursive agreement or, in Scanlon's account, reasonable rejection do any real work, or is it redundant or, worse, a mere cover? If we don't identify norms as moral because they are products of (real or hypothetical) deliberative procedures or because they are reasonably rejectable but for deeper and independent reasons, doesn't this make the role of a joint agreement (or reasonable rejectability) circular? Alternatively, if the deliberative procedure is regarded *solely* as a useful heuristic—an aid in gathering information—but not central to the constitution or shaping of a moral norm, doesn't this make constructivism trivial, reducing it to something like: It's important to keep the moral conversation going? It's a very short step from there to the conclusion drawn by McMahon that "discursive agreement" at best plays what he calls a "piecemeal role"—a useful heuristic but one that any plausible moral theory should easily be able to take onboard. (I will return to McMahon's criticism in greater detail below.)

To see more clearly the similarities and differences between Habermas and Scanlon, some further features of Scanlon's contractualism need to be pointed out. First, contractualism does not purport to provide a unifying account of *all* moral phenomena, including our obligations to the environment, other species, or even to our own individual selves. Rather, Scanlon is interested in what he describes as the "morality of right and wrong" or the aspect of morality concerned with what it is that we owe to one another (Scanlon 1998, 171, 178). Nevertheless, what it means to call an act morally wrong (in this narrower sense) is to be explained by the basic idea of justifiability to others (or "reasonable rejectability") and *not* the other way around. Contractualism "holds that thinking about right and wrong is, at the most basic level, thinking about what could be justified to others on grounds that they, if appropriately motivated, could not reasonably reject" (Scanlon 1998, 5).

Second, though this point is not always appreciated in discussions of his position, Scanlon claims that closely associating the idea of morality (again in the narrower sense) with the idea of justifiability to others means that the sorts of considerations or reasons that are central to his view are what he calls "personal" or "agent-relative" reasons and not "impersonal" or "agent-neutral" reasons: "Impersonal reasons do not, themselves, provide grounds for reasonably rejecting a principle" (Scanlon 1998, 220; also Scanlon 2003, 186; 2004, 128). What we are asked to consider (as individuals) is whether another agent (who similarly cares about justification to others) would have a reason to object, not whether there exist impersonal reasons (e.g. reasons that make no essential reference to the agent to whom the reason applies—a reason, for example, to promote happiness *per se* rather than a reason to promote his own happiness) (Ridge 2001, 475). By focusing on the personal reasons individuals might have for objecting to a norm or principle in this way Scanlon attempts to capture and express the basic idea of justifiability to others that is central to his account.

Finally, Scanlon states that it is ultimately the notion of reasonableness contained in the idea of reasonable rejectability that performs a great bulk of the work in his contractualist account (Scanlon 2004, 134). Moreover, the notion of reasonableness is substantive (like the notion of fairness) and so there is little hope of being able to capture it in a "tightly constructed procedure" (as, for example, Rawls's attempts in the construction of the Original Position) (Scanlon 2004, 242). Rather, he writes: "On the version [of contractualism] I am defending … we must sometimes exercise judgment as to whether certain considerations are or are not relevant to the reasonable rejectability of a principle, since these grounds are not completely specified in advance" (Scanlon 1998, 218; also 157–158, 206). Nonetheless, Scanlon maintains that it is still the fact that a principle is reasonably rejectable—and not the various substantive grounds that contribute to the person's individual judgment—that defines (or constitutes) the content of morality: "On this view, the idea of justifiability to others is taken to be basic in two ways. First, it is by thinking about what could be justified to others on grounds that they could not reasonably reject that we determine the shape of more specific moral notions such as murder or betrayal. Second, the idea that we have reason to avoid actions that could not be justified in this way accounts for the distinctive normative force of moral wrongness" (Scanlon 1998, 5).

As in the case of Habermas's discourse morality, various critics have claimed that the deliberative procedure or contractualist furnishings in Scanlon's account cannot do any real justificatory work (Pettit 2000, 2006). Rather, it is the particular *reasons* individuals invoke in rejecting a principle that marks it as morally wrong—e.g. the pain inflicted on an innocent person, for example—and not the fact that it is rejectable. So why shouldn't we look directly to those reasons rather than the additional furnishings for the account of moral wrongness? Addressing this criticism highlights one of the most basic issues in the debates about the nature of morality and task of moral theory mentioned in my opening remarks: Those who argue we should appeal directly to the substantive reasons themselves (rather than the idea of reasonable rejectability) are almost invariably consequentialists (as is Pettit) and they apparently take for granted (but don't defend) the view that morality is primarily concerned with impersonal reasons (among which the central or dominant impersonal reason is that of maximizing an aggregate good such as happiness or well-being). However, this is precisely what contractualism denies and this denial is a primary motivation for construing morality around the idea of justifiability to others on the basis of personal (and interpersonal) reasons. Though Scanlon does not dispute the existence of impersonal reasons, he does argue that they are brought into an account of morality (or moral wrongness) in the wrong way when they are appealed to directly rather than indirectly within the framework of reasonable rejectability (Scanlon 2003; Freeman 2006; Ridge 2001). Thus, a persuasive defense of the claim that contractualism is redundant or circular would first require an independent (non-question-begging) argument for the competing view of morality that assumes the centrality of impersonal reasons. But consequentialists have arguably thus far not met this demand and so one could at least claim a dialectical stalemate. Scanlon and other contractualists might also argue that (at least from a phenomenological viewpoint) the idea of reasonable rejectability invoked in their account better expresses the fundamental idea of mutual respect and recognition.

To conclude this brief excursus on Scanlon, I want to suggest that once his contractualism is considered in connection with these more specific points, its status as a form of constructivism becomes clearer. It should also make apparent how his contractualism might in fact be closer to Habermas's own theory than is often supposed. We can thus turn to some of the specific features and criticisms of Habermas's discourse morality.

C. Habermas's discourse morality up close

Like Scanlon's contractualism, Habermas's discourse morality is offered both as an account of what it means to make a moral claim (at least in the restricted sense of a claim about what we owe to each other) and as a test or procedure that should play some role in our actual moral deliberations. In particular (and again like Scanlon), Habermas offers his discourse morality both as a response to certain (modest) forms of moral skepticism and as an alternative to consequentialism. Like Scanlon, it thus does not fit easily within a sharp distinction between meta-ethical reflection and normative theory. It is, rather, offered as a defense of "cognitivism" in the sense that it is a form of moral rationalism (in the Kantian tradition) and as a "proceduralist" account, in contrast, for example, to some virtue-based accounts of morality. The aim is to capture in a deliberative procedure the idea of an impartial adjudication of competing moral claims. For this reason, I think it is appropriate to view it as a form of (moral) constructivism.

Habermas describes Principle U as a pragmatic "rule of argument" (or "inference rule") (MCCA, 66, 197) that is intended to govern what he calls a "moral discourse" (in contrast to other practical forms of discourse—prudential, ethical, legal-political, etc.). As such, it is not itself a "first-order" (directly action-guiding) moral norm but rather a higher-order normative principle that specifies the features of a moral discourse and defines the conditions of a (constructivist) deliberative procedure. To recall from above, Principle U states that a norm is valid (or morally justified) "if and only if all affected can accept the consequences and the side effects its *general* observance can be anticipated to have for the satisfaction of *everyone's* interests (and these consequences are preferred to those of known alternative possibilities for regulation)" (MCCA, 65).[5] I take this to mean that a controversial or contested moral norm can only retain its *prima facie* status (or can only be first granted status as a moral norm) to the extent that it could be agreed to by all affected in a discourse in which the aim is to determine whether the norm satisfies Principle U. As I read Habermas, he is a constructivist since the moral validity or correctness of a norm depends on whether the norm in question either actually is, or could reasonably be regarded (by those affected) as, the "outcome of a deliberative procedure that incorporates all the relevant requirements of correct reasoning" (Freeman 2007, 7)— namely, the conditions specified in Principle U.

So conceived, discourse morality has been criticized in a number of different ways. Some have argued that Habermas's attempt to provide a justification or grounding for Principle U in connection with (formal) pragmatic presuppositions of language (or speech acts) has not been successful (Benhabib and Dallmayr 1990; Wellmer 1991; Finlayson 2000; Ingram 2010, 136). Others have argued that, especially with reference to Principle U, discourse morality is too formal and must be recast in a more substantive manner (Benhabib 1990; Gunnarsson 2000; Gilabert 2005). A different objection holds that Habermas's discourse morality is incoherent because it relies on a problematic notion of "strong dialogicality" (McMahon 2000). So, even if some case has now been made for Habermas's constructivist understanding of discourse morality, many other important criticisms and challenges confront it. I will now turn to a consideration of some of these.

(1) The derivation of Principle U

In his initial attempt to provide a justification for U (in "Notes"), Habermas claimed to provide a "logical derivation" of Principle U from the pragmatic presuppositions of argumentation (MCCA, 97). In response to some early and strong criticism, he quickly modified his initial claim (Benhabib 1986, 307; Benhabib 1990; Finlayson 2000). In response, and perhaps with some recasting of the original aim, Habermas now claims that the argument for Principle U is best construed as an "abduction" or "argument from the best explanation" rather than a strict logical derivation (IO, 43). One important feature of the later view is that Habermas explicitly renounces (like Scanlon and Rawls) the strong rationalist attempt to derive a basic moral principle from non-moral premises alone.[6] In other words, it is not an attempt to answer the question "why be moral?" by showing that the skeptic is, in some relevant amoral sense, irrational if he or she rejects U.[7] Rather, the aim of a justification of Principle U is to answer skeptical or more contextualist challenges to the claim that moral judgments might be based on reasons all could accept—including the skeptic—and so are "rational" or "objective" in this sense. What Habermas believes the abductive argument for Principle U shows is that a person can reject Principle U only at the price of denying or exempting herself from the communicative conditions of social action in general—something the skeptic presumably does not do. Though this is clearly a variant of Karl-Otto Apel's claim that attempts by the skeptic to exempt herself from the basic moral principle amount to a "performative contradiction," it is not best construed as an appeal to a non-moral norm or principle of rationality. In other words, it is not the claim that one can reject morality only at the price of irrationality (see Gunnarsson 2000, 14f.)

In Habermas's revised account (and in a parallel account offered by Rehg) the argument for Principle U identifies two sets of norms that must be combined (IO, 45; Rehg 1994; Baynes 1992, 114): First, there is an identification and formulation of what have come to be called "Alexy's rules of argument" in connection with the pragmatic presuppositions of argument—all competent speakers are allowed to participate, all have an equal opportunity to contribute to the argumentation, and all force or coercion is excluded except the "force of the better argument" (Alexy 1990; MCCA, 89). Secondly, there is a claim that when these rules are combined with a relatively weak idea of what it means to "justify a norm of action," one can arrive (abductively) at Principle U. Much of the discussion has focused on the second step and the question of whether Habermas's appeal to the weak idea of justifying a norm of action is sufficiently weak or whether it is more substantive and surreptitiously appeals to elements of Principle U (Benhabib 1990; Gunnarsson 2000; Rehg 1994). As I understand it, Habermas's claim is that social actors (in a wide range of societies and social contexts) already possess some implicit understanding that a justification or account is required when a perceived social conflict or disagreement about the existing terms of social cooperation arises. But this is still a quite formal feature, associated with the idea of communicative action in general, that Habermas has in mind when he appeals to the "weak" idea of "what it means to justify a norm" and not a stronger and ultimately question-begging notion of, say, the equal consideration of interests (see BNR, 887). Of course, the justifications individuals give in many contexts often do draw upon more substantive assumptions. But it is the formal feature of communicative action—the weak obligation to give an account—that Habermas appeals to in the second step of his argument. It is a thin, but non-negligible, idea of norm-justification in which individuals are viewed as mutually accountable agents.

The derivation of Principle U is completed only when the two steps are brought together. The very demanding (but non-moral) pragmatic presuppositions of argument are combined with the thin notion of an action-theoretic obligation to give an account to yield the demanding obligation regarding the justification of moral norms contained in Principle U. Habermas makes this two-step argument more explicit in a later clarification in *The Inclusion of the Other*:

> A moral obligation cannot follow from the so to speak transcendental constraint of unavoidable presuppositions of argumentation alone; rather it attaches to the specific objects of practical discourse, namely to the norms introduced into discourse to which the reasons mobilized in deliberation refer. I emphasize this when I specify what U can be rendered plausible *in connection with* a (weak, hence nonprejudicial) *concept of normative justification*.
>
> (IO, 45; also BNR, 87)

This clarification of Habermas's two-step argument also allows him to address an otherwise compelling objection made by Albrecht Wellmer. Wellmer argued that Habermas's attempt to derive Principle U from the pragmatic presuppositions of argumentation had confused norms of rationality with the norms of morality in a potentially dangerous way:

> Obligations to rationality refer to the acknowledgement of arguments, moral obligation to the acknowledgement of persons. It is a requirement of rationality to acknowledge even the arguments of my enemy if they are good ones; it is a requirement of morality to permit even those people to speak who are not yet capable of arguing well. Overstating the point a little, we might say that obligations to rationality are concerned with arguments regardless of who voices them, whereas moral obligations are concerned with people regardless of their arguments.
>
> (Wellmer 1991, 185)

But it should now be clear that Habermas does not confuse these two types of norms. Rather he makes the demanding norms of argumentation relevant for the justification of moral norms by combining the former with the weak idea mutually supposed by social agents—and so persons—about what it means to give a justification for an action-norm.

This interpretation of the derivation of Principle U makes it possible to clarify another potential confusion concerning his defense of a discourse morality. Speaking in rather sweeping terms, Habermas remarks that,

> every morality revolves around equality of respect, solidarity, and the common good. Fundamental ideas like these can be reduced to the relations of symmetry and reciprocity presupposed in communicative action. In other words, the common core of all kinds of morality can be traced back to the reciprocal imputations and shared presuppositions actors make when they seek understanding in everyday situations.
>
> (MCCA, 201)

But this claim would seem to depend on two different senses of communicative action if he wants to avoid confusion. Not all moralities—not even all moralities based on some notion of equality—can be derived from a "thin" or weak interpretation of communicative action (together with the rules of argumentation) introduced above. If that were the case, the derivation of Principle U would not be unique but would be just one possible moral principle among others. On the other hand, if a stronger understanding of communicative action is granted—one that situates it within thicker descriptions of the contexts of action— then other (and competing) moral principles may be derivable from it.[8] Thus Habermas remarks, "Knowledge of how to participate in argumentation must be joined with knowledge drawn from the experience of a moral community" (BNR, 87).

It is thus important to keep in mind that communicative action can be understood either weakly or strongly depending on how thinly or thickly the context of action is described.[9] On the weak reading, communicative action refers only to the quite thin and abstract idea of the "yes/no" position-taking that, according to Habermas, is built into communicative action. This does contain a weak normative content since it appeals to a (thin) notion of the freedom/authority of speaker/hearer to assume the "yes/no" stance in the exchange of speech acts. On the strong reading, the description of the action upon which the discourse is "superimposed" might have "thicker" moral content: that is, the norm or norms in question are more deeply embedded in a context of action in which at least one actor is calling into question the appropriateness of a contested moral norm (as in, say, "marriage is between one man and one woman"). In this case, the discourse is not only framed by the more abstract and "thin" notion of communicative action, but also by the thicker context of action in which substantive norms are contested. Moral discourses will almost always (inevitably) be about the latter sorts of norm, and Principle U can be "derived" or "abducted" from the "superimposition" of discourse (rules of argumentation) on such conflicts of action as well, even though the weaker reading of communicative action is sufficient for the derivation (MCCA, 201).

This distinction in communicative action has another important advantage. The features of communicative action identified in the weak interpretation are not specific to modern societies in the sense that it assumes a fairly strong notion of individual autonomy. Rather, it assumes only a weaker notion of "accountability" (*Zurechnungsfähigkeit*). Nevertheless, it is in fact only in a modern society or "post-conventional" setting that the explosive and unsettling force of Principle U is likely to be felt. That is, to the extent that a community is more or less homogeneous, norms are less likely to be contested and so the requirement for a discursive resolution (in the demanding sense of Principle U) may not even arise. This is one point at which Habermas's thesis about modernity becomes especially relevant:

> The more differentiated the structures of the lifeworld become, the easier it is to discern the simultaneous growth of the autonomous individual subject and his dependence on interpersonal relationships and social ties. The more the subject becomes individuated, the more he becomes entangled in a densely woven fabric of mutual recognition, that is, of reciprocal exposedness and vulnerability. Unless the subject externalizes himself by participating in interpersonal relations through language, he is unable to form that inner center that is his personal identity. This explains the almost constitutional insecurity and

chronic fragility of personal identity—an insecurity that is antecedent to cruder threats to the integrity of life and limb.

(MCCA, 199)

The implication of this thesis for discourse morality is relatively straightforward. Insofar as U entails that it is left to those affected as participants in a discourse to settle what counts as a moral norm, the outcome of such deliberative procedures will differ depending upon the normative content participants bring to a discourse (or the moral community to which they belong) (BNR, 87–88). It is only under the "fragmenting" force of modernization, and the development of the normative ideas of moral individualism, moral equality, and "reasonable disagreement" that are in complex ways associated with it, that the more demanding requirements of Principle U also begin to increase exponentially in their explosive power. It is also in such a "post-conventional" context that moral norms will of necessity assume an increasingly abstract form (as prior "agreements" based on substantive moral traditions are disrupted by the increasing pluralism of worldviews).

If this interpretation is correct, much of the controversy will accordingly not be about Principle U *per se* or its derivation. Rather, the debates will be about what morality is or can (or must) be in a pluralist and increasingly "individuated" lifeworld. Or, perhaps better stated, in contexts where the discourse participants themselves bring in a much more diverse and heterogenous set of contested moral norms and considerations that tend to explode the very idea of what morality has been taken to be (e.g. a fairly determinate code of conduct for living one's life well). Under such conditions of a reasonable pluralism and increasing "burdens of justification" moral principles—that is, what might reasonably be viewed as the outcome of a moral discourse—become increasingly abstract and general (converging, perhaps, on a debate about a basic core of human moral rights and their best interpretation). Everything else—that is, everything that cannot be reasonably viewed as the conclusion of a moral discourse—becomes instead a matter of "ethics" or a "conception of the good." Further, in contrast to the reading offered by Joseph Heath, distinctions between questions of the right (or morality) and the good (or values) are not assumed prior to a moral discourse; they are rather the outcome or anticipated conclusion of a moral discourse (Heath 2001, 234f.). This does not mean that conceptions of the good do not continue to inform a moral discourse, but insofar as it is not reasonable to expect that a given conception of the good will meet with the agreement of all in a discourse, that conception itself can no longer serve as a moral norm or be invoked as the basis for a moral norm.

(2) Further criticisms of discourse morality

With this interpretation of Principle U and its place in a discourse morality in view, some of the other criticisms of Habermas's discourse morality can be more briefly considered. First, several critics have objected to the heavily procedural and formal character of discourse morality (Taylor 1993; Benhabib 1990, 345; Gilabert 2005) and have suggested that it must be revised and/or recast in a way that incorporates more substantive norms and values. Some of these criticisms are due, at least in part, to a misunderstanding of Habermas's proceduralism (see further Chapter 6). Any plausible proceduralism must incorporate some values and will not be completely "value-free." In Habermas's case, it is the thin and abstract notion of autonomy or "accountability" introduced in connection with the idea of "communicative freedom" or the yes/ no-position-taking of actors with respect to claims raised in speech acts (Günther 1998). (At a subsequent and slightly more determinate level, this core idea of autonomy or communicative freedom is characterized in connection with the co-original notions of private and public autonomy—it also has other variations, as in the quotation above about individuation.) Though Principle U is (or defines) a procedure for ascertaining valid moral norms, it incorporates this highly abstract notion of autonomy and so its proceduralism is not "value-free." It is also via this abstractly described authority to take a "yes/no" position—or what Stephen Darwall relatedly calls "second-personal authority"—that the claim that morality is "tailored to suit the fragility of human beings individuated through socialization" can be developed. Principle U, in turn, captures this insight in the requirement that valid (moral) norms must be capable of achieving a joint agreement among those engaged in a practical discourse about need-interpretations. It is a norm's connection with such an agreement that in turn confers on it the status of a *moral* norm. However, the procedure specified in this constructivism is not devoid of any substantive ideals; rather, like at least some other forms of constructivism, the substantive ideal(s) are mirrored in the procedure itself. Habermas's claim (like Scanlon's and Darwall's) is that the procedure captures a normative ideal of respect or mutual recognition (which itself expresses the value of "second-personal authority" or "communicative freedom") (see Southwood, 126).

In a related criticism, Erin Kelly (2000) questions whether a discourse morality construed in a formal manner is capable of generating any determinate outcomes. She argues that Scanlon's contractualism is ultimately more attractive since it explicitly embraces a (substantive) notion of reasonableness and she argues further that discourse morality must also incorporate some (moral) notion of reasonableness if it is to be able to produce any determinate outcomes. I agree with Kelly in part: there must be something that plays a roughly equivalent role in discourse morality to the role played by reasonableness in Scanlon's contractualism. But this can be found in Habermas's notion of reciprocal perspective-taking as a feature of a practical discourse: participants in discourse aimed at reaching agreement (if possible) must not only exercise judgment about whether a norm's general observance will satisfy their own need-interpretations, they must also ask, first, whether these need-interpretations can be justified to others (if they are to be considered relevant in an assessment of the norm in question) and, second, whether they (in seeking to reach a joint or collective agreement) are giving sufficient weight to the competing need-interpretations of others. Neither of these requirements can be guaranteed by specifying formal features—the rules of argumentation—alone; they depend upon many other cognitive and empathic skills as well. However, it might also be a virtue of discourse morality that success in reaching any determinate outcomes does not rely *solely* on such individual capacities (however important they may be). Rather, it depends as well on the institutionalization of various types of discourse and the multiple overlaps among them. (More on this in the conclusion below.) On the other hand, it is less clear how much determinate outcome is really to be expected from moral discourse.

Scanlon's contractualism also does not offer very much. It is misleading, in any case, to regard discourse morality as an individual or collective decision-procedure that when applied to a moral problem will generate a unique answer.

Finally, Christopher McMahon has developed a very different line of criticism in several essays on Habermas's discourse morality. He correctly points out that Principle U calls for a joint agreement (in a strong sense) among all affected that a norm is in the equal interest of all. A joint agreement means not only that there is a happy convergence between individual judgments about what is right but requires that each person makes her moral judgment dependent on the judgments of others in a more robust sense. But, McMahon asks, why should Principle U involve such a strong collective requirement? He suggests that on one "epistemic" reading of discourse morality, it may in fact be the case that such collective input would diminish the chance of cognitive bias and error. But this epistemic reading does not support the demand for a strong notion of consensus—or what he calls "strong dialogicality." Rather, he argues that it supports only the heuristic demand that, before making an individual judgment, one should seek out all the relevant information. On the other hand, McMahon finds a "moral" argument for imposing "strong dialogicality" implausible, and it would make the argument for Principle U circular or question-begging (McMahon 2011, 207). As he interprets it, the requirement that all affected must jointly agree for a norm to be valid rests on Habermas's mistaken assumption that each person stands in a privileged (and infallible) position with respect to his or her own need-interpretations (McMahon 2011, 206; 2000, 525). If each person is alone an infallible judge, no one else possesses the right or authority to dismiss a particular claim as mistaken or irrelevant without that individual's consent. The requirement of a joint agreement—or strong dialogicality—then follows from this idea of an individual veto right. McMahon further argues that, given a broadly Wittgensteinian view of rule-following that Habermas shares, this idea of an infallible first-personal perspective is ultimately incoherent (McMahon 2000, 527). If the existence of a (valid) norm depends on a unanimous agreement, then there would be no way for an individual to follow a rule with which he did not agree. Indeed, there would be no way to distinguish between correctly following (or violating) a norm and merely believing that to be the case.

Though he has interesting and suggestive things to say about how Principle U might be construed, I think that McMahon's claim that the requirement of joint agreement rests on a claim about the first-personal authority of need-interpretations is mistaken. Rather, any assumption about first-personal authority must be understood in a defeasible way and so it is possible (and perhaps not even uncommon) that an individual can be mistaken about what is in his or her own best interest (see Taylor 1985b). Nor, as I suggested above, should the requirement of joint agreement be interpreted in a way that suggests that individuals must suspend their judgment until all agree. Rather, each person must be convinced by reasons that a contested norm is equally in the interests of all. Nevertheless, if there is not a joint agreement among all—that is, if each participant is not convinced by the reasons that others are able to give—then the contested norm is not morally valid.[10] This interpretation of joint agreement does not rule out the possibility that participants might agree to disagree or that they might agree to settle some disagreements with reference to higher-order norms on which all can in turn agree. But it does assume that a notion of joint agreement (or strong dialogicality) at whatever level or however counterfactually anticipated is required for a norm to be morally valid.

McMahon also rejects the requirement of "strong dialogicality" because it entails a "constitutive" rather than a heuristic or "epistemic" interpretation of Principle U. Thus, he claims that it is not the agreement *per se*, but rather the underlying substantive reasons themselves that contribute to the moral impartiality of a norm: "The interaction ['joint agreement'] does not itself constitute this impartiality," (McMahon 2002, 115). But this reading is simply another version of the appeal to impersonal reasons that we saw directed at Scanlon's contractualism earlier and so does not need to be accepted: Appeal to impersonal reasons begs the question when it is used to dismiss moral constructivism (Freeman 2006). Thus, while McMahon's suggestion that discourse morality should be viewed as an attempt (like Rawls's) to characterize "the reasons of fairness" seems correct, in dismissing the idea of a joint agreement he misses the way in which moral constructivism tries to capture that idea of fairness or mutual recognition (see also Southwood, 124). The demand for joint agreement, in short, does not rest on a mistaken assumption about the infallibility of first-personal need-interpretation but, to repeat, mirrors in the deliberative procedure this exacting demand of respect or mutual recognition—a view that Rawls, Scanlon, and Habermas all share, albeit in different ways.

III. Conclusion: A dialectic of moral and political constructivism?

In concluding this chapter, I return to the suggestion made above, namely, that Habermas's discourse morality might be located between a liberal moral realism as articulated, for example, by Larmore (among many others) and forms of contextualism that (I will assume here without further argument) are not attractive. Is there any conceptual space to be occupied between these two alternatives? A variation on this question has been posed to a moral constructivist even more sharply in connection with a recent discussion by Samuel Freeman (2007). Freeman asks: who specifically is the audience to whom Scanlon's moral contractualism—or Habermas's discourse morality—might be directed? If it is to citizens of a liberal polity then, Freeman claims, it cannot provide an appropriately stable or reliable moral basis for a liberal constitution because it fails the publicity condition of (Rawls's) *political* constructivism: It is not reasonable to assume that all citizens would endorse a constructivist account as the best or correct "comprehensive" morality. According to Freeman, it could count at most as one among other reasonable private or personal moralities which could in turn become part of a reasonable overlapping consensus. On the other hand, however, a gnawing skepticism persists among many critics that Rawls's own "free-standing" political conception, insofar as it takes for granted the values of a liberal political culture, does not adequately address the question of the moral foundations of a liberal-democratic constitution in an increasingly pluralist and fragmented world (Forst 2012, 92f.). It is here that the liberal "moral realist" stakes his claim and argues that political constructivism comes up short (Larmore 1996). It is here too that more proceduralist positions attempt to gain a foothold

(Waldron 1999). But, finally, it is here that the advantages of discourse morality more fully emerge. Rather than entrusting the weight of moral constructivism *solely* to individual judgments about reasonableness (or what is or isn't reasonably rejectable)—as important and indispensable as those individual moral judgments are—discourse morality differs from Scanlon's contractualism by turning attention *additionally* to the equally indispensable need for multiple and overlapping forms of practical discourse dispersed throughout a formal and informal public sphere—that is, through a vibrant and robust civil society and a complex and interlocking set of institutions for deliberation and decision-making in a formally constituted political government. Like Scanlon's contractualism, discourse morality is (in some sense) a "comprehensive" moral doctrine—it is not, for example, limited only to questions of what *citizens* (in contrast to "all affected") can legitimately demand of one another. It is nonetheless a constructivism that has as its broader aim an operationalizing of the deliberative procedure in such a way that "comprehensive moral doctrines" (or, perhaps more accurately, their contested substantive norms) can themselves become the content of a broad and public moral discourse. In this sense, and in contrast to more contextualist readings of Rawls's political constructivism , it does seem to fulfill a demand that reasonable citizens can appropriately expect of one another, at least when it is a question of why they (morally) ought to accept basic principles of political legitimacy (and "constitutional essentials").[11] It is then not limited to being one comprehensive morality among others. On this interpretation, discourse morality is uniquely positioned to fill a void between comprehensive moral doctrines and prospective principles of political legitimacy, though it must (at the same time) compete for allegiance among other proposals within the public sphere broadly conceived (see Ferrara, 96).

As I suggested above, on this interpretation of discourse morality, moral discourses do not (strictly speaking) take place exhaustively or definitively in any given location or within any limited period of time. They occur, to the extent they happen at all, in the context of a capacious and open-ended understanding of the public sphere. This might seem to make discourse morality border on the trivial—an injunction to "keep the conversation going"—but I don't believe this is the case: Principle U asks whether a proposed moral norm can meet with a very demanding agreement; this is not a "discourse" that can be held within the sole confines of any single home or church or civic group (let alone in *foro interno* or "monologically")—and so it requires that citizens do not simply rest content with the support provided to political principles from within their own personal comprehensive doctrines (an idea suggested by Rawls's metaphor of "modules"). Rather, it is a discourse that arguably best takes place in a context in which other discourses are simultaneously occurring as well and where the deliberations and decisions in one can become "inputs" for deliberations and decisions within others (and where these in turn become inputs to still further discourses).

Of course, as I also suggested above, it is likely that in such a context moral norms will of necessity become more abstract and thin and, most likely, quite few in number: they devolve into the question of what is required to show mutual respect to one another, where this question is in turn debated as we *simultaneously* learn about the real consequences of a given norm's general observance for the need-interpretations of each. It is unlikely, however, that we will ever reach an end to such a discourse or that we will arrive at a definitive list of moral norms or rights. Rather, such discourses are more likely to give rise to "a dialectic between fact and norm" concerning the freedom and equality of each, as Habermas puts it in the related legal context (BFN, 409f.). In this respect, morality also depends on politics (as well as on law and a robust civil society) for new insights concerning need-interpretations and for new information concerning the likely consequences of a norm's general observance, just as politics must look for its own moral legitimation (contrary to at least some readings of Rawls) to a dynamic "moral core" that, on this view, is best interpreted constructively.[12] Morality takes shape and develops in the context of an ongoing discourse (and, often too, heated debates and at times violent protest in civil society) about the basic moral rights required to guarantee each individual equal concern and respect. Discourse morality presents morality as a learning process that complements Habermas's parallel description of the political constitution as a self-correcting learning process (TT, 122; BFN, 444).

Further reading

Two excellent book-length discussions of discourse morality are Günther (1993) and Rehg (1994). Rehg's article (2011) on discourse ethics in Fultner is a good introduction as is Heath (2014). Gunnarsson (2000) offers a very helpful discussion of Habermas's project and compares it to the views of Gauthier (1987) and McDowell (2002). Benhabib and Dallmayr (1990) contains important early discussions of Habermas's theory. The various essays by Finlayson (especially 2000, 2005 and 2013) are also quite good. Kelly (2000) offers an instructive comparison between Scanlon and Habermas and argues for Scanlon's more substantive account.

Notes

1 Some of this overemphasis may be due to the wider reception of his moral theory—in contrast to some of his other work—in two early collections (Benhabib and Dallmayr 1990, and Darwall 1997). Gordon Finlayson has rightly attempted to correct for this in several of his essays (see especially Finlayson 2009, 2000).

2 Heath (2014, 20); Heath contrasts an early (and middle) "Durkheimian" period in Habermas to a later (post-1988) Kantian period that he believes has lost its roots in communicative action (language) and its dependence on corroboration with empirical work in moral psychology. For some indication that Habermas's appreciation of Kantian morality occurs fairly early, despite his criticisms, see PPP, 117–118.

3 Compare Freeman's definition of constructivism: "moral [and other normative] principles are correct (true, reasonable, universally valid, and so on) when they are the outcome of a deliberative procedure that incorporates all the relevant requirements of correct reasoning. In this regard, constructivism affords priority to the objectivity of judgment in determining moral truth: moral truths are the judgments that would be made by correctly reasoning from an *objective point of view*, which is a deliberative procedure incorporating all relevant requirements of practical reasoning" (Freeman 2007, 7); compare also James (2007, 302).

4 For this reason, this interpretation differs slightly from the more Kantian justification of a discourse morality pursued by Forst (see Forst 2012, c. 1 and 2; and Habermas's brief remarks on Forst in R4, 297) as well as the project of an "ultimate grounding" (*Letztbegründung*) developed by K.-O. Apel (in Benhabib and Dallmayr 1990).

5 For slightly different formulations, see also, "Every valid norm must satisfy the condition that the consequences and side effects its general observance can be

anticipated to have for the satisfaction of the interests of each could be freely accepted by all affected (and be preferred to those of known alternative possibilities for regulation)," Remarks, JA, 32; and "A norm is valid when ['if and only if,' according to 'Proceedings' version] the foreseeable consequences and side effects of its general observance for the interests and value-orientations of each individual could be jointly accepted by all concerned without coercion," IO, 42.

6 This is nicely discussed in Gunnarsson (2000); there is some debate about whether Habermas ever embraced the strong rationalist justification Gunnarsson describes.

7 Thus I disagree with a widespread interpretation of Habermas's project: see Gunnarsson (2000); Finlayson (2000); and many others. Whether this was part of the original project in "Discourse Ethics" is open to dispute; but it is fairly clear that this is not how Habermas currently understands his project (see JA, 76).

8 By a "strong" or "thick" interpretation of communicative action, I have in mind something like Taylor's "strong evaluators" or MacIntyre's notion of a tradition; see also Gunnarsson (2000, 132) on weak and strong evaluations. This reading of Habermas's notion of "thin" communicative action is however not identical with Taylor's "weak evaluator"; for more on Taylor's view and its difference from Habermas, see Baynes (2010).

9 The confusion can be seen in the following passage where Habermas fails to distinguish between a weak and a strong sense: "Without being able to draw upon prior acquaintance with the intact relations of recognition sustained by the 'strong' traditions of the moral community to which they belonged under premodern conditions, the participants could not even form the intention to reconstruct a post-traditional morality from the sources of communicative reason alone. They already know what it means to have moral duties and to justify an action in light of binding norms" (BNR, 87–88); elsewhere Habermas distinguishes between a "weak" and a "strong" sense of communicative action in a slightly different way (OPC, 327).

10 This interpretation will however require the introduction of an idea of reasonableness (or some other "acceptability requirement" on reasons offered in a discourse) if this idea of discourse morality is to gain any traction (see Estlund 2008, chapter 3).

11 This reflects Habermas's criticism that Rawls's idea of an overlapping consensus leaves too much to the idea of a contingent convergence among (reasonable) comprehensive doctrines.

12 For Habermas's own discussion of Larmore's brand of moral realism, see TT, 122. An engaging criticism of this approach to the problem of deep (moral) disagreement or what he calls "deep politics" is found in Talisse (2009).

Six

Democracy and the *Rechtsstaat*

Habermas's *Between Facts and Norms*

One version of the project of radical democracy, which has roots in Rousseau and Marx, has been expressed in the vision of a rational self-organization of society based on the collective exercise of "free public reason." Jürgen Habermas has aligned himself with this version in the past and, with some important qualifications, he continues to do so in his major work on democratic theory, *Between Facts and Norms* (hereafter, BFN). Two departures from his earlier position, however, particularly stand out: First, Habermas takes great pains to distance himself from the holistic or totalistic conception that often accompanies this version of democracy and in which society is regarded as a kind of macro-subject integrated via a central agency (the state) or organizing principle (labor).[1] Second, BFN assigns to law and the legal community generally a more positive and prominent role in the legitimation process.[2] The first shift results from Habermas's long engagement with Niklas Luhmann's systems theory; the second reflects an increased appreciation for Talcott Parson's identification of the "societal community" (and especially law) as a primary institutional complex responsible for social integration in highly differentiated and pluralist societies (see Luhmann 1995; Parsons 1970). The project of radical democracy can neither replace a market economy nor do away with a highly bureaucratized administrative state (or "state apparatus") but must rather find ways in which society can enjoy the benefits offered by these two social "subsystems" while at the same time taming them and rendering each accountable to a democratically legitimated rule of law. Radical democracy, in short, must practice an art of "intelligent self-restraint" that acknowledges the differentiations of modern and highly complex societies by realigning itself in a more creative manner with the liberal *Rechtsstaat* (see Habermas 1989a, 63–64).[3]

In addition to this reassessment of the political and legal implications of systems theory, BFN also engages current debates in "Anglo-American" political theory—especially concerning the nature and limits of liberal democracy. It should thus be possible to form an initial judgment about how Habermas's "discourse theory of law" and model of "procedural democracy" might fare when confronted by some of the more pressing issues in liberal democratic theory. In these discussions three issues stand out: First, there is a longstanding debate about the relation between democracy and other political ideals (such as political equality, the rule of law, and the guarantee of basic rights and liberties). Are these political values in deep conflict with the ideal of democracy or can they be made compatible with one another? Second, there has been a lengthy discussion about the ideal of liberal neutrality (see Baynes 1992a and Patten 2014). Is the claim that the liberal state should not act in ways intended to promote a particular conception of the good defensible when, on the one hand, the diversity of distinct cultures and life-forms are increasingly threatened by global markets and, on the other, the ethical foundations of liberal society are being called into question by non-liberal regimes? Third, as an extension of the critique of neutrality, the "dilemma of difference" (Minow 1990) poses a distinct challenge to liberal ideology: Must any attempt to address "difference" under the liberal ideals of equality, impartiality, and toleration necessarily perpetuate injustices and do violence to those categories and classes not traditionally recognized as within the norm? This issue has been raised particularly (though not exclusively) in recent feminist jurisprudence (see Young 1990 and Menke 2011).

In what follows, I will first indicate the ways in which BFN continues some basic themes introduced in TCA (section I). It is not possible to understand the project of BFN without keeping in mind the core arguments of his magnum opus. I will then outline some of the main elements of BFN, especially his reinterpretation of Kant's "system of rights" in a way that indicates how the private and public autonomy of citizens mutually presuppose one another (II) and his proposal for a procedural democracy centered around a two-track conception of deliberative politics (III). In the final section I will return to the three challenges to liberal democracy just mentioned in order to see how they might be addressed within the framework of Habermas's model of deliberative politics (IV).

I. Communicative reason and the tension between facticity and validity

A central thesis of TCA is that the conceptions of reason or rationality used in most social theory do not provide a basis for addressing the Hobbesian problem of social order or, beyond that, for adequately describing the processes of modernization (see Chapter 3). Neither the model of instrumental rationality (familiar in rational choice theory) nor the model of functional rationality (found, for example, in Marxism and systems theory) can account for the contribution of the normative self-understanding of social actors (which are subsequently reflected in social institutions) to processes of social reproduction and integration. These self-interpretations employ idealizations (or "fictions") that cannot be regarded by the participants as "mere" fictions without undermining their social efficacy. Habermas traces these idealizations back to the presuppositions actors must make whenever they seek to communicate with one another—presuppositions regarding an objective world, the identity of linguistic meaning, the mutual accountability of actors, and the context-transcending validity of claims to truth and rightness (BFN, 4).

Communication is not reducible to getting someone to believe something. For Habermas, it consists (paradigmatically) in reaching an understanding with someone about something, where "reaching an understanding" draws upon (unavoidable) presuppositions constitutive for a weak and fragile (but nonetheless socially effective) form of mutual recognition: To reach an understanding with someone about something implies that one is also prepared to provide warrants for the claims raised with one's utterances should they be contested and that one recognizes the other as someone who is free to take a yes/no position with respect to those claims.

Communicative reason refers, then, to this rationally binding/ bonding illocutionary force present in all communicative action and "communicative freedom" refers to the "right" or capacity to take a yes/no position with respect to any speech-act offer (BFN, 119).

A second theme carried over from TCA is that processes of cultural reproduction, social integration, and socialization unavoidably depend on the idealizations that have their basis in these notions of communicative action and reason. The transmission of knowledge and values, the maintenance of social orders, and the formation of individual identities and life-plans cannot proceed without reference to the common presuppositions of an objective world, identical meaning, accountable actors, and the validity of claims to truth and rightness. Although such idealizations invariably involve counterfactual assumptions they are nevertheless effective in actual processes of social integration and reproduction.

> The ideal moment of unconditionality is deeply ingrained in factual processes of communication because validity claims are Janus-faced: as claims, they overshoot every context; at the same time, they must be both raised and accepted here and now if they are to support an agreement effective for coordination— for this there is no acontextual standpoint. The universalistic meaning of the claimed validity exceeds all contexts, but only the local, binding act of acceptance enables validity claims to bear the burden of social integration for a context-bound everyday practice.
>
> (BFN, 20–21)

This reference to counterfactual idealizations that are actually effective for social coordination—to a context-transcending reason existing in society—is the origin of the tension between "facticity" and "validity" that structures Habermas's BFN. In a more sociological vein, Habermas analyzes various ways in which societies have reckoned with this tension through reliance on shared background assumptions in everyday interactions or through the creation of strong institutions (such as religion) that fuse the moments of validity and facticity together (BFN, 23f.). The claim Habermas pursues in the new work is that, in the wake of secularization and disenchantment, highly differentiated and pluralist societies are compelled to rely less on traditions and "strong institutions" to bridge the tension between facticity and validity and thus must look elsewhere to fulfill the tasks of social reproduction and integration. In this situation law offers a unique means for dealing with this tension (even as the idea of positive law contains its own "internal" tension between coercive enforcement and valid norm):

> In the dimension of legal validity, facticity and validity are once again intertwined, but this time the two moments are not fused together—as they are in lifeworld certainties or in the overpowering authority of archaic institutions withdrawn from any discussion—in an indissoluble amalgam. In the legal mode of validity the facticity of the *enforcement* of law is intertwined with the legitimacy of the genesis of law that claims to be rational because it guarantees liberty. The tension between these two distinct moments is thus intensified and behaviorally operationalized.
>
> (BFN, 28)

When the social tension between facticity and validity moves into the legal medium itself—in what Habermas calls the "internal" tension—it is reflected in the law's claim to reach judgments that are both rational and certain (or predictable) as well as in its claim to issue legitimate orders that can be coercively enforced. At the same time the legal system itself becomes the principal means by which modern societies are able to address the "external" tension between a political order's claim to be legitimate and its reliance on the *de facto* recognition of its members. To summarize Habermas's thesis: in highly differentiated and pluralist societies the task of social coordination and integration falls to institutionalized procedures of legitimate law-making that transform into binding decisions the more diffuse public opinions initially produced *via* the anonymous communication network of a loosely organized and largely autonomous public sphere.

It might be useful to illustrate this "external" tension between facticity and validity by reference to Rawls's recent account of public reason as the core of a liberal principle of legitimacy. Rawls claims that the justification of principles for regulating the basic social structure must be "political, not metaphysical"—that is, it cannot appeal to anything "outside" the practice of public justification among free and equal citizens. Yet, it must not be "political in the wrong way"—that is, it cannot be a mere *modus vivendi* or stand-off between competing interest positions or incompatible conceptions of the good (Rawls 1999, c. 22). In this connection Rawls introduces a "liberal principle of legitimacy" which reads: "Our exercise of political power is fully proper only when it is exercised in accordance with a constitution the essentials of which all citizens as free and equal may reasonably be expected to endorse in the light of principles and ideals acceptable to their common human reason" or, as he also puts it, "acceptable to them as reasonable and rational" (Rawls 1996, 137; 1999, 578). Yet if institutions satisfying this criterion are also to be stable, the ideals implicit in this "common human reason" cannot exist only at the level of ideal theory, but must be the focus of an "overlapping consensus" within the public political culture (Rawls 1996, Lecture IV). The moment of validity present in the idea of public justification requires the stabilizing "facticity" of a wide overlapping consensus (see Cohen 1993, chap. 2). However, to the extent that Rawls acknowledges a certain tension between facticity and validity—between the question of stability and the conditions of justification or acceptability—he tends to assume that this tension is sufficiently overcome within a liberal political culture, or at least that we must proceed *as* if it were. Habermas, by contrast, makes the tension explicit in order to consider how, in modern societies, it might be bridged through a political process in which (broadly stated) the public reasons generated in a process of discursive opinion-formation are channeled and transformed into collectively binding decisions.

Despite this and other important differences, there is nonetheless a deeper affinity between the respective appeals to "public reason" (Rawls) and "communicative reason" (Habermas) as a response to the question of legitimacy. Both conceptions invoke a basic notion of autonomy as a capacity for reason-giving whether it is grounded in a conception of the fundamental moral powers of citizens (Rawls) or in the presuppositions shared by those who act communicatively (Habermas).[4]

II. Discourse theory, the principle of democracy and the system of rights

Habermas next turns to the centrally important question of the legitimacy of law: What makes legal authority legitimate? In effect, Habermas advocates a sophisticated version of consent theory (one which depends not on actual or hypothetical consent, but one in which the legal-political order retains roots in processes of communicative sociation). He rejects a narrower legal positivist position, advocated as well by Luhmann, that law is legitimate if it has been enacted in accordance with established legal procedures. At the same time, however, appeal to natural law theory is precluded on the basis of his own commitment to radical democracy. As Habermas puts it, "Nothing is given prior to the citizen's practice of self-determination other than the discourse principle, which is built into the conditions of communicative association in general, and the legal medium as such" (BFN, 127–128). Thus, just as he earlier argued that modernity must generate its own normativity out of itself (PDM, 7), he now (relatedly) claims that legality must account for its own legitimacy. In brief, Habermas's strategy is to show that the legitimacy of law is based on a rationality immanent to law, even though that rationality is dependent on and open to dimensions of (communicative) reason that reach beyond the legal medium. "In modern societies as well the law can fulfill the function of stabilizing expectations only if it preserves an internal connection with the socially integrative force of communicative action" (BFN, 84; see Baynes 2007).

Habermas approaches the question of the legitimacy of legality through a central difficulty in Kant's political thought frequently discussed in the secondary literature. The difficulty is reflected in the question whether Kant is best understood as a natural rights theorist or a social contract theorist. Habermas concurs with those who argue that Kant is closer to the natural right tradition in that his "Universal Principle of Right (*Recht*)" is generally regarded as a "subsidiary formula" (Nell 1975) of the categorical imperative and hence derived from and subordinate to the moral law. This implies, however, that the Universal Principle of Right, as well as the system of public and private law (*Recht*) Kant generates from it, do not ultimately depend on the consent (actual or hypothetical) of the parties to the social contract.[5]

In a provocative and original reading, Habermas suggests that the tension between a social contract and a natural rights reading arises from an ambiguity in Kant's concept of autonomy or self-rule. As Kant took over this notion from Rousseau, it suggests the idea of both individual *and* collective self-legislation: "a person is subject to no laws other than those that he (either alone or at least jointly with others) gives to himself" (Kant 1991, 50). For Kant, the concept of individual autonomy is effectively synonymous with morality, while the notion of collective self-determination is captured in his idea of the social contract. However, insofar as Kant's argument for the establishment of civil society (or the state) relies solely on the Universal Principle of Right, which guarantees equal subjective liberty for all, the notion of collective self-determination is subordinated to a moral principle (or natural right). As Habermas argues, this initiates a dialectic in the tradition of legal dogmatics between legal positivism (objective law as command of the sovereign) and natural law (which stresses subjective liberties) in which the idea of popular sovereignty or collective self-determination is gradually effaced. However, such an effacement undermines attempts to account for the legitimacy of law for it ultimately removes law from the process of democratic law-making and/or deprives the right to subjective liberty of any relation to a conception of public autonomy (BFN, 89; see also Maus 2002). It fails, in other words, to reconcile the public and private autonomy of citizens in a manner that could in turn secure the legitimacy of legality.[6]

Of course, Habermas is not interested in Kant's system of rights only for historical reasons. He uses this problematic in Kant to clarify the basic structure of his own discourse theory and to respond to some earlier criticisms.[7] He now insists, for example, on a sharper delineation between the principle of discourse—"Just those action norms are valid to which all possibly affected persons could agree as participant in rational discourses" (BFN, 107)—and its specification as a rule of *moral* argumentation, that is, as Principle U (see Chapter 5).[8] The principle of discourse is now described as a more general principle that applies to all action norms prior to any distinction between moral and legal norms. Principle U is then introduced *simultaneously* with the principle of democracy—roughly equivalent to Kant's idea of the social contract—which specifies a general procedure for legitimate law-making (see BFN, 110). The principle of democracy states that "only those statutes may claim legitimacy that can meet with the assent of all citizens in a discursive process of legislation that in turn has been legally constituted" (BFN, 110). Although distinct, the two principles are not hierarchically ordered as in Kant; rather, they are complementary and, in important ways, the principle of democracy (as a principle of legitimation for positive law) supplements various "deficits" that necessarily accompany a post-conventional rational morality. These include, for example, the cognitive indeterminacy that arises with a moral principle requiring that all relevant features of a situation be taken into consideration as well as the motivational uncertainty that results from the fact that moral insight does not guarantee compliance. In both cases legal norms are thus able to complement moral norms even though the former must also remain open in various ways to processes of moral argumentation (BFN, 112f.).

Even more important than this complementary relation between the basic moral principle and a principle for legitimate lawmaking is Habermas's parallel claim that the principle of democracy is not subordinate to a system of rights. On the contrary, Habermas claims that they are "equiprimordial" or "co-original" (*gleichursprünglich*) (BFN, 122) and "reciprocally explain each other" (BFN, 94). The system of rights is the "reverse side" (BFN, 94) of the principle of democracy, and "the principle of democracy can only appear as the heart of a system of rights" (BFN, 121). These remarks indicate Habermas's commitment to a reconciliation of democracy with other political values, especially a system of basic rights and liberties. Since, according to Habermas, earlier efforts to achieve such a reconciliation have not been successful (BFN, 84), I will summarize what I take to be the main steps in his own attempt.

Habermas's general strategy is to recall attention to the "intersubjective meaning" of legally granted subjective liberties or individual rights (BFN, 89). Echoing Hegel as well as Kant, he emphasizes the fact that rights are not primarily things individuals possess but relations that have their basis in a form of mutual recognition—however circumscribed and artificial.

At a conceptual level, rights do not immediately refer to atomistic and estranged individuals who are possessively set against one another. On the contrary, as elements of the legal order they presuppose collaboration among subjects who recognize one another, in their reciprocally related rights and duties, as free and equal citizens. This mutual recognition is constitutive for a legal order from which actionable rights are derived. In this sense 'subjective' rights emerge co-originally with 'objective' law, to use the terminology of German jurisprudence.

(BFN, 88–89)

Basic rights do not exist in a determinate form in a prior state of nature. They are something individuals mutually confer on one another insofar as they undertake to regulate their common life *via* positive law and thus to regard one another as free and equal consociates under law.

More specifically, Habermas's claim is that the system of rights (along with the principle of democracy) can be developed from the "interpenetration" (*Verschränkung*) of the discourse principle and the legal form (BFN, 121). As I understand it, this "derivation"— Habermas speaks of a "logical genesis" (*logische Genese*)—of a system of rights occurs in two stages: First, the notion of law cannot be limited to the semantic features of general and abstract norms. Rather, bourgeois formal law has always been identified with the guarantee of an equal right to subjective liberty.[9] This is reflected in Kant's Universal Principle of Right (*Recht*) as well as Rawls's First Principle both of which guarantee the greatest amount of liberty compatible with a like liberty for all. For Habermas this link between positive law and individual liberty means that insofar as individuals undertake to regulate their common life through the legal form they must do so in a way that grants to each member an equal right to liberty.

However—and this is the second step—although the legal form is conceptually linked to the idea of subjective rights, it alone cannot ground any specific right (BFN, 128). A system of rights can be developed only if and when the legal form is made use of by the political sovereign in an exercise of the citizens' public autonomy. This public autonomy in the last analysis refers back to the discourse principle which implies the "right" to submit only to those norms one could agree to in a discourse. Of course, in connection with the principle of discourse this "right" has only the "quasi-transcendental" status of a communicative act and does not carry with it any coercive authorization. It can acquire a coercive authorization only when, as the principle of democracy, it is realized in the legal medium together with a system of rights.

> The principle of discourse can assume through the medium of law the shape of a principle of democracy only insofar as the discourse principle and the legal medium interpenetrate and *develop* into a system of rights bringing private and public autonomy into a relation of mutual presupposition. Conversely, every exercise of political autonomy signifies both an interpretation and concrete shaping of these fundamentally 'unsaturated' rights by a historical legislator.
>
> (BFN, 128)

Habermas's underlying idea is when the rather abstract principle of discourse is brought to bear on the equally general notion of legality or the legal form it yields a distinction between the "principle of democracy" and the "system of rights" (or subjective liberties). Neither of these two political ideals stands alone; rather even conceptually each depends on the other. Habermas hopes in this way to have reconciled democracy and individual rights in a manner that does not subordinate either one to the other. "The system of rights can be reduced neither to a moral reading of human rights [as in Kant and the tradition of natural rights—KB] nor to an ethical reading of popular sovereignty [as in Rousseau and some communitarians—KB] because the private autonomy of citizens must neither be set above nor made subordinate to their political autonomy" (BFN, 104). Rather, the co-originality or "equiprimordiality" of the system of rights and the principle of democracy, which also reflects the mutual presupposition of citizens' public and private autonomy, is derived from this "interpenetration" of the legal form and the "quasi-transcendental" discourse principle that "must" occur if citizens are to regulate their living together by means of positive law.

In connection with the strategy outlined above, Habermas introduces five basic categories of rights (BFN, 122–123):

(1) Basic rights that result from the politically autonomous development of the right to the greatest possible measure of equal individual liberties.

(2) Basic rights that result from the politically autonomous development of the status of a member in a voluntary association of consociates under law.

(3) Basic rights that result immediately from the actionability of rights and from the politically autonomous development of legal protections.

(4) Basic rights to equal opportunities to participate in the processes of opinion- and will-formation in which citizens exercise their political autonomy and through which they generate legitimate law.

(5) Basic rights to the provision of living conditions that are socially, technologically, and ecologically safeguarded, insofar as the current circumstances make this necessary if citizens are to have equal opportunities to utilize the civil rights listed in (1) through (4).

The first three categories cover those rights traditionally identified with the "subjective liberties" that secure the private autonomy of citizens and are constitutive of the legal medium in which citizens confront one another as legal addresses—freedom of speech, conscience, and the person under category (1); rights to association under (2); and rights to legal protection, due process etc. under (3). These are, however, "enabling" rights and thus, according to Habermas, cannot properly be construed as a limitation upon the legislator's sovereignty (BFN, 128). The fourth category, by contrast, points to the role of legal subjects as authors of law and thus secures their public autonomy in the form of rights to political participation. Finally, the last category, to which Habermas assigns a more derivative status, includes various rights to welfare and other (material) conditions necessary for an effective opportunity to exercise the first four categories of rights.

Two final observations on this system of rights are worth noting: First, Habermas claims that the system of rights is universal not in the sense that it specifies a pre-given set of natural rights, but in the sense that it presents a general schema or "unsaturated" placeholder (BFN, 125) that legal subjects must presuppose if they want to regulate their living together by positive law. It is thus constitutive of the legal medium, yet at the same time it is not fixed or determinate. The system of rights must be "developed in a politically autonomous manner" by citizens in the context of their own particular traditions and history (BFN, 129).

Second, in connection with Albrecht Wellmer's argument that he underestimates the role of a "right not to be rational," Habermas acknowledges that there is a paradox involved in the "juridification of communicative liberty" (BFN, 130; see Wellmer 1991, 29). The rights securing public autonomy, just like those guaranteeing private autonomy, must take the form of "subjective liberties" (or civil rights). This means that it is up to citizens themselves to exercise their communicative liberty. "Subjective liberties entitle one to drop out of communicative action, to refuse illocutionary obligations; they ground a privacy freed from the burden of a reciprocally acknowledged and expected communicative freedom" (BFN, 120). At the same time, however, this juridification of communicative freedom also reveals the fact that the legitimacy of legality cannot be guaranteed by the legal form alone but depends on sources beyond its control, namely the realization of a rational public opinion and will-formation in an autonomous public sphere (BFN, 130–131).

With his derivation of the system of rights that secures the private and public autonomy of citizens, Habermas believes that he has accounted for the legitimacy of legality. It is based neither on the legal form alone (as maintained by positivists) nor on its conformity to an extra-legal set of natural rights or natural law. Rather, the legitimacy of law derives from the fact that it has a rationality of its own, secured in the mutual guarantee of the private and public autonomy of citizens, that ultimately refers back to the rational bonding/binding illocutionary force inherent in communicative reason and action.

III. The *Rechtsstaat*, procedural democracy, and "weak" and "strong" publics

If the legitimacy of law depends on the fact that "it preserves an internal connection with the socially integrative force of communicative action" (BFN, 84), then the system of rights (including the rights of public autonomy) must be institutionalized, and the communicative power that comes about whenever, in Arendt's phrase, people act in concert must be mobilized and effectively secured within the legal medium itself. This requirement reveals still another aspect of the internal tension between facticity and validity: To become socially effective law requires a centralized political power with the capacity to enforce collectively binding decisions—no legitimate law without democracy.[10] At the same time, however, law is the sole medium through which the communicative power of citizens can be transformed into administrative power—no genuine democracy without law.

Habermas first introduces a set of "principles of the constitutional state" (*Rechtsstaat*) that specify general institutional guidelines for both the *generation* of communicative power (through the institutionalization of the system of rights) and the *exercise* of power (by ensuring a connection between communicative power and administrative power).[11] These include the principle of popular sovereignty, the guarantee of legal protection, the legality of administration, and the separation of state and society (BFN, 168ff.). Habermas's discussion attempts to locate these classical doctrines within the framework of his own discourse theory. Taken together, the principles should explain the idea of the constitutional state by showing how "legitimate law is generated from communicative power and the latter in turn is converted into administrative power via legitimately enacted law" (BFN, 169).

Although his discussion cannot be pursued in any detail here, it is clear that Habermas seeks to establish two general points (BFN, c.4; see Zurn 2007). First, in contrast to Arendt, the notion of communicative power should not be understood too substantively as the (more or less spontaneous) expression of a common will but rather should be seen as the product of an overlapping and intermeshing of a variety of (more and less institutionalized) pragmatic, ethical-political, and moral discourses (BFN, 168). Communicative power neither presupposes a shared ethical-political self-understanding nor orients itself to the ideal of a rational consensus in the manner constitutive (for Habermas) of moral argumentation. Rather, it is identified with the realization of a rational public opinion and will-formation in a process of lawmaking that comprises a complex network of processes of reaching understanding *and* bargaining (BFN, 180). This interpretation of communicative power should also warn against an overly hasty and too direct identification of moral argumentation (which aims at consensus) with political discourse.

Second, the legitimate *exercise* of power can only occur through the medium of law but in a way that nonetheless remains tied to communicative sociation: Rule by the people must be a rule of law, but the rule of law must be joined to rule by the people or, as Frank Michelman has expressed it, rooted in a "jurisgenerative politics" (Michelman 1988, 1502). A discourse theoretical approach offers a way of understanding this connection between the rule of law and popular sovereignty without appealing to a "transcendent" notion of reason or overburdening citizens' capacities for public virtue. It also provides for a less concretistic interpretation of the classical principle of the separation of powers in that the functions of the legislature, judiciary, and administration can now be differentiated according to various forms of communication and a corresponding potential for reasons:

> Laws can regulate the transformation of communicative power into administrative power inasmuch as they come about according to a democratic procedure, ground a comprehensive legal protection guaranteed by impartial courts, and shield from the implementing administration the sorts of reasons that support legislative resolutions and court decisions. These normative reasons belong to a universe within which legislature and judiciary share the work of justifying and applying norms. An administration limited to pragmatic discourse must not change anything in this universe by its contributions; at the same time, it draws therefrom the normative premises that have to underlie its own empirically informed, purposive-rational decision-making.
> (BFN, 192)

This analysis of the principles of the constitutional state and their justification—which I have only been able roughly to indicate—is nevertheless one-sided unless it is accompanied by an account of the *process* by which citizens are to govern themselves or engage in a "jurisgenerative politics." It is at this point that the model of a "procedural democracy" is introduced (see further Chapter 7). Within the context of North American discussions, however, this label could be misleading since the term "procedure" is not used in contrast to a "substantive" conception of democracy (as it is, for example, in John Ely's influential account) (Ely 1980). Rather, as Habermas uses the term it designates the attempt to realize the rights of public and private autonomy through an institutional design that incorporates various practical discourses. Procedural democracy is thus closer to what has been called a "public reasons" approach (see Cohen 1993 and Freeman 2007).

Habermas introduces his model of procedural democracy by way of a contrast between two highly stylized alternatives: liberal and republican (or communitarian). These have become familiar reference points in recent discussions. Cass Sunstein, for example, has recently summarized the liberal model well: "Self-interest, not virtue, is understood to be the usual motivating force of political behavior. Politics is typically, if not always, an effort to aggregate private interests. It is surrounded by checks, in the form of rights, protecting private liberty and private property from public intrusion" (Sunstein 1991, 4). By contrast, republicanism characteristically places more emphasis on the value of citizens' public virtues and active political participation. Politics is regarded more as a deliberative process in which citizens seek to reach agreement about the common good, and law is not seen as a means for protecting individual rights but as the expression of the common praxis of the political community.

Habermas's procedural democracy attempts to incorporate the best features of both models while avoiding the shortcomings of each. In particular, with the republican model, it rejects the vision of the political process as primarily a process of competition and aggregation of private preferences. However, more in keeping with the liberal model, it regards the republican vision of a citizenry united and actively motivated by a shared conception of the good life as unrealistic in modern, pluralist societies.[12] Since, as we have seen, political discourses involve bargaining and negotiation as well as moral argumentation, the republican or communitarian notion of a shared ethical-political dialogue also seems too limited (BFN, 285). "According to discourse theory, the success of deliberative politics depends not on a collectively acting citizenry but on the institutionalization of the corresponding procedures and conditions of communication, as well as on the interplay of institutionalized deliberative processes with informally constituted public opinions" (BFN, 298). What is central is not a shared ethos, but institutionalized discourses for the formation of rational political opinion.

The idea of a suitably interpreted "deliberative politics" thus lies at the center of Habermas's procedural democracy (see further, Chapter 7). In a deliberative politics attention shifts away from the final act of voting and the problems of social choice that accompany it. The model attempts to take seriously the fact that often enough preferences are not exogenous to the political system, but "are instead adaptive to a wide range of factors—including the context in which the preference is expressed, the existing legal rules, past consumption choices, and culture in general" (Sunstein 1991, 5). The aim of a deliberative politics is to provide context for a transformation of preferences in response to the considered views of others and the "laundering" or filtering of irrational and/or morally repugnant preferences in ways that are not excessively paternalistic (see Goodin 1985). For example, by designing institutions of political will-formation so that they reflect the more complex preference structure of individuals rather than simply register the actual preferences individuals have at any given time, the conditions for a more rational politics (that is, a political process in which the outcomes are more informed, future-oriented, and other-regarding) can be improved.[13] One could even speak of an extension of democracy to preferences themselves since the question is whether the reasons offered in support of them are ones that could meet the requirements of public justification. What is important for this notion of deliberation, however, is less that everyone participate— or even that voting be made public—than that there is a warranted presumption that public opinion be formed on the basis of adequate information and relevant reasons and that those whose interests are involved have an equal and effective opportunity to make their own interests (and the reasons for them) known.

Two further features serve to distinguish Habermas's model of procedural democracy and deliberative politics from other recent versions. First, this version of deliberative politics extends beyond the more formally organized political system to the vast and complex communication network that Habermas calls "the public sphere."

> [Deliberative politics] is bound to the demanding communicative presuppositions of political arenas that do not coincide with the institutionalized will-formation in parliamentary bodies but extend equally to the political public sphere and to its cultural context and social basis. A deliberative practice of self-legislation can develop only in the interplay between, on the one hand, the parliamentary will-formation institutionalized in legal procedures and programmed to reach decisions and, on the other, political opinion-formation along informal channels of political communication.
>
> (BFN, 274–275)

The model suggests a "two-track" process in which there is a division of labor between "weak publics"—the informally organized public sphere ranging from private associations to the mass media located in "civil society"—and "strong publics"—parliamentary bodies and other formally organized institutions of the political system (see also Fraser 1992). In this division of labor, "weak publics" assume a central responsibility for identifying, interpreting, and addressing social problems:

> For a good part of the normative expectations connected with deliberative politics now falls on the peripheral structures of opinion-formation. The expectations are directed at the capacity to perceive, interpret, and present encompassing social problems in a way both attention-catching and innovative.
>
> (BFN, 358)

However, decision-making responsibility, as well as the further "filtering" of reasons *via* more formal parliamentary procedures, remains the task of a strong public (e.g. the formally organized political system).

Second, along with this division of labor between strong and weak publics and as a consequence of his increased acknowledgment of the "decentered" character of modern societies, Habermas argues that radical-democratic practice must assume a "self-limiting" form. Democratization is now focused not on society as a whole, but more narrowly on the political-legal system (BFN, 305). More specifically, he maintains that it must respect the boundaries of the political-administrative and economic subsystems that have become relatively freed from the integrative force of communicative action and are in this sense "autonomous." Failure to do so, he believes, at least partially explains the failure of state socialism (see Habermas 1990a). The goal of radical democracy thus becomes not the democratic organization of these subsystems, but rather a type of indirect steering of them through the medium of law. In this connection, he also describes the task of an opinion-forming public sphere as that of laying siege to the formally organized political system by encircling it with reasons without, however, attempting to overthrow or replace it.

This raises a number of difficult questions about the scope and limits of democratization. Given the metaphorical form often adopted in his discussion, it is not obvious what specific proposals for mediating between weak and strong publics would follow from his model. Some have questioned, for example, whether he has not conceded too much to systems theory and Nancy Fraser, in an instructive discussion of Habermas's conception of the public sphere, raises the question whether there might not be other possible "divisions of labor" between strong and weak publics.[14] Habermas's response seems to be that an answer to most of these questions will not be found at the level of normative theory, but depends upon the empirical findings of complex comparative studies (see also the discussion of systems theory in Chapter 3).

However, a more general question that arises in connection with this model of democracy is whether Habermas's confidence in the rationalizing effect of procedures alone is well-founded. In view of his own description of "weak publics" as "wild," "anarchic," and "unrestricted," the suspicion can at least be raised whether discursive procedures will suffice to bring about a rational public opinion

(BFN, 307). To be sure, he states that a deliberative politics depends on a "rationalized lifeworld" (including a "liberal political culture") "that meets it halfway."[15] But without more attention to the particular "liberal virtues" that make up that political culture and give rise to some notion of shared purposes, it is difficult not to sympathize with critics who charge that his account seems quite thin (Buchwalter 2001). Some of his later remarks on a "constitutional patriotism" that must not be understood too abstractly offer some further suggestions (IO, 225–226). Nevertheless, the question remains whether Habermas's almost exclusive attention to questions of institutional design and discursive procedures provides an adequate basis for dealing with this paradox or whether he must not supplement his model with a more specific account of the "liberal virtues" or "ethical foundations" that must "meet these halfway" (BFN 461, 500).

IV. Three challenges to liberal democracy

We are now in a position to consider how Habermas's model fares with respect to the three challenges raised in the introduction: the project of reconciliation, the question of liberal neutrality, and the dilemma of difference.

(1) From the discussion in section II it is clear that BFN represents a major effort to reconcile democracy with other political ideals. Since Habermas claims that no one has yet succeeded in this project, it is worth considering how his view differs from some other recent attempts.

In *Democracy and Its Critics* Robert Dahl acknowledges the potential conflict between a "procedural" democracy and a "substantive" set of basic rights and attempts to resolve it by arguing that the right to self-government through the democratic process is basic and that other political rights can be derived from this fundamental right (Dahl 1989, 169–170).

> These specific rights—let me call them *primary political rights*—are integral to the democratic process. They aren't ontologically separate from—or prior to, or superior to—the democratic process. To the extent that the democratic process exists in a political system, all the primary political rights must also exist.

> To the extent that primary political rights are absent from a
> system, the democratic process does not exist.
>
> (Dahl 1989, 170)

This strategy faces two serious objections. First, it is not clear
whether other "non-political" rights can be accounted for in a
similar manner and, even if so, whether this would not amount to
an instrumentalization of private autonomy for the sake of public
autonomy. Second, although it is a "substantive" not "procedural"
account, Dahl's strategy suffers from a reliance on an "aggregative"
conception of democracy that is in the end similar to Ely's procedural
conception referred to above. This is suggested, for example, in his
endorsement of a fairly utilitarian reading of the "principle of equal
consideration of interests" in contrast to the autonomy-based
conception implicit in Habermas's account.[16]

In "Equality, Democracy and Constitution" Ronald Dworkin also
attempted to reconcile democracy and basic rights (Dworkin
1990). He begins with John Ely's observation that many of the
"disabling provisions" of the US Constitution (roughly the Bill of
Rights) may be seen as "functionally structural" to the democratic
process and thus not in conflict with it. The right to freedom of
expression is an example:

> Since democratic elections demonstrate the will of the people
> only when the public is fully informed, preventing officials
> from censoring speech protects rather than subverts democracy.
> … So a constitutional right of free speech counts as functionally
> structural as well as disabling in our catalogue.
>
> (Dworkin 1990, 328)

However, as Ely concedes, this strategy will not work for all the
"disabling provisions"—for example, the Establishment Clause of
the First Amendment or rights that regulate the criminal process—
and so, Dworkin concludes, "Ely's rescue of democracy from the
Constitution is only a partial success" (Dworkin 1990, 328).

Dworkin's own response to the "supposed conflict between
democracy and a constitution" (Dworkin 1990, 330) begins by
distinguishing between a "statistical reading of democracy" (i.e. the

aggregative conception discussed above) and a "communal reading of democracy" (e.g. Rousseau's general will) (Dworkin 1990, 330). He then argues for a specific version of the latter which he calls "democracy as integration." This model is specified in connection with three principles: the principle of participation (requiring that each citizen has an equal and effective opportunity to make a difference in the political process), the principle of stake (requiring that each person be recognized or shown equal concern), and the principle of independence (specifying that individuals be responsible for their own judgments). Dworkin then concludes that on this model many of the disabling provisions Ely rejected may be regarded as functionally structural and, hence, not anti-democratic: "On the communal conception, democracy and constitutional constraint are not antagonists but partners in principle" (Dworkin 1990, 346).

Dworkin's model is clearly preferable to aggregative conceptions. The three principles appeal directly to the ideals of autonomy and mutual recognition, and the analysis of democracy (as well as law) in connection with the integrity of a community's practices and attitudes points away from a metaphysical or substantialist conception of community. On the other hand, as he recognizes, his "principle of stake" threatens to become a "black hole into which all other political virtues collapse" (Dworkin 1990, 339). His response, however, which is to claim that the principle requires not that each citizen actually be shown equal concern but only that there exists a "good faith effort," seems to downplay the public autonomy of citizens.

Habermas's proposal, as we have seen, reconciles popular sovereignty and constitutionalism by claiming that public and private autonomy mutually presuppose one another. A virtue of the model is that it relates these ideals at an abstract level: Public and private autonomy are two dimensions of the fundamental "right" to communicative liberty as this is expressed in the legal form. If one begins with this notion of communicative liberty, it is possible to regard the constitution as a sort of "public charter" and the system of rights as a form of "precommitment" that citizens make in undertaking to regulate their common lives by public law.[17] As such the proposed reconciliation of democracy and rights neither undervalues public autonomy, nor overtaxes private autonomy. It is not based on a shared conception of the good, but on a more abstract form of recognition contained in the idea of free and equal consociates under law.

At the same time, the principal strength of this approach may also prove to be its greatest weakness. Given the abstract character of the reconciliation of public and private autonomy, it is difficult to determine how it might contribute to more specific constitutional debates, for example, regarding the interpretation of the Establishment Clause of the First Amendment, or the more specific scope and content of the right to privacy, Habermas would no doubt claim that the system of rights is "unsaturated" and needs to be filled in both with reference to a political community's particular tradition and history and in response to the ongoing deliberations within the public sphere (BFN, 128–129; TT, chap. 8). This may be so, but it also seems reasonable to expect that the general proposal for a reconciliation of democracy and basic rights should offer some further guidance to more specific debates about rights (e.g. would it support a constitutional right to abortion as a condition for securing the public autonomy of women?). It is possible that Habermas's account could provide some direction regarding these questions, but much more work needs to be done in this "middle range" between general conceptions and the enumeration of specific rights and liberties.

(2) Despite his emphasis on "weak publics" and pluralist civil society Habermas's model of procedural democracy and deliberative politics endorses a "nonrestrictive" or "tolerant" version of the principle of liberal neutrality (BFN, 308ff.; see also BNR, chap. 9). This principle has been criticized by communitarians and others who argue that it is excessively individualistic or atomistic in its conception of the citizen and/or that it presupposes its own conception of the good and thus is inherently self-defeating (since it cannot allow for the promotion of values required for a liberal society) (see Taylor 1989). In particular, it has been argued that the principle of liberal neutrality is not compatible with the state's pursuit of measures intended to promote or maintain a diverse civil society and robust public sphere (Walzer 1990). Is Habermas's own endorsement of a principle of state neutrality consistent with his affirmation of the value of a robust public sphere?

It is important that the meaning of liberal neutrality, at least on its best interpretation, not be misunderstood. First, the principle of neutrality is not itself a neutral or non-moral principle. It does not imply a merely procedural neutrality with respect to whatever conceptions of the good life citizens may happen to have. Rather, it is an ideal introduced in conjunction with a principle of right (for example, Kant's Universal Principle of Right or Rawls's Principle of Equal Liberty) and thus one that is biased against conceptions of the good that are incompatible with the basic rights and liberties specified by that principle (Rawls 1999, 431). Second, the principle of neutrality does not even require that the state treat equally any permissible conception of the good citizens may have or that the policies pursued by the state must have the same effect upon any and all (permissible) conceptions of the good life. This form of neutrality, which has been called neutrality of effect or consequential neutrality, is both impractical and undesirable. Rather, what liberal neutrality entails is "neutrality of aim" or "neutrality of grounds" in the sense that arguments and considerations introduced in support of specific principles or policies should not appeal to particular conceptions of the good life but should regard all citizens and their (permissible) conceptions with equal concern and respect (Rawls 1999, chap. 21 and Baynes 1992a).

Even on this interpretation the principle can be contested. Can policies be neutral in their justification in this way or must not such claims to neutrality inevitably appeal to some (permissible) conceptions of the good over others? One version of neutrality, suggested by Bruce Ackerman's notion of "constrained conversation" and Rawls's "method of avoidance," is susceptible to this challenge since by unduly restricting the issues that can be placed on the political agenda or raised in public discussion there is the danger of reinforcing the status quo and inhibiting mutual understanding. This strategy also suggests that there is a relatively fixed and clear distinction between those matters appropriate for public discussion and those that are not.

An alternative interpretation of liberal neutrality is able to avoid this objection. On this interpretation, the principle of neutrality is not understood as part of a general strategy of avoidance, but as part of what is required in showing equal concern and respect in a stronger sense: The state should not act in ways intended to promote a particular conception of the good life since that would constitute a failure to show each citizen equal concern and respect. Unlike the method of avoidance, this interpretation of neutrality does not require keeping controversial issues off the political agenda in order to avoid moral conflict. Rather, it is quite consistent with the view that the state act in ways intended to promote rational discussion in order to help resolve potentially divisive social and moral conflicts (see Gutmann and Thompson 1996). On this interpretation neutrality is compatible with the attempt to secure a form of mutual respect or "militant toleration" in which difference is not only tolerated, but in which individuals seek to understand one another in their differences and arrive at a solution to a matter at hand in view of their common recognition of one another as free and equal citizens (see especially Patten 2014).

It might be objected that this view leads beyond liberal neutrality to a liberal or "modest" perfectionism. In fact, a similar argument for a more robust and pluralist public sphere has been made by Michael Walzer (Walzer 1990). As paradoxical as it may seem, in view of the tremendous "normalizing" effects of the market economy and bureaucratic state there is little reason to assume that either a robust and pluralist public sphere or the other general social conditions for a more deliberative politics can be secured without the (self-reflective) intervention and assistance of the state. However, while I have suggested that the state may be justified in acting in ways to secure such forums, I do not see that this requires embracing a perfectionist account of liberalism rather than the alternative principle of neutrality outlined above and embraced by Habermas. For, on this interpretation, the actions of the state are justified not because of their contribution to a particular way of life or conception of the good, but because robust and pluralist deliberative forums are necessary conditions for the effective exercise of basic rights of public and private autonomy. The state may at times be justified in acting in ways aimed at promoting or securing the conditions for a pluralist civil society not because it regards a pluralist society as good for its citizens, but because it regards such conditions as requirements of practical reason in the sense that informed and reasonable deliberation could not be achieved without them.

(3) Finally, issues raised in the critique of liberal neutrality re-emerge in a heightened form in the "dilemma of difference." For

the claim is now that the pursuit of "justice" through the bourgeois legal form (e.g. general law aimed at guarantee of equal rights) necessarily devalues difference and does violence to individuals, groups, and practices which deviate from the established norm (see Young 1990 and Minow 1990). The dilemma of difference, which has been most extensively discussed in recent feminist jurisprudence, is inextricably entwined with the fundamental principle of legal equality. "Treat equals equally" requires a judgment about the respects in which two things are equal and what it means to treat them equally. But this gives rise to the following dilemma:

> By taking another person's difference into account in awarding goods or distributing burdens, you risk reiterating the significance of that difference and, potentially, its stigma and stereotyping consequences. But if you do not take another person's difference into account—in a world that has made that difference matter—you may also recreate and reestablish both the difference and its negative implications. If you draft or enforce laws you may worry that the effects of the laws will not be neutral whether you take difference into account or you ignore it.
>
> (Minow 1993, 232)

Attempts to secure legal equality have generally pursued either an "assimilationist model" (which emphasizes the extent to which we are all alike) or an "accommodation model" (which seeks to create "special rights" on the basis of "real" differences). As some feminists point out, however, both models founder upon the same problem. In attempting to determine which differences deserve legal remedies and which should be ignored, the background norms which establish terms of relevance and in light of which judgments of similarity and difference are made frequently go unchallenged.[18]

One response has been to resist making judgments of sameness and difference altogether (see MacKinnon 1987). However, once the problem is framed in the above manner, that is, not as a problem of judgments of sameness and difference per se, but as a critique of the underlying norms and criteria guiding them, attention shifts to the processes through which those norms have been defined. And here, I think, the strength of Habermas's approach emerges: The effort to secure equal rights and the protection of law for each citizen must go hand in hand with efforts to secure the exercise of the public autonomy of all citizens. Public and private autonomy mutually suppose one another and must be jointly realized to secure processes of legitimate law-making. With this model in view, one could then take up the suggestion of some feminists that the point is not for the law to be "blind" to difference, nor to fix particular differences through the introduction of "special rights," but "to make difference costless."[19]

With respect to these three challenges to liberal democracy, I conclude that the abstract and highly procedural character of Habermas's version of the project of radical democracy is both its strength and its weakness. Its strength is that, in connection with his theory of communicative reason and action, Habermas generates a unique and powerful argument for a model of democracy in which the public and private autonomy of citizens are given equal consideration. It generates an intersubjective account of basic rights and a procedural democracy more attractive than any of the liberal or republican accounts currently available. It also offers a strong argument for the design of institutions that will facilitate discussion based on mutual respect. On the other hand, the highly abstract character of the proposal suggests that more work still needs to be done if it is to contribute more directly to specific debates about basic rights, the "dilemmas of difference," or what counts as the appropriate correspondence (or "meeting halfway") of liberal virtue and institutional design that, as Habermas concedes, is required if his notions of procedural democracy and deliberative politics are to be effectively realized in the modern world.

Further reading

Rosenfeld and Arato (1998) is an important collection of essays on BFN and includes a lengthy reply by Habermas. Schomberg and Baynes (2002) contains a number of essays on BFN. Zurn (2011) is a good introduction to Habermas's legal theory and Zurn (2007) is a book-length study, especially helpful for situating his views in relation to Dworkin, Ackerman, Michelman, and others. Baxter

(2011) is a full-length study that also critically examines Habermas's relation to Luhmann's work. Cohen (1999) is an informed discussion of Habermas by a leading political theorist of deliberative democracy.

Notes

1 Habermas has since suggested that traces of this holistic conception can still be found in his *Structural Transformation of the Public Sphere*; see his "Further Reflections on the Public Sphere" in Calhoun (1992, 433f.).

2 This assessment of law reflects a somewhat more positive attitude than the position expressed in TCA which regarded law more ambivalently as both an "institution" responsible for integration and a "medium" through which the lifeworld could be colonized (TCA 2, 365).

3 I have left the German "*Rechtsstaat*" in order to preserve the two senses of "constitutional state" and "rule of law" present in the German term.

4 In this sense both can be seen as attempts to "detranscendentalize" Kant's conception of practical reason; the comparison with Rawls is developed further in Chapter 6.

5 For an example of such a moral interpretation of Kant's political theory, see Riley (1983); for an interesting discussion on the relation between politics and morality in Kant that is closer to Habermas's view, see Pallikkahayil (2010) and Maus (2002).

6 For an interesting and parallel reading of Rousseau's primary political concern as an attempt to incorporate two distinct notions of public and private liberty or (social autonomy and civic freedom) into a coherent system, see Neuhouser (1993).

7 Many have commented on the ambiguity in Habermas's discourse ethics as to whether U is a moral principle or principle of political justice—see, for example, Wellmer (1991, 148) and Finlayson and Freyenhagen (2011, Introduction).

8 For Habermas's earlier formulation of the relation between the discourse principle and the principle of universalizability, see "Discourse Ethics" (MCCA, 65–66). His new position still leaves open the question about the precise "derivation" of D from the "pragmatic presuppositions of argument" since, in the earlier work, D seemed to be dependent on the derivation of U.

9 Some support for this claim can already be found in the fact that the German "*Recht*," like the French "*droit*," means "subjective right" as well as "objective law."

10 For further defense of this claim, see Baynes (2007).

11 Habermas already observed this distinction between the generation of power and the exercise of power in his important essay on Arendt's Communication Concept of Power in Habermas (1983).

12 Habermas cites Frank Michelman's "Law's Republic" as an example of this sort of republicanism; he might also have referred to some of the writings of Charles Taylor. Habermas's own position seems closer to the "Madisonian" republicanism of Cass Sunstein (Sunstein 1988).

13 Specific proposals for realizing the ideals of deliberative politics could range from something like James Fishkin's idea of a "deliberative opinion poll" to alternative procedures of voting and modes of representation; see Fishkin (1990) and Young (1990).

14 Fraser asks whether other divisions of labor might not be possible; Baxter is more critical on this proposed distinction; Cohen and Rogers explore alternative models.

15 BFN 302; compare also Habermas's corresponding remark that a postconventional morality "is dependent upon a form of life that meets it halfway. ... There must be a modicum of fit between morality and socio-political institutions" (MCCA, 207–208) and the interesting essay on this topic by Klaus Offe (Offe 1992).

16 On the principle of equal consideration of interests, see Dahl (1989, 85).

17 For this notion of "precommitment" and the Constitution as a "public charter," see Freeman (1992) and Zurn 2007, 131f.

18 See Littleton (1993); Rhode (1989); and Habermas's own discussion of the "dialectic of legal and factual equality" in BFN, 509f.

19 This position, which she calls the "acceptance model," is proposed by Christine Littleton in Littleton (1993). I do not mean to suggest (nor does Littleton) that this is an easy task for, as Charles Taylor points out in a related discussion, there can arise conflicts between the "politics of equal dignity" and "the politics of difference"—conflicts, for example, between equal opportunity and cultural membership—that cannot easily be resolved (Taylor 1992, 37).

Seven

Deliberative democracy, public reason, and democracy beyond the nation-state

I. Habermas and the basic idea of a deliberative democracy

Habermas has been a leading political theorist in advocating a deliberative conception of democracy. The aim of this conception is to specify a broad set of procedures and conditions for reaching collectively binding decisions that are both legitimate and presumptively correct (or rationally acceptable). In general, deliberative theorists focus on the (formal and informal) processes that precede the final act of decision-making, rather than concentrating on a more narrowly circumscribed process of aggregating voter preferences. Legitimacy on this conception derives not simply from the act of voting, but from wider processes that lead up to that act as well (Manin 1987). As with other normative conceptions, it is primarily conceived as a set of *ideal* procedures in light of which existing institutions and practices could be criticized and assessed.

Joshua Cohen has offered a concise and useful formulation of such an "ideal deliberative procedure" that lies at the core of his own conception of deliberative democracy.

> A democratic conception can be represented in terms of the requirements that it sets on such [an ideal] procedure. In particular, outcomes are democratically legitimate if and only if they could be the object of a free and reasoned agreement among equals. The ideal deliberative procedure is a procedure that captures this principle.
>
> (Cohen 1989, 22)

Knight and Johnson have offered a comparable ideal: "We view deliberation as an *idealized process* consisting of *fair procedure* within which political actors engage in *reasoned argument* for the *purpose of resolving political conflict*" (Knight and Johnson 1994, 285). Among the "fair procedures" Knight and Johnson include the requirement of "manifestly free and equal access to relevant deliberative arenas for purposes of establishing procedures, setting the agenda, and making final decisions" (285). Finally, Samuel Freeman defines a deliberative democracy as "one in which political agents or their representatives (a) aim to collectively deliberate and vote (b) their sincere and informed judgments regarding (c) measures conducive to the common good of citizens" (Freeman 2000, 382). Central to all these views is the idea of "a process of public reasoning about the common good" (Freeman 2000, 336) and it is this feature that most distinguishes it from the liberal-pluralist or "aggregative" alternative.

In contrasting it to a liberal-pluralist conception of democracy, Knight and Johnson suggest that four distinct features can be found in what they call the "standard case" of deliberative democracy: (1) A deliberative conception views the democratic process as one that is concerned with the common good, where this is not identified exclusively with a notion of aggregate interests or collective goods (Knight and Johnson 1994, 281; Cohen 1989, 24–25). Although politics is not exclusively focused on the common good, this idea is given a more prominent normative role than it is within liberal conceptions. (2) In response to the longstanding question of whether law is best conceived as *voluntas* (will or decision) or *ratio* (reason), deliberative conceptions come down on the side of *ratio*. A central means by which the common good is discerned or "fashioned" (Knight and Johnson 1994) is within a deliberative process that places a high premium on reason and argumentation. Further, the relevant notion of reason is not simply instrumental, but includes as well the idea that its exercise is "truth-tracking" or at least "reasonable" in a more substantive sense.[1] (3) A central assumption of a deliberative conception is that the deliberations that take the common good as their focus do not simply treat individual preferences as exogenous elements of the political system. Rather, it assumes that in the process of reasonable deliberation, the search for a common good will often result in the transformation and/or "laundering" of merely private preferences. "Preferences do not exist independently of the institutions through which they are expressed; their formation is at least partially endogenous to the process of agenda formation, which must, therefore, be seen as a deliberative rather than as a purely aggregative mechanism" (Beitz 1989, 12–13; Sunstein 1991). (4) Finally, deliberative democracy invokes a different conception of citizen motivation than that found in the liberal-pluralist model. What motivates citizens is not simply self-interest constrained by the recognition of some principles for mutual advantage, but an interest in finding the common good and a "higher-order" desire to justify claims to others who share such an interest.

The conception of a "procedural democracy" and "deliberative politics" introduced by Habermas in *Between Facts and Norms* shares all four of these features of a deliberative democracy in some form. Politics is concerned, at least in part, with the common good and processes of deliberation have as their primary focus, at least some of the time, the common good or "generalizable interests." This conception of democracy is also "cognitive" or "epistemic" in that it is concerned with specifying procedures for collective decision-making that have a presumption of generating reasonable or rational outcomes (BFN, 285). Habermas also argues that democratic procedures should specify not simply a means for aggregating pre-political preferences but the conditions of deliberation in which agreement about "generalizable interests" can be pursued, at least in part through the transformation of preferences. Finally, though Habermas puts less emphasis on this aspect, the realization of a deliberative politics assumes that individuals have motivations other than those of self-interest. Democratic procedure requires a "rationalized lifeworld" including a liberal political culture and corresponding civic virtues that, as he puts it, "meets it halfway" (BFN, 461). What stands out in his conception, however, is that with respect to each of these features of a deliberative democracy he is inclined to give them a more procedural interpretation. This is particularly evident in his attempt to distinguish his position from both the liberal-pluralist and republican alternatives (BFN, chap. 4; IO, 239f.). It will be helpful then to consider in more detail the sense in which Habermas's conception of democracy is—and is not—procedural.

"Procedural" and "proceduralist" are among the most commonly used adjectives in Habermas's *Between Facts and Norms*. He broadly contrasts his preferred "proceduralist legal paradigm" to both the liberal and welfarist paradigms (BFN, 409). He speaks of a "procedural understanding of the constitution" (BFN, 246), a "proceduralist" view of constitutional adjudication, a "proceduralist" understanding of law (BFN, 409), a "proceduralist" theory of politics (BFN, 273), and a "procedural" interpretation of popular sovereignty (BFN, Appendix I). He also describes his own conception of democracy as "proceduralist." Within the context of German discussions, it is clear that Habermas's primary concern is to distance himself from material value-ethics interpretations of the law and political process, interpretations inspired by the work of Max Scheler and Nicolai Hartman (BFN, 254). Habermas also uses the term "procedural" to distinguish his own conception of the democratic process from liberal and republican alternatives. This is partly to differentiate his position from one that takes as fixed and given a "pre-political" set of (natural) rights and from one that has the democratic process derive its legitimacy "from the prior agreement of a presupposed substantial-ethical community"—that is, from a prior agreement on a conception of the good. Thus, Habermas writes, "a consistent proceduralist understanding of the constitution bets on the intrinsically rational character of the procedural conditions grounding the supposition that the democratic process as a whole facilitates rational outcomes. In that case reason is embodied solely in the formal-pragmatic facilitating conditions for deliberative politics" (BFN, 285; Gledhill 2012).

However, within the wider context of legal and democratic theory, the term "procedural" is ambiguous and there are many different conceptions that have been described as "proceduralist" that differ importantly from Habermas's own. For example, in his influential essay, "Is Democracy Special?," Brian Barry describes his own conception as proceduralist which he understands to mean a rejection of,

> the notion that one should build into 'democracy' any constraints
> on the content of the outcomes produced, such as substantive
> equality, respect for human rights, concern for the general

welfare, personal liberty, or the rule of law. The only exception (and these are significant) are those required by democracy itself as a procedure.

(Barry 1979, 155–156)

While the question of what is "required by democracy itself as a procedure" is itself a matter of much debate, Habermas's conception of democracy is not procedural in this sense. It clearly entails more substantive normative content than Barry would want to include.

Further, even normatively richer procedural conceptions, such as Peter Singer's conception of democracy based on a notion of "fairness as compromise" or John Ely's "process-oriented approach" to the constitution and constitutional review, fall short of Habermas's conception (Singer 1974; Ely 1980). For these conceptions, the democratic process consists in a set of rules and procedures that are supposed to weigh equally preferences whose formation is largely exogenous to the democratic process itself. Each person should be granted the opportunity to register her preference and no person's preference should count for more than another person's. These conceptions thus operate with an ideal of political equality understood in terms of the equal opportunity to influence political outcomes. A procedure is "fair" if it captures this notion of equal power. The difficulty with such conceptions, however, is that they remain relatively indifferent to the initial preferences that enter into the procedure (Beitz 1989, 82). A fuller and thus more adequate account must consider the formation and quality of preferences as well. To do this, the ideal of political equality must initially be conceived at a more abstract level and cannot be identified directly with the more narrowly procedural idea of the equal opportunity to influence outcomes.[2]

Habermas's conception of democracy thus assumes a more abstract ideal of political equality and its aim is to mirror or capture this more abstract ideal in a set of ideal procedures thereby considered "fair." The ideal of political equality is, however, not equated with a set of procedures that secures an equal opportunity (for any given preference) to influence outcome. "Rather, the claim that a norm lies equally in the interest of everyone has the sense of rational acceptability: all those possible affected should be able to accept the norm on the basis of good reasons" (BFN, 103). In this sense, Habermas's procedural conception is closest to what Charles Beitz has called "complex proceduralism":

> Like other forms of proceduralism, [complex proceduralism] holds that democratic procedures should treat *persons* as equals; but it will not follow that the appropriate criterion for assessing procedures is the simple principle of equal power over outcomes. Instead, complex proceduralism holds that the terms of democratic participation are fair when they are reasonably acceptable from each citizen's point of view, or more precisely, when no citizen has good reason to refuse to accept them.
>
> (Beitz 1989, 23)

In Habermas's conception too there are certain abstract ideals—and ultimately the idea of communicative freedom—or capacity of each person to take a "yes" or "no" position on a speech-act offer—that are identified prior to any proposed set of (ideal) procedures. Habermas nonetheless continues to describe his conception as "procedural" for two reasons: First, he claims that the fundamental ideal that forms the "dogmatic core" of his theory is not itself simply one value among others but reflects a basic norm implicit in the very idea of communicative action (BFN, 445–446). Second, he claims that this ideal—developed in *Between Facts and Norms* in connection with the co-equal and mutually interdependent ideas of public and private autonomy—can in turn be used to describe a set of (ideal) democratic procedures. It is because the procedures sufficiently mirror this basic ideal, however, that we are entitled to confer a presumption of reasonableness or fairness upon them (BFN, 295). In sum, for Habermas, ideal procedures attempt to capture or express an ideal of citizens as free and equal engaged in reasoning about their common good.

1. The "co-originality thesis": Democracy and liberal values

Habermas's procedural or "discourse" conception of democracy, as outlined in Chapter 4 of *Between Facts and Norms*, provides a basis for reconsidering the longstanding dispute concerning the relation between democracy and other liberal values or, in Benjamin Constant's phrase, the liberty of the ancients and the liberty of the moderns. Habermas argues that neither the "principle of democracy" nor the basic scheme of (liberal) rights should be seen as primary. Rather, as he puts it, the principle of democracy and the basic scheme of rights are "co-original" (or equiprimordal) and emerge together via the "interpenetration of the discourse principle and the legal form" (BFN, 121; see Chapter 6 and Rummens 2006). As Habermas sees it, this enables his conception to avoid the two extremes of a legal positivism that leaves basic rights up to the political sovereign, on the one hand, and a subordination of popular sovereignty to a prior moral principle as in, for example, Kant and the natural law tradition, on the other. "The universal right to equal liberties may neither be imposed as a moral right that merely sets an external constraint on the sovereign legislator, nor be instrumentalized as a functional prerequisite for the legislator's aims" (BFN, 104). The "co-originality thesis" thus regards public autonomy (roughly, the idea that citizens can be bound only by laws that they give to themselves) and private autonomy (roughly, civil and political rights) as reciprocally dependent on each other such that neither can claim a prior or independent status.

   In an extended comparison between Habermas's views and his own, Joshua Cohen endorses this idea of the "co-originality" of public and private autonomy (Cohen 1999). However, Cohen is less convinced by the specific arguments in support of it. In particular, he suggests, first, that Habermas's account appeals to a "comprehensive doctrine" or philosophy of life that is inappropriate given the "fact of reasonable pluralism" and, second, that it is deficient in its support for an *equal* right to liberty. Cohen's alternative account of the relation between basic liberties and democracy is highly instructive and strengthens the co-originality thesis. However, given that Habermas has elsewhere acknowledged that there is a substantive "dogmatic core" to his theory—the idea of communicative freedom or autonomy—it is not necessary to read him in the more procedurally minimalist manner that Cohen proposes. In fact, the description of Habermas's distinctive use of the term "procedural" above is offered as an alternative to such an interpretation.

   Cohen's first reservation—that it is a comprehensive doctrine—is initially plausible in that Habermas's account of political legitimacy is presented within the wider framework of his theory of communicative action. However, an alternative reading is possible: The "interpenetration of the discourse principle and the legal form" can itself be seen as a restriction of the more abstract idea of autonomy (in communicative action *simpliciter*) to the political-legal context and thus as first introducing the idea of citizens or "legal consociates." In Habermas's own variation on the social-contract tradition, the guiding question thus becomes, "What basic rights must free and equal citizens mutually accord one another if they want to regulate their common life legitimately by means of positive law?" (BFN, 82, 118). Further, this question must finally be addressed from the internal perspective of citizens committed to regulating their lives in common and not only from the external standpoint of one preferred philosophical theory. Thus, unlike earlier contract theorists (including at least some readings of Rawls), this question cannot be settled by appeal to the particular interests of hypothetical parties nor by appeal to a set of "natural" (pre-political) rights but, in the final analysis, only to considerations about what citizens would consent to in view of their status as free and equal persons:

> Under conditions of postmetaphysical thinking, we cannot expect a further-reaching consensus that would include substantive issues. This restriction to presuppositions that are formal in this sense is tailored for the specifically modern pluralism of worldviews, cultural forms of life, interest positions, and so forth. Naturally, this does not mean that a constitution-making practice of this kind would be free of all normative content. On the contrary, the performative meaning of this practice, which is merely set forth and explicated in constitutional principles and the system of rights, already contains as a doctrinal core the (Rousseausian-Kantian) idea of the self-legislation of voluntarily associated citizens who are both free and equal.
>
> (BFN, 406)

As I will argue below in connection with the idea of public reason, this interpretation more or less parallels Rawls's idea that a "political conception" must not be "political in the wrong way."

According to Cohen's second reservation, Habermas's commitment to equal liberties is deficient since it rests on a claim that the system of rights can be derived *exclusively* from "the interpenetration of the discourse principle and the legal form." Since, on his view, the discourse principle imposes a fairly general requirement of impartiality Cohen is doubtful that its conjunction with the idea of the "rule of law" (or "legal form") will yield a sufficiently broad set of liberal rights (including, rights to conscience, bodily integrity, privacy, property, etc.). Although it must be admitted that Habermas's argument here is not as clear as it might be, Cohen reads Habermas's proceduralism in an excessively minimalist manner. If, as I have argued, the discourse principle itself presupposes an (abstract) ideal of persons as free and equal, then it may impose more constraints than Cohen assumes. Further, the notion of the "legal form" that Habermas invokes, derived from legal debates in twentieth-century German law, is also more substantive in character than the idea of the "rule of law" more narrowly conceived and already includes something like the idea of equal subjective liberties (BFN, 84–89; Baynes 2012, 134–136). Thus, the "interpenetration" strategy could arguably generate something close to the liberties specified, for example, in Rawls's Principle of Equal Liberty. On the other hand, however, Cohen is correct to note that, on Habermas's account, the "interpenetration of the discourse principle and legal form" yields only a general scheme of basic rights and not a concrete set of liberties (Cohen 1999, 393). Although this scheme is more detailed than Cohen assumes, it does not by itself provide a means for assigning specific weight to the reasons that citizens must consider when determining the more specific scope of the basic liberties—it will arguably leave open, for example, the question of whether the scope of liberty (or equality) require a legal right to abortion. On Habermas's account, these are questions that citizens within a given polity must determine for themselves within the framework of a deliberative politics. Of course, citizens would have to give consideration to precisely the kinds of reasons—and the appropriate weighting among them— that Cohen raises in his own reflections on the relation between democracy and rights to civil and expressive liberties—including religious liberty (see Cohen 1998).

2. The role of consensus

The idea of consensus plays an important role in Habermas's conception of a deliberative democracy as it does in other deliberative conceptions. As Joshua Cohen has expressed it, "Ideal deliberation aims to arrive at a rationally motivated *consensus*—to find reasons that are persuasive to all who are committed to acting on the results of a free and reasoned assessment of alternatives by equals" (Cohen 1989, 23). The aim of reaching agreement on the basic principles and terms of social cooperation reflects the conviction that the democratic process should not simply provide a mechanism for aggregating personal or pre-political preferences, but should provide a context for reasoned debate and discussion about the merits of policies and proposals in a way that recognizes the freedom and equality of each citizen. It is also claimed that a search for consensus is one way in which what James Madison called the "mild voice of reason" can find expression within the political process. The ideal of consensus, then, follows from a commitment to the freedom and equality of citizens as well as from a desire to improve the "reasonable quality" (BFN, 304) of democratic outcomes.

Nevertheless, the value placed on a search for agreement or consensus has not gone unchallenged. Some critics understandably claim that in a society characterized by the "fact of pluralism" it is both impractical and unreasonable as a goal, while others have pointed to the pernicious effects that could follow from an insistence on consensus. For example, Donald Moon, who describes his own version of "political liberalism" as "a variant of traditional consensus theories of legitimation, but one that does not share their faith in supposing that nonconsensuality can be overcome," notes the risk in consent theory of "excluding certain voices, and so generating a false consensus" (Moon 1991, 211). Similarly, in a critique of deliberative theories, Iris Young has also argued that the demand for consensus can exclude the viewpoints of others and promote cultural bias (Young 1997). Finally, James Bohman and William Rehg have criticized the prominent role given to the search for consensus in Habermas's theory, arguing that a "weaker interpretation of epistemic deliberation" is required within multicultural societies (Bohman and Rehg 2002, 46).

Although these criticisms may apply to some models of deliberative democracy, in general they rest on a misunderstanding of the role of consensus. Neither Habermas nor Cohen, for example, claim that *all* social conflict or disagreement can be resolved in a consensus—not even, as Knight and Johnson point out, "in the ideal case" (Knight and Johnson 1994, 282). Cohen, for example, is quite explicit that, "even under ideal conditions there is no promise that consensual reason will be forthcoming" (Cohen 1989, 23). The bulk of the political process, Habermas acknowledges, depends on compromise and on the outcome of fair procedures, including, as prominent among these, majority rule, even if it simultaneously insists upon the importance of a background "meta-consensus" (BFN, 282; see List and Dryzek 2003). It is thus necessary to be more precise about the role (and underlying motivation) of consensus within Habermas's conception of democracy. Several brief observations are in order.

First, none of the theorists we have been considering suggest that political legitimacy requires or rests on a *de facto* consensus or agreement. For just the reasons Moon notes, such a consensus may be "false." Deliberative theorists like Habermas speak rather of an ideal consensus that can be reached only if certain demanding conditions have been met. In this sense, the search for consensus functions primarily as a regulative idea that can only be approximately realized in practice. However, once the role of consensus is formulated in this way, it might suggest that the real normative work is not being done by the idea of consensus per se but by other ideals lying behind it. As I have suggested, the search for consensus reflects a commitment to the view that "the principles of political association should be justifiable to all whom they bind" (Larmore 1996, 137). There is, I think, a great deal of truth to this claim; nonetheless, the idea of consensus remains important to the extent that it draws attention to such a "meta-consensus" on something like core "constitutional essentials" and basic justice, even while acknowledging that any specific interpretation of these constitutional essentials can itself become a matter of public debate and scrutiny (see List 2002).

Second, recognition of the (derivative) value of consensus as a regulative idea does not mean that agreement, even after extended deliberation, is to be reasonably expected on a wide range of preferences or policies. There can be, however, no pre-set answer to the question of the scope or range of agreement since the search for consensus itself may lead to new insight and the discovery (or creation) of new bases for agreement. This, at least, is the hope that deliberativists hold out: Unlike the liberal-pluralist alternative, it takes the aim of consensus seriously, but, unlike the republican (or civic humanist) alternative, it does not assume that deep agreement or a "shared common ethos" is required or even plausibly to be expected. Rather, the search for consensus on the common good— or "justice" or "constitutional essentials"—remains the focus of deliberation, even if an actual consensus does not come about.

However, there is a further role of consensus in deliberative accounts that does seem to require actual agreement in order for (good faith) deliberation to take place. If citizens are to regard the outcome of deliberative procedures as legitimate and "fair" (even if not necessarily correct or just) it would seem that they must all agree that certain values have been at least sufficiently realized. This follows from the fact that, according to the deliberative model, the legitimacy or fairness of the procedures is not solely a procedural question (Cohen 1989). As I suggested in connection with Habermas's view above, the conception of equality to which he appeals is not the equal consideration of interests procedurally defined, but the equal status of citizens as co-authors of the legal order to which they are bound—that is, a conception of democratic equality. If citizens are not able to agree on a minimal political "core morality"—or if it is not publicly known and embedded in the democratic institutions of the society—then it is not clear how the outcomes could claim to be legitimate at all (even, again, if they are not correct or just according to some citizens' judgment).

Critics might reply (and have replied) that this last role of a political-moral consensus does not take the fact of *moral* pluralism seriously enough (Caney 1999). Disagreement is not limited to ethical questions, as Habermas has sometimes suggested, but extends to moral questions, or questions of justice, as well. This is in fact simply what Jeremy Waldron refers to as the "circumstances of politics" (Waldron 1999, 7) and Alessandro Ferrara labels 'hyperpluralism' (Ferrara). Similarly, some critics will find Rawls's idea of an overlapping consensus—a political consensus that can emerge despite a plurality of reasonable comprehensive doctrines—to be similarly suspect. Clearly, many questions of justice are as contestable as ethical questions. However, as I argue in the next section, unless there is reason to expect agreement on even a minimal core morality it is not clear how any further compromise could be regarded as fair, or how any other distinction between a reasonable (as opposed to an unreasonable) disagreement could be sustained.[3]

II. The idea of public reason—the Rawls/Habermas exchange

The idea of public reason figures prominently in the conceptions of political legitimacy proposed by both Habermas and Rawls. However, in their exchange each criticizes the other for shortcomings in their respective approach: Rawls suggests that Habermas's idea of public reason is part of a comprehensive philosophical doctrine and thus unacceptable as a basis of political legitimacy in a society characterized by a plurality of comprehensive views. Habermas, by contrast, suggests that Rawls's model of public reason, with its reliance on the idea of an overlapping consensus, remains too beholden to the contingencies of a *de facto* agreement to serve as a suitable basis of political legitimacy (IO, 84). But even if Rawls is not always clear about his conception of public reason, their positions are not as far from one another as is often supposed. In particular, though Rawls suggests that his model of public reason is circumscribed and perhaps even constituted by what he calls the "domain of the political," when his conception of the political is properly understood—when, that is, it is not "political in the wrong way"—it does not differ significantly from Habermas's own account of public reason. In the end, both accounts of public reason incorporate a core set of liberal values tied, in Rawls's case, to the notion of citizens as free and equal persons with the two basic moral powers and, in Habermas's case, to a notion of communicative autonomy.

To begin, the idea of public reason also plays a crucial role in Habermas's account of political legitimacy. Basic political norms (e.g. what Rawls calls the "constitutional essentials" and matters of basic justice) are legitimate only if they conform to a demanding ideal of public reason, that is, only if they could be agreed to by all citizens as participants in a practical discourse for the same (publicly available) reasons. Thomas McCarthy and others have argued that this conception of political legitimacy, together with the idea of public reason, is too strongly oriented to the idea of consensus or "rational agreement" and that he should move more in the direction of Rawls's notion of an overlapping consensus which allows for "reasonable disagreement" and "reasonable pluralism" within a public culture (McCarthy 1998). Political legitimacy neither can nor should depend on such a demanding idea of rational agreement but rather should draw upon the idea of a "mutual accommodation" among diverse worldviews and corresponding forms of life. This revision would also give rise to a more thoroughly "proceduralist" interpretation of political legitimacy.

On the other hand, in his own contribution to the exchange Habermas argued that Rawls's notion of an overlapping consensus cannot serve the purpose to which he puts it and that he needs a stronger, more systematically grounded notion of practical reason to support his own liberal principle of legitimacy (IO, chaps. 2 and 3). This principle reads as follows: "Our exercise of political power is fully proper only when it is exercised in accordance with a constitution the essentials of which all citizens as free and equal may reasonably be expected to endorse in the light of principles and ideals acceptable to their common human reason" (Rawls 1996, 137). According to Habermas, however, Rawls interprets this principle of legitimacy in connection with the *de facto* emergence of an overlapping consensus rather than, as one should, in terms of a more abstract and normatively secure (communication-theoretical) idea of rational agreement or acceptability (appropriately tailored or restricted to the domain of legal consociates). In contrast, then, to both McCarthy and Habermas, I want to give some reasons for suggesting that the views of Rawls and Habermas on public reason are closer to one another than is often supposed.

First, according to McCarthy, Habermas has not offered a conception of public reason (and, hence, political legitimacy) that can adequately respond to the value pluralism that characterizes liberal-democratic societies. On the one hand, there is typically no homogeneous ethico-political culture that could provide the necessary background for an agreement on "constitutional essentials and matters of basic justice." On the other hand, the model of discourse that Habermas proposes does not make sufficient allowance for "reasonable disagreements" about moral/ethical questions. Rather, cases supporting the idea of a reasonable value pluralism are either interpreted as "interim reports" on an ongoing moral disagreement, where it is claimed there is only one right answer, or they are too quickly treated as a matter of negotiation and compromise, in just the way that conflicts of "interest" are to be handled (McCarthy 1998, 150). The result is a certain inadequacy within Habermas's theory in responding to the value pluralism characteristic of modern societies. McCarthy's suggestion is that, to accommodate the fact of reasonable pluralism, Habermas must relinquish the strong claims concerning rational agreement (*Einverständniss*), make room for a notion of mutual accommodation and, consequently, give his theory a still more "procedural twist" (McCarthy 1998, 151). By making greater use of his own distinction between direct and indirect justification of a norm, for example, Habermas could allow for the idea of a "reasonable disagreement" on values, while nonetheless still providing citizens with a strong procedural reason for accepting as legitimate those norms and decisions they oppose at a substantive level (McCarthy 1998, 128).

As I have attempted to show above, however, despite his own frequent use of the term procedural, neither Habermas (nor Rawls) are proceduralists "all the way down" (see also Cohen 1994). Rather, both attempt to mirror in a set of procedures a prior substantive value or set of values—autonomy in the case of Habermas, and the idea of citizens as free and equal persons in the case of Rawls. It is these values or ideals that then confer a presumption of reasonableness or fairness on the proposed procedures (BFN, 266, 295; OPC, 406). More important, however, is the question of the conditions under which an agreement should count as reasonable. But here too the differences may not be as great as first appears. The idea of the reasonable is invoked at many levels within Rawls's theory, but its most basic use is with respect to persons: A citizen is reasonable if she is willing to accept and abide by fair terms of cooperation and willing to accept the "burdens of judgment," that is, to acknowledge and abide by the limits of public reason (Rawls 1996, 49n.1). This basic virtue of the citizen is itself understood in connection with what Rawls calls the basic moral powers of the person: the capacity for a sense of justice and the capacity for a conception of the good. These moral powers are part of a moral psychology or conception of the person that, along with the idea of social cooperation, form one of the "fundamental intuitive ideas" found in a liberal political culture and from which his political conception is drawn. According to Rawls, although this idea is not itself part of a comprehensive doctrine or theory of human nature, it is nonetheless a normative reflection, informed as well by moral and social-scientific theory, on the basic capacities of human agency (Rawls 1996, 86–87). The further notions of a "reasonable comprehensive doctrine," a "reasonable overlapping consensus," and "reasonable pluralism" all draw upon this prior notion of reasonable persons: a doctrine, for example, is reasonable if its more specific elements fall within the "burdens of judgment" of reasonable citizens and an overlapping consensus is reasonable just in case it is a consensus among reasonable comprehensive doctrines. Finally, a reasonable disagreement is a disagreement that persists even after reasonable people, exercising good faith and recognizing the "burdens of judgment" nonetheless fail to agree on a particular matter. According to Rawls, such disagreements will be a permanent feature of a liberal democratic society.

Even with these brief remarks, it should be relatively clear that what Rawls describes as the reasonable is not the conclusion or outcome of an agreement or overlapping consensus that just happens to exist. Rather, the prior idea of the reasonable informs what can count as a reasonable comprehensive doctrine and thus what could finally be part of a (reasonable) overlapping consensus. The idea of the reasonable, in other words, is something that is specified in advance of any existing overlapping consensus, rather than something that results from it. It might be objected, in response, that this reading does not follow Rawls's own recent distinction between "moral autonomy" and "political autonomy" (or, relatedly, between "persons" and "citizens") and thus still gives Rawls's position a too Kantian interpretation—one his "freestanding" political conception is meant to avoid (see Forst 2002, 158). However, though Rawls's own formulations sometimes lend support to such a reading, this cannot be his considered position. He is himself explicit that a "political" conception is still a "moral conception" (Rawls 1996, xliv, li). In short, even his conception of the political autonomy of citizens still assumes the "fundamental intuitive ideas," including the idea of citizens as free and equal with their two basic moral powers—and these fundamental ideas are themselves contained in (Rawls's idealized version of) our own practice of social cooperation with its guiding principle of reciprocity.

A related question often raised in connection with Rawls's political liberalism—and one raised by Habermas—concerns the role that the idea of an overlapping consensus plays in its justification (in contrast to its stability or likelihood to endure over time) (IO, 69, 89f.). According to Rawls, the idea of an overlapping consensus is first introduced at a second stage, in connection with the question of social stability, not at the first stage when the initial justification of the principles of justice is at issue. This does not mean, however, that the overlapping consensus is not at all relevant to the process of justification. Rawls's considered view seems to be that if it turns out that the political conception justified at the first stage (or what he calls *pro tanto* justification) is not stable— that is, could not become the object of a reasonable overlapping consensus—then this would somehow call into question its earlier claim to being justified (Rawls 1996, 387; Hedrick, 41).

In his own interpretation of Rawls, however, Habermas takes a different tack. That is, he attributes a *more* significant justificatory role to the idea of an overlapping consensus than Rawls seems to have in mind. Habermas apparently does not consider that the idea of the reasonable must already be presupposed prior to the identification of those comprehensive doctrines that might be eligible candidates for a reasonable overlapping consensus. Rather he regards the notion of the reasonable as itself the outcome of a contingent or "lucky" convergence: "Only the lucky convergence of the differently motivated nonpublic reasons can generate the public validity or 'reasonableness' of the content of this 'overlapping consensus' that everyone accepts. Agreement in conclusions *results* from premises rooted in different outlooks" (IO, 84). Now, while it is true that each citizen may and even should look to his or her own comprehensive doctrine to see whether he or she has reason to affirm the content of the overlapping consensus, it is not the case either that the justification of the content rests exclusively upon these "nonpublic" reasons or that a contingent overlapping consensus produces or defines the "reasonableness" of that content (see also Forst 2012, chap. 2). Interestingly, in a later essay on the place of religion in the public square Habermas himself endorses a position essentially the same as Rawls's own idea of a freestanding political conception as a "module" that can be embedded in a person's own comprehensive doctrine but that does not need that doctrine for its own justification (BNR, 112).

This (modest) repositioning of the reasonable within Rawls's conception of political liberalism suggests how Rawls may in fact be closer to Habermas's own position. It is the basic idea of the citizen as reasonable and rational and, behind this, the idea of the basic moral powers of the person that importantly shapes the subsequent employment of the reasonable in Rawls's work. In ways that closely resemble Habermas's basic assumptions about communicative freedom—the capacity to take a position on a speech-act offer—Rawls's idea of the reasonable acquires at least some of its normative authority from the fundamental human capacity to respond to and act from reasons: the legitimacy of a political order depends on what citizens can endorse in view of their "common human reason" (though a great deal more philosophical argument—contained in *A Theory of Justice* and *Political Liberalism*—is required to show what kind of political order might possibly satisfy this requirement).

An important consequence of the Rawls–Habermas exchange is that it highlights the importance of democratic theory for Rawls's own reflections about justice. As Joshua Cohen has argued in an instructive essay, the principles of justice—or "justice as fairness"—are in an important sense principles "for a democratic society" (Cohen 2002). By this Cohen means not only that they are appropriate (and perhaps even required) for a society that is democratically organized; rather, he means that they are principles that in their content reflect the idea of society among free and equal citizens who are prepared to publicly acknowledge and affirm the principles governing the basic institutions in which they live. Further, they are principles that can appropriately guide the deliberations of citizens in their attempts to publicly recognize and affirm their equal status. Here it is perhaps especially significant that Rawls describes his difference principle as a principle of "democratic equality" (TJ, 65). To insist that inequalities in some primary social goods are only permissible if they work to the advantage of the least well off is one way in which the equal status of citizens can be affirmed and so serves to express the idea of democratic society as a society among equals.

Such an interpretation of Rawls's democratic commitments offers some resources for Rawls to respond to the final criticism offered by Habermas mentioned above. Habermas suggests that since on Rawls's account the citizens have a fully developed theory of justice delivered to them (by the philosopher?) they "cannot reignite the radical democratic embers of the original position within the civil life of their society" (IO, 169; and, even more forcefully, Wolin 1996). Rather, since they are constrained from the outset by the prior agreement of the parties, they cannot conceive their own democratic constitution as an ongoing project. However, based on Rawls's own reply, Habermas's reading of Rawls on this point may not be compelling. Although it is true that his two principles are more determinate than Habermas's own structurally analogous "system of rights," they are offered not from the perspective of an expert philosopher, but as attempt by a philosopher to make a substantive contribution to a public debate among citizens about appropriate principles for a democratic society. Moreover, even Habermas's own conception of deliberative democracy does not mean that citizens (with each new generation?) start from scratch. Rather, they too must presuppose the "system of rights" and are guided in their collective deliberations by a given constitutional tradition in arguing for their respective claims about what is for the common good. It thus does not seem that acknowledging the constraints of justice in their deliberations must necessarily denigrate its democratic character or prohibit them from seeing their constitution as an ongoing project (see also TT, 122). In short, both Rawls and Habermas can be read as attempting to clarify the conditions for the practice of deliberative democracy against a broader set of (existing) social practices (James 2005; Baynes 2014).

III. The practice of public reason

Habermas's idea of public reason is offered not simply as a notion for more abstract political theorizing, but is also intended to have consequences for political practice. In this concluding section I will briefly consider some more practical implications of his idea. In particular, I want to indicate some ways that it might inform both the practice of toleration and the practice of *political* public reasoning.

(1) As many commentators have pointed out, toleration is an important yet elusive liberal virtue (Heyd 1996; Forst 2011a). It asks that we live with what we might find deeply repugnant from a personal point of view. In this respect, it is an attitude that, despite its almost banal ring, is both extremely demanding and yet indispensable to a liberal political culture: On the one hand, we may personally (and justifiably) feel quite opposed to the practice or way of life we are asked to tolerate, yet, on the other hand, we are asked actively to affirm the right of others to engage in that practice or way of life (even though we need not have any regret should that practice or way of life cease to exist).[4] How is it possible to cultivate such an attitude, particularly in a pluralist society where we are bound frequently to encounter attitudes and ways of life with which we disagree? And, secondly, what are the appropriate limits of such an attitude: is it necessary to tolerate the intolerable? Is not this paradoxical virtue simply one more symptom of an impoverished liberalism that finds itself obliged to defend practices it finds morally offensive? These are not easy questions to answer but several brief observations can be made. Habermas's distinction between a political culture and the larger societal culture, as well as Rawls's parallel distinction between what he calls the "political public" and the larger background culture, is important here inasmuch as the first term in these pairs helps to set the basic frame and limits of the tolerable. In this respect it helps to define the minimal "core morality," the violation of which need not be tolerated, either from a legal or a moral point of view (Larmore 1996, 12–13). Of course, this does not mean that, as a matter of policy, questions such as the legal regulation of hate speech or violent pornography are now immediately settled; rather it suggests that this core morality provides the general framework within which a political community is first properly bound to address those topics (see BNR, 258f.). At the same time, however, matters that do not concern the "core morality" of the political culture are ones that all citizens have an obligation to tolerate as a matter of public morality. It may also be that, as part of

an attitude of toleration, citizens also have an obligation to try to reach a greater mutual understanding of one another's perspective. The exercise of toleration thus may (*but need not*) develop into stronger forms of appreciation and "civic friendship."

(2) In the context of his exchange with Rawls, Habermas has defended a conception of public reason and corresponding conception of "reasonableness" as an important political virtue and one that is probably as demanding as the virtue of toleration. In connection with his version of "political liberalism" based on the idea of an "overlapping consensus" among divergent comprehensive moral or religious worldviews, Rawls has argued that, as a duty of civility, citizens have a moral obligation, when they consider how to cast their vote, to regard themselves as "ideal legislators" and ask whether the reasons in support of the proposed legislation or policy are ones that it is reasonable to think other citizens could also endorse. In response to criticisms of his initial formulation, he now endorses what he calls an "inclusive" model of public reason which allows citizens to act from reasons drawn from their comprehensive moral or religious convictions so long as they believe the positions they support could "in due course" also be supported on the basis of public reasons that all affected could acknowledge on the basis of their shared conception of themselves as free and equal persons (Rawls 1999, 584, 592). Rawls goes on to indicate that this duty applies only to political discussions within the "public political forum" and not to discussion within the larger "background culture" of civil society (Rawls 1999, 576). Thus, while it is permissible for a person to advocate laws, say, prohibiting same-sex marriages in various associations and fora of civil society, it would be inappropriate for that same person to make such an argument in a political forum where it is not reasonable for him or her to assume that the co-participants (and co-citizens) could share the same grounds of the argument.[5] Nonetheless, it is clear that this still represents a quite demanding requirement for public reason.

In his own reflections Habermas is led to a similar conception of public reason and, if anything, gives it an even stronger interpretation.[6] He writes: "Anything valid should also be capable of a public justification. Valid statements deserve the acceptance of everyone for *the same reasons*."[7] Thus, for Habermas, though it may indeed be possible for individuals to embed their shared political conceptions within their own comprehensive moral or religious worldviews, this connection between private moralities and public reason does not provide a sufficiently stable or normatively appropriate basis for the legitimate exercise of coercive political authority. Rather, citizens must simultaneously both presuppose and strive to articulate a basic political consensus (focused on the idea of a core morality mentioned above) that all citizens can endorse as valid for the same (publicly available) reasons. The legitimate exercise of political power requires that the reasons that justify at least the basic principles of justice and "constitutional essentials" be ones that all citizens can endorse for the same reasons—that is, in view of their shared conception of themselves as free and equal persons. The shared political conception must be "freestanding" in this sense. Moreover, the political virtue of reasonableness requires that citizens, in regarding themselves as "ideal legislators," seek to find for the policies and legislation they support reasons that they reasonably believe others could reasonably endorse.

Two important objections to this account of the civic virtues need to be addressed: First, are they themselves exclusionary and/or sectarian in conception? And, second, is it at all plausible to think that they can be effectively promoted and sustained within the two-track model of deliberative democracy advocated by Habermas?

(1) The first objection, which has been raised from some quite diverse perspectives, is that the virtues of toleration (and reasonableness) are not innocent but rather function in ways that are both exclusionary and sectarian. Although this objection raises a number of extremely complex issues, when properly understood, these virtues do not have to have the exclusionary consequences its critics have claimed. While Kirstie McClure, for example, may be right that the practice of toleration asks, say, religious believers to regard the truth claims of their faith as matters of private belief, it does not follow that it constitutes an unjustifiable or unacceptable harm against them (McClure 1996, 199). There is no guarantee that within a liberal polity matters of religious faith and practice or, for that matter, other individual or collective ways of life will remain unchanged. Rather, the question must be whether or not individuals have their equal rights and liberties denied them in their treatment

by the state. It does not seem to constitute a harm or violation of a right to, say, freedom of speech, if one is told that he or she is not morally entitled, in certain political fora, to press claims against others that others do not (and cannot reasonably be expected to) acknowledge. Similarly, the claim that citizens act unreasonably if they promote policies and legislation on the basis of non-public reasons does not per se imply that they themselves are the victims of exclusionary or sectarian politics. On the one hand, to claim that it is a violation of a moral duty to pursue positions on the basis of non-public reasons within the more narrowly circumscribed political public sphere does not mean that there are not many other fora available within civil society in which those views can be aired and discussed. Secondly, I have again not broached the difficult topic of when (or whether) it is permissible to respond to such moral infractions with legal remedies (e.g. the legal regulation of hate speech) (but see Cohen 1996). Rather, my more general and limited point has been to claim that the civil duty of toleration does not necessarily imply an (unjustifiable) exclusion of others or their points of view.

A slightly different version of this objection can be found in the claim that the "discipline of public reason" is too harsh in that it will require individuals to argue their opinions in a form that will strike them as foreign or insincere. If comprehensive doctrines and philosophies of life must be left at the entrance to political assembly and arguments presented in terms of public reasons that others could acknowledge citizens may not even recognize themselves in their positions and, ironically, this requirement of reciprocity may inhibit the aim of mutual understanding. According to Daniel Weinstock, Rawls's assumption that public reason functions like a "module" that can be attached (or detached) from any (reasonable) comprehensive doctrine rests on a questionable psychology of beliefs since the "fit" between public and "private" reasons may be much tighter for many citizens (Weinstock 2000). Thus, to take just one example—my own, not Weinstock's—consider Catharine MacKinnon's arresting description of our gendered society:

> Men's physiology defines most sports, their needs define auto and health insurance coverage, their socially designed biographies

define workplace expectations and successful career patterns, their perspectives and concerns define quality in scholarship, their experiences and obsessions define merit, their objectification of life defines art, their military service defines citizenship, their presence defines family, their inability to get along with each other—their wars and rulerships—defines history, their image defines god, and their genitals define sex.

(MacKinnon 1987, 36)

It is difficult to imagine how this criticism of the sexism in social life could be as effective if it were to be expressed in the language of public reason (rather than in connection with a comprehensive view of the good life)—or how it could be expressed with the same conviction.

However, this version of the objection misses the point of—and motivation for—the idea of public reason, at least in Habermas and Rawls. First, as indicated above (and as Weinstock also notes), the expectation that reasoning be public (or that reciprocity be exercised) applies only to certain political fora and not within the wider "background" culture or in what Habermas calls "civil society." Such a wide constraint would surely undermine, as Weinstock argues, both mutual understanding and individual autonomy. More importantly, however, Rawls's account of public reason leaves citizens free to find the deeper roots of their convictions about the political values in their comprehensive views and thus does not ask them to sacrifice their non-political identity when they are asked to argue (again in certain contexts) from their shared pool of public reasons. It does assume, however, that they are capable of drawing a distinction between their common political identity as citizens and whatever further identities they may possess.

(2) The second objection is equally challenging: Is it in fact reasonable to assume that in a civil society characterized as "wild" and "anarchic" the social and cultural conditions will exist that would be required for the promotion and maintenance of the civic virtues of toleration and reasonableness? Habermas is himself quite aware of this challenge: "On account of its anarchic structure, the general public sphere is ... more vulnerable to the repressive and exclusionary effects of unequally distributed social power, structural

violence, and systematically distorted communication than are the institutionalized public spheres of parliamentary bodies" (BFN, 307–308). There can thus be, it seems, no guarantee that the associations arising within civil society will not be "tribalistic," inegalitarian, or ones that contribute to a culture of group bias and discrimination. Can a liberal political culture be fashioned and sustained under such conditions? It is unlikely that a definitive answer can be given to this question one way or the other. Many empirical as well as normative assumptions are involved. However, at least until we have more evidence to the contrary perhaps we should not be overly pessimistic about the possibilities for wider civility even in the face of a civil society that is deeply pluralistic and "anarchic." On the one hand, the form of civility that is required for a democratic polity may not need to be as "thick" as some communitarians and others have supposed. What is required, it would seem, is a liberal political culture that is based on, and incorporates in its own norms of civility, the "core morality" mentioned above. The bonds of civility do not have to reach so deeply into particular and often sectarian worldviews that it objectionably threatens their (at any rate always fluid) identities, and it may be possible to embrace the central elements of a core morality from the perspective of otherwise very different worldviews. This is the important lesson to be learned from Rawls's idea of an overlapping consensus that Habermas embraces as well (BNR, chap. 10).[8] It also captures what Habermas elsewhere describes in connection with a "constitutional patriotism" that would be the counterpart to a liberal neutral state (IO, 225).

On the other hand, it is perhaps also the case that we have not sufficiently explored the ways in which government, through its regulatory policy, can help to promote the minimal bonds of civility. This indeed may be one of the major differences between the liberal egalitarianism of the welfare state and Habermas's "two-track" model of a deliberative politics with its crucially important distinction between "weak" and "strong" publics (see BFN, chap. 9). The largely interventionist and regulatory practices of the liberal welfare state, some have argued, may be counterproductive to their own intended effects (Margalit 1996). What is required—though it is by no means an easy task—is a focus on the (limited) ways in which the state, in cooperation with institutions of civil society, can help to foster the virtues necessary for a liberal political culture.[9]

IV. Democracy beyond the nation-state

In an essay marking the two-hundredth anniversary of Kant's essay "Perpetual Peace," Habermas invokes Kant's call for a "cosmopolitan order" (*Weltbürgerliche Zustand*) that would bring about a definitive end to the bellicose "state of nature" between nation-states (IO, chap. 7). At the same time he faults Kant for equivocating between a commitment to a global constitutional order or "world republic" and a weaker voluntary federation among sovereign states. If states are to be subject to enforceable law and obligated by more than (largely impotent) moral norms, a loose federation will not suffice. In the same essay Habermas seems to agree with calls for a "cosmopolitan democracy" that include a reformed and strengthened United Nations (including a "world parliament" with directly elected representatives in a "second chamber") (IO, 187). Changes on the international scene since Kant's time also provide this utopian vision a greater degree of realism: The variety of phenomena that, taken together, have recently been grouped under the heading "globalization" raise important questions about the possibility of achieving democracy within the limited framework of the nation-state. The increased number and expanding influence of multinational corporations, growing international flow in labor and capital, expanding population migration, and large-scale ecological threats challenge in new ways the nation-state's claim to legitimacy, even on the domestic front. In short, can the nation-state, given its apparently diminished capacity to act, maintain its legitimacy in the face of the growing demands of its citizenry? At the same time, the widening (if fragile) recognition of human rights, the more active role of the United Nations and other international organizations, and a developing global civil society (including worldwide informational media) make it meaningful at least to ask whether a "post-national constellation" is not emerging in which the locus of democratization is no longer centered exclusively on the territorial nation-state.

In several important essays published since *Between Facts and Norms* Habermas has joined the growing debate concerning the possibility—and shape—of a cosmopolitan democracy. Indeed, there is much in his "two-track" model of democracy, with its strong division of labor between "weak" and "strong" publics, that suggests why this might be so: On the one hand, there is no inherent reason why his idea of a weak public sphere cannot also be realized in the context of a global civil society and, on the other, there are also some reasons for extending his discursive account of strong publics—the formal institutions of decision-making—in connection with the idea of a more multi-layered and dispersed conception of sovereignty and the related idea of "subsidiarity" and an emergent "anomalous" administrative law (see Baynes 2012). Similarly, his claim that there has been at most only a historical (not a necessary) convergence between the political *demos* (or state) and a relatively homogenous nation or people (*Volk*) also supports the claim that the former need not be limited to the traditional (territorial) idea of the nation-state. At the same time, however, Habermas has modified his earlier cautious endorsement of a "world republic" and now prefers to speak of a "constitutionalization of international law" or "global governance without a world government" (PNC, 109; DW, 139f.). He thus also distances himself from the views of some cosmopolitan democrats who argue for a more unified federal world order (BNR, 323). In these later essays, Habermas advocates a "multilevel federal system" that distinguishes among three global actors according to their respective functional roles and tasks: a supranational political body (or reformed UN) limited to the maintenance of peace and protection of basic human rights; an intermediate level occupied by regional bodies devoted to a "global domestic politics," including large-scale economic and environmental policies and which he refers to as a "transnational negotiating system"; and nation-states that have acquired a more modest and self-limiting identity (DW, 134f. and 174f.; BNR, 322f.). He has also expressed some cautious optimism about developments in transnational law as long as they can be linked to newly emerging forms of democratic accountability as well (Habermas 2012; Baynes 2012).

In this context Habermas has also voiced support for strengthening the role of the United Nations (though now limited to the two goals of maintaining peace and protecting human rights) and for the further strengthening of the International Criminal Court (ICC) with a mandate to prevent at least gross violations of human rights. At the same time, however, he is more cautious than some advocates of cosmopolitan democracy about the likelihood of achieving on a global scale the kind of civic solidarity (as a "solidarity among strangers") that is for him a necessary condition for a more robust deliberative politics (DW, 177; Cronin 2011). In this respect, he reflects a limited agreement with some of his more civic republican critics such as Charles Taylor or David Miller. His own constructive proposal (in addition to his support for a European constitution) calls for the development of "transnational negotiating systems" in which various players (including nation-states, international governmental institutions, and non-governmental organizations) might together fulfill the function of a "strong public," while citizens motivated by a cosmopolitan consciousness and active in various ways in a global civil society, together with a more vigilant global mass media, would constitute a "weak public." (Habermas 2012, 58).

As with the two-track model introduced at the level of the nation-state, the challenge again is for imaginative institutional design leading to a more responsive and accountable "strong public" than is possible today at the level of the nation-state alone (see Fraser et al. 2008). However, the basic structure of this proposal for cosmopolitan democracy remains the same: a dynamic division of labor between a free-wheeling public sphere that functions as a kind of "receptor" for identifying and thematizing social problems—and ensuring that they are placed on the political agenda—and the more formally organized (though multi-layered and dispersed) strong publics responsible for "translating" publicly generated reasons into socially effective policies via accountable administrative bodies (Nanz and Steffek 2007). This is certainly an extremely abstract model of democracy and many of its more specific institutional details are missing, but, contrary to some of his critics, Habermas's vision of a renewed public sphere is by no means simply an abdication either to the triumph of liberalism as traditionally conceived or to capitalism in its latest "global" phase (Scheuerman 2008).

As noted above (in Chapter 6), an important feature of Habermas's deliberative model of democracy is his sharp division of labor between a "weak public" and a "strong public" or between the formation of public opinion in the vast array of associations that together constitute civil society and the more formally organized institutions of decision-making (including mass political parties as well as the institutions of government).[10] Indeed, a main feature of Habermas's work since the early 1990s has been his controversial claim that radical democracy must be "self-limiting" in the sense that, while a "weak public" should attempt to influence the deliberations and decision-making of a "strong public," it should nonetheless not attempt to displace (or replace) those formally organized bodies (Habermas 1990a; BFN). Rather, drawing on a proposal by Bernard Peters, Habermas uses the metaphors of sluices, dams, and canals to describe how a vast network of institutions and associations lying on the periphery might shape opinion and influence decision-making in the political core without replacing those formal institutions or depriving them of their own important function (Peters 1993; Scheuerman 2002). Though I won't pursue the details further here, this model is obviously influenced by his systems-theoretic conviction that the formally organized institutions of the market and political power serve important functions even if they must simultaneously be tamed by the "communicative power" formed in civil society (see BFN, chap. 7).

Since a "strong public" at the global level corresponding to the state-apparatus at the national level will most likely be more plural and dispersed among a variety of transnational bodies, there is perhaps even more reason to look to the role of civil society in making global governance public and more accountable (DW, 141). Thus, the increasing juridification of global governance—whose positive aspects Habermas describes as a constitutionalization of international law—must itself be accompanied by a strengthened role of a global civil society that has a similar taming effect on the development of transnational or global law. This would in turn allow for the emergence of a form of democratic global governance even in the absence of a world government and would aptly capture Habermas's two-track model at the level of a post-national constellation.

In fact, the last few decades have witnessed an increasing attention to the emergence of a global or transnational civil society that might perform just such a role (Keane 2003; Kaldor 2004; Smith and Brassett 2008). Jan Aart Scholte, a long-time scholar of civil society, has recently characterized it as "a political space where voluntary associations seek, from outside political parties, to shape the rules that govern one or another aspect of social life" (Scholte 2011, 214) and he has expressed guarded optimism about its increased role in global governance. He has also studied for over two decades the ways in which various associations comprising a global civil society have worked to make other international organizations (such as the UN, the World Bank, the IMF, and WTO, among many others) more transparent and accountable to their stakeholders. Many organizations have granted at least consultative status to NGOs and draw on their expertise in other ways in their policy deliberations. The WTO, particularly since its Third Ministerial Meeting in Seattle in 1999, has aggressively cultivated its relationship with NGOs, created an informal NGO Advisory Board, and has, as a result, made its deliberations more transparent and accountable (Williams 2011; Erman and Higgott 2010). At the same time, through their efforts to increase public awareness about activities and policies of various international organizations, NGOs have at least helped to make some of those meetings more responsive and have arguably had some positive effect on the formation of public policy itself (Scholte 2004; Dryzek 2006). Although at this point the conclusions are still mixed and their influence is uneven, NGOs and other civil society associations have certainly had some success in making the deliberations of these organizations more accessible to a wider public, in providing forums for discussion of their policies, and in making them more responsive to their stakeholders.

Working in close connection with Habermas's own two-track model, Patrizia Nanz and Jens Steffek have also stressed the importance of a global civil society for democratic and accountable governance and they have identified specific ways in which civil society might enhance transparency, increase the quality of deliberations, and make deliberations more inclusive (Nanz and Steffek 2004, 2007). It would also be useful, in connection with Habermas's multi-level model of global governance, to explore the different roles and contributions of civil society with respect to each level.[11] For example, at the supranational level, a global public sphere can help maintain peace and secure human rights by appeal to a moral conscience focused on basic human rights as has arguably been the case in the various uprisings and protests of the Arab Spring and beyond. With respect to the "global domestic politics" of "transnational negotiating systems," by contrast, the role of NGOs and other organizations within civil society becomes much more complex and would have to take into consideration extremely difficult questions concerning the relevant domains of expertise, the appropriate identification of "stakeholders," and the fair opportunity for inclusion and voice (Scholte 2011). There is also even greater danger for a hegemonic imposition of dominant interests (DW, 142).

Nonetheless, despite these increased complexities and challenges, a robust and vigilant global civil society, together with a transnational public media, does not seem less suited to play such a role than its national counterpart and can arguably make some claim to provide a more appropriate source of legitimacy than some of its competitors (such as global private corporations and markets, or various international organizations, or some subset of international legal and juridical bodies alone) (Steffek 2010). Of course, if this proposal for a public and democratic global governance is to offer an attractive model, more needs to be said and much more will need to happen: active associations of civil society are still predominantly those located in the northern hemisphere and those with strong ties to economically developed states, they still have often very limited access to international organizations, inadequate resources, and in some cases questionable democratic accountability within their own structure (Scholte 2004). Still, coupled with the increased pressures for a rule of law at the transnational level, a more robust and active civil society offers one realistic account for how global governance might be made more public and, hence, more democratic. If that is indeed an emerging trend in global governance, it would still require a more vigilant and active role of associations of civil society in holding governments and international organizations accountable and a more involved mass media that informed its public about the actions of civil society in both their successes and their failures. A discernible trend does not alone constitute a realized ideal.

Many difficult questions about the prospects—indeed, even the very idea—for a global democracy remain. In particular, the question of how to detach democratic accountability from its historical links with the territorial nation-state is especially relevant for the idea of "disaggregated sovereignty" within a vast system of vertical and horizontal networks or (if it amounts to the same thing) what Habermas calls "the organizational forms of an international negotiation system" (PNC, 109). Habermas's suggestion that democratic legitimacy might be linked more to an "expectation of rationally acceptable results" of diverse and overlapping deliberative fora than the decisions of a territorially delimited political body is certainly worthy of further consideration (despite the fears of a "technocratic" or "expert-oriented" elitism) (see Schmalz-Bruns 2007; and Niesen 2008).[12] Similarly, questions about the appropriate role of the principle of symmetry (or "all-affected principle")—the claim that all those affected by a political decision should have an equal voice in that decision—within a conception of democracy become even more troublesome at the global level (Held 2004, 99; see also Fraser et al. 2008; Benhabib 2011).

However, as difficult as these questions are, they do not themselves offer any support for the view that we can have transnational rule of law without global democracy and they do not seem to threaten the twofold thesis I have briefly sketched here in connection with Habermas's position: first, the claim that if the mutual supposition of the rule of law and democracy is valid at the level of the nation-state, there would seem to be at least *prima facie* grounds for expecting the same relation of mutual supposition at the global level as well; and, second, the claim that global governance can be made more public and more democratic through a strengthening of institutions and associations of a global civil society that indirectly influences the quality of the deliberations and decisions of the various international organizations. Of course, there is no guarantee that globalization will develop along these lines and some indications that indeed it may not (see Cronin 2011; Niesen 2008). Still, the Habermasian project offers a not implausible scenario for how a realistic utopia in the best sense of that term might unfold, namely, by "taking men as they are and laws as they might be" (Rousseau).

Further reading

Bohman and Rehg (1997) and Elster (1998) both contain important essays on deliberative democracy. Bohman (1996) is a defense of a deliberative conception much indebted to the work of

Habermas. Estlund (2008) contains an important criticism of Habermas's position.

Finlayson and Freyenhagen (2011) is a valuable collection of the "debate" between Rawls and Habermas. Forst (2012) contains several essays on the similarities and differences between the two and defends a position of his own. Hedrick (2010) is also a very good introduction to many of the issues between Rawls and Habermas.

Cronin (2011) is an excellent introduction to Habermas's position on cosmopolitan democracy and a "world constitution." Bohman (2007) is an important book on the topic, influenced by Habermas but developing a distinctive position of his own. Scheuerman (2008) is a good critical overview and Niesen and Herborth (2007) is an important collection on his international politics as well.

Notes

1 There is a rapidly growing literature on how best to interpret this epistemic dimension: see Elster (1998), Bohman and Rehg (1997), Besson and Marti (2006), and Peter (2008); though Peter's criticisms of views, such as Estlund's, that assume a procedurally independent standard of justice seem right, she overstates the differences between her own preferred conception and the views of Habermas and Joshua Cohen. The differences begin to fade when one realizes that their notion of an "independent standard" is a contrast between the ideal procedure and its (always potentially imperfect) implementation.

2 See, for example, Habermas's remark linking the notion of equal respect with the idea of reasons acceptable to all (BFN, 103).

3 Habermas's basic strategy in response to this challenge is to "go abstract" and argue that in an increasingly pluralist society the bases of agreement shrinks to the terms of fair procedure. But a procedural conception, as noted, attempts to mirror an abstract ideal of equal respect. In fact, the example cited by Bellamy and Hollis—the case of the Lincoln/Douglas debate over slavery—shows precisely why not just any compromise can be considered fair (Bellamy and Hollis 1999a, 74–75). (The notion of a "core morality"—a term adopted from Larmore—is compatible with the dialectic of moral and political constructivism described at the end of Chapter 5 since citizens can embed that core in differing and more comprehensive moral frameworks.)

4 See Scanlon (1996) and Habermas's related remarks in R3, 393 and BNR, 260.

5 Rawls, it seems to me, is in fact unclear as to whether this constraint applies to all citizens or only to legislators and candidates for public office (see Rawls 1999, 576 and 577, where he suggests that all citizens are to think of themselves *as if* they were legislators).

6 Habermas, "'Reasonable' versus 'True', or the Morality of Worldviews," (in IO, chap. 3). Though this is not the most charitable way to read Rawls, it is one that is widely shared; see for example Raz (1990).

7 IO, 86; see also OPC, 321, where he writes: "*Agreement* [Einverständniss] in the strict sense is achieved only if the participants are able to accept a validity claim for the *same* reasons."

8 See Rawls's *Political Liberalism* (1996) as well as the argument for mutual respect based on a principle of reciprocity despite deep moral disagreement, contained in Gutmann and Thompson (1996).

9 See on this the interesting proposal concerning the use of the "intangible hand" of the state for such a purpose in Pettit (1997).

10 This feature of Habermas's model has not generally been noted by those who engage Habermas's cosmopolitan views; two notable exceptions are Bohman (2007) and Dryzek (2006).

11 In related work, they have also proposed criteria for empirically measuring the effects of global civil society within global governance (Nanz and Steffek 2005).

12 "The democratic procedure no longer draws its legitimizing force only, indeed not even predominantly, from political participation and the expression of political will, but rather from the general accessibility of a deliberative process whose structure grounds an expectation of rationally acceptable results" (PNC, 110; see also Habermas 2009, 147).

Eight

A "sobered" philosophy

The discourse of modernity, postmetaphysical thinking, and a post-secular society

Habermas has had a career-long interest in the question of the relationship of philosophy to other disciplines, especially the social sciences, and in the question of the place of philosophy within the wider public culture (see "Why Still Philosophy?" in PPP). As he expresses it in a later essay, a "sobered" philosophy that has relinquished more ambitious aims still serves an important role within the academy and within public culture generally (TJ, 277). The relationship between specialized academic philosophy (*Schulphilosophie*) and mundane knowledge or wisdom (*Weltphilosophie*) within society as a whole has, in fact, been part of the discourse of philosophy at least since Kant (TJ, 283). But the question of what responsibility philosophy has either to or for mundane knowledge and, beyond that, to human "common sense" remains a hotly debated topic within philosophy itself (PDM, 208; FK, 108; PT, 18).

Given this interest, it is not surprising that in the mid-1980s Habermas decided to engage critically a philosophical discussion emerging especially in France that, at least in his opinion, was fulfilling its public function in precisely the wrong sort of way. Postmodernism is a difficult term to define but in philosophy it generally refers to a critique of reason that has roots in Nietzsche and was renewed again in a reception of Heidegger in France beginning in the mid-1960s. It has come to be associated primarily with figures such as Jacques Derrida, Michel Foucault, and François Lyotard. What especially troubled Habermas about the work of these philosophers—as well as its more popular reception—is that it involved what he described as a "totalizing critique of reason" that, if correct, threatened to leave many more mundane practices and assumptions—like truth telling, accountable agency, or respect for informed critique and argument in the public sphere—unintelligible. At least that was how he saw it.

On Habermas's view, the legitimate need to criticize some of the excesses and failures of the modern or "Enlightenment" ideal of reason had given rise to a series of philosophical efforts—in many cases quite obscure—to criticize "logocentrism" or the "philosophy of the subject" and provide a philosophically compelling explanation of what had gone wrong. In some respects, this is what Habermas had also attempted to do in TCA. But on his view the philosophy of the subject could not be overcome by way of a deeper or more radical critique but instead had simply to be set aside in favor of a theory of communicative action and reason more explicitly pragmatist and modest about its own resources. By contrast, Habermas saw in the postmodern critique of the philosophy of the subject either its continuation (in fairly esoteric forms of metaphysical thinking) and/or the outright dismissal of the achievements of the Enlightenment project—or project of modernity—in the attempts to move beyond its dark side.

A brief comparison with Richard Rorty's own reception of postmodernism might be instructive here not only because Rorty is much less hostile to postmodernism than Habermas but also because it indicates some of the deeper similarities and differences among the various interlocutors. In an illuminating essay contrasting Habermas and Derrida on the question of the "function of philosophy," Rorty proposes to split the difference between the two (Rorty 1998). He reads Derrida principally as a "private ironist" interested in promoting new forms of self-creation, freed from the constraints of any disciplinary conventions. Habermas, by contrast, is portrayed as a public philosopher who champions the liberal-democratic values of individual rights and resisting cruelty. Problems only arise for each when he takes himself to be doing something more: an attempt to ground democratic freedoms in universal communicative reason, in the case of Habermas; or an effort to expose how all attempts to secure reason presuppose conditions that inevitably thwart such efforts, in the case of Derrida (Rorty 1998, 317). Rorty's proposed solution is to live and let live—if, that is, each would exercise self-restraint with respect to his own project. Philosophy can be practiced both as "private irony" and as a public call to fight cruelty and defend rights. In both cases, though, it should avoid slipping into renewed efforts of transcendental critique (whether as "reconstructive science" in Habermas or as an attempt to expose the impossible conditions of possibility in Derrida).

At first glance Habermas might be expected to embrace Rorty's suggestion since, as we have seen, in many respects he shares his pragmatist convictions. He too is suspicious about various forms of realism and metaphysics that seek a deeper guarantee to ordinary practices than what can be found in those practices themselves. However, there are several reasons why Habermas is not likely to be content with Rorty's suggested division of labor.[1] First, the sorts of disturbances that give rise to the need to clarify the deeper resources of critique are not due solely to the excesses of philosophical inquiry. They arise from disturbances within social practices (or within the lifeworld itself). Second, the division of labor Rorty proposes is itself too static. It is not as if, on the one hand, the interpretation of democratic rights and liberties is settled (as Rorty at one point suggests) (Rorty 1998, 326). Challenges to these arise not only in the deeper recesses of the academy but, equally as often, in the context of conflicts in social life itself. Similarly, what Rorty assigns to private irony—new experiments in self-creation—for Habermas can and do have implications for how public debate should be understood. The contrast between Rorty's remarks about keeping religion within the private sphere and Habermas's reflections on a "post-secular society"—discussed below— is a case in point. Finally, and most importantly, the sorts of universalizing claims that Rorty thinks we should avoid are, on Habermas's view, already implicit in our more mundane social practices. Habermas's insistence that our practices of justification involve a "context-transcending truth claim" or a regulative norm of truth that goes beyond current justification is not an unnecessary philosophical distraction but a claim about an ideal built into those social practices.[2]

While Rorty's reception of postmodernism might initially have seemed like a promising path to reconciliation between Habermas and the postmodern theorists he criticizes, it is itself too compartmentalized and unstable. Habermas's response to Rorty's suggestion that we shouldn't scratch where it doesn't itch is simple:

it itches (QC, 194). The problems philosophy confronts can't always be dismissed as simply of their own making. But, at another level, Habermas shares Rorty's pragmatist intuitions. In contrast to the postmodern critique of reason, it is possible to avoid the deep paradoxes or increasingly esoteric claims it has produced. As Habermas attempted to show in TCA, sufficient resources for a critique of modern reason can be found in practices tied to communicative action (PT, 142). Habermas's treatment of the discourse of modernity (I), as well as his sketch of a form of "postmetaphysical thinking" (II) and his proposal concerning a "post-secular society" (III) can each be viewed as an attempt to elaborate and extend his alternative account of communicative reason. It also illustrates in more detail the conception of philosophy connected with his particular version of Kantian pragmatism.

I. The philosophical discourse of modernity

The Philosophical Discourse of Modernity (1985) is Habermas's most polemical work. Habermas often reads philosophical texts aggressively to find ways to articulate his own views—most good philosophers do that—but in this case it is as if he reads the texts in order to create a distance between himself and them. Roughly, as we have seen in Chapter 3, TCA seeks to bring about a "paradigm shift" from the philosophy of the subject to an intersubjective or communicative account of reason. Yet, each of the authors he criticizes in this work—especially Heidegger, Derrida, and Foucault—has also claimed to have moved beyond metaphysics—and so beyond the philosophy of the subject. Habermas's polemic is not only that they have failed but that in their attempt to go beyond metaphysical thinking each has in his own way become ensnared in that metaphysics. This leads Habermas to conclude that the best way to become "postmetaphysical" is not to try to beat metaphysics at its own game—to offer a yet deeper explanation of the conditions of possibility that made such a (disorienting or misleading) metaphysics possible—but, in a more straightforwardly pragmatist gesture, to return to an analysis of our social practices.

The polemical approach is unfortunate because in some cases—perhaps especially in the case of Foucault—the projects may have much more in common if they are read more charitably. In many cases it has fallen to Habermas's students—Wellmer, Honneth, Benhabib, and others—to develop more sympathetic interpretations of these figures. Still, even if Habermas's readings are sometimes disappointing, they are not completely surprising and on occasion they are also very illuminating. PDM appeared shortly after TCA and at a time when the wider political and cultural trends were against an understanding of modernity and its emancipatory potential that Habermas defended. The rise of neoconservatism—with the elections of Margaret Thatcher, Helmut Kohl, and Ronald Reagan— questioned just this claim about the emancipatory potential of modernity.[3] It is also not hard to see Habermas's polemic as stemming at least in part from the two very different post-war receptions of Heidegger in Germany and in France, respectively, as he later suggested (Thomassen 2006, 117).

This contextualization does not excuse Habermas's strong polemic. Most of those whom Habermas labeled "young conservatives" were equally opposed to the neoconservative trend.[4] Since his interpretations of these figures are thus not likely to be considered definitive to many, the aim here will only be to highlight some of Habermas's main criticisms. A more extensive assessment of his claims is beyond the scope of this chapter. As others have shown, in many cases it is possible to find deeper alliances between Habermas and those whom he criticizes (see, for example, Kompridis (2006) on Heidegger; Menke (2001) on Derrida; Honneth (1991), Kelly (1994), Allen (2008), and Koopman (2013) on Foucault).

(1) Horkheimer and Adorno's influential *Dialectic of Enlightenment* is a challenging text, but Habermas focuses on one of its central themes: "Myth is already enlightenment; and enlightenment is already mythology" (Horkheimer and Adorno, xviii). Even this thesis is not easy to interpret, though the claim seems to be that while mythology (e.g. Homer's *Odyssey*) already exhibits elements required for individual emancipation (the self's distancing from its origins), the Enlightenment as "instrumental reason" in the service of self-preservation is itself myth (or a form of ideology). At any rate, according to Habermas, the basic thesis of *Dialectic of Enlightenment* is relatively clear: "Reason itself destroys the humanity it had first made possible" (PDM, 110). This is because reason, understood as

the rational control and domination of nature in the name of "self-preservation," eventually undercuts and destroys the (more substantive) reason that initially allowed for a richer and more meaningful culture (including morality, religion, and art) in which "subjectivities" could orient themselves. By contrast, a "rationality in the service of self-preservation gone wild" or, as Horkheimer expressed it elsewhere, "self-preservation without a self" destroys the possibility for a more humane living by subordinating everything else to a domination of nature (PDM, 112). Even "inner nature" (or the formation of subjectivity or a self) is subordinated to this demand. However, according to Habermas, the form of critique that Adorno and Horkheimer invoke here is no longer "immanent critique" (roughly, the attempt to use bourgeois ideals to expose their failure or shortcomings) (see PDM, 116). Rather the "totalizing critique" they practice calls into question the very reason by means of which immanent critique might proceed: "It is turned not only against the irrational function of bourgeois ideals, but against the rational potential of bourgeois culture itself, and thus it reaches into the foundations of any ideology critique that proceeds immanently" (PDM, 119).

Habermas's concern in the chapter is twofold. First, he wants to distinguish the form of totalizing critique found here from what he finds in Nietzsche. Whereas Adorno and Horkheimer attempt to preserve a form of ideology-critique however paradoxical, Nietzsche abandons the rational critique of ideology in favor of a heightened form of aesthetic critique. Any distinction between validity and power is relinquished in favor of an "aestheticized" will to power (PDM, 98). In the last analysis, Nietzsche's critique of culture assumes the form of a perspectivalism in which competing claims are interpreted as conflicts of power that cannot be rationally adjudicated.

Second, Habermas argues that even their paradoxical form of ideology-critique would only be appealing if it could be shown that there is no alternative to it (PDM, 128). More specifically, unless their "one-sided" interpretation of cultural modernity (as "instrumental reason in service of self-preservation") is a moderately convincing interpretation, other options for ideology critique might be identified (PDM, 114). Such an alternative is, of course, what Habermas has in mind with his claim that the *Dialectic of Enlightenment* "does not do justice to the rational content of cultural modernity that was captured in bourgeois ideals" and the alternative sketch of (cultural) modernity he presents: a decentered worldview that focuses not only on science and instrumental rationality, but also on the distinctive rationalities or "logics" associated with law and morality and art and art criticism respectively (PDM, 113). In short, contrary to the claim of the *Dialectic of Enlightenment* the "rational content" of modernity is not exhausted by instrumental reason directed at the domination of nature. For Habermas, this is at best a misdirected extension of *one* dimension (science and technology) to the exclusion of other achievements of the Enlightenment (autonomous morality and law, on the one hand, and a "liberated aesthetic subjectivity," on the other).

(2) The strong critique of Heidegger and especially the late Heidegger is not surprising. Habermas's extreme disappointment in a thinker who deeply influenced him, as we noted, stems from Heidegger's refusal to accept any personal responsibility for his participation in the National Socialist movement. I suspect that the harsh criticism of the later Heidegger—after the *Kehre* (or turn)—also stems at least in part from the lasting influence that *Being and Time* had on Habermas. That work can also be read as a form of transcendental pragmatism that is in some important respects close to Habermas's own (Lafont 2000; Crowell and Malpas 2007). In PDM (and elsewhere) Habermas defends the strong thesis that the reasons for Heidegger's *Kehre* were due almost exclusively to external (political) factors and not the result of philosophical problems internal to his earlier work. This is, to say the least, a controversial thesis. What seems less disputable is that after the *Kehre* Heidegger advocates a form of thinking or thoughtful remembrance (*Andenken*) that is not subject to the same standards of public criticism and accountability as other forms of reason. Heidegger frequently makes the claim that discursive modes of argument and truth depend for their possibility on a prior notion of truth as "unconcealment" (Lafont 2000, chap. 3; Wrathall 2010). This revival of a specialized form of thought that is the privilege of philosophy is what Habermas has consistently rejected since introducing his notion of philosophy as "critique" in KHI. On Habermas's view it also suggested an unbridgeable chasm between "world-disclosing" knowledge and more mundane "inner-worldly"

learning (PDM, 154; PT, 42; TJ, 25). Others have argued that this latter claim is a very uncharitable reading of Heidegger (Wrathall 2010, 34f.). But even if one does not accept the view that external motivations were largely responsible for later developments in Heidegger's work, Habermas is by no means alone in his claim that his later philosophy promotes a style of thinking that substitutes a notion of solicitude or surrender to the call of Being for a model of discursive thought and rational argument (Tugendhat 1994; Philipse 1999; Lafont 2000). For Habermas, it is thus not difficult to see in it the dismissal of a more dialectical relation between world-disclosing knowledge and inner-worldly learning—that is, the form of Kantian pragmatism endorsed by Habermas. It is for Habermas also an indication of the elitist or "mandarin" attitude that he believes characterized Heidegger (PDM, 147; NC, 147).

(3) Habermas's discussion of Derrida is more surprising since the latter's critique of "logocentrism" in many ways parallels Habermas's own critique of the philosophy of the subject. Both reject the idea of philosophy as "first philosophy" or the view that philosophy has to ground or legitimate the other sciences by establishing a secure foundation in reason. However, what seems to trouble Habermas is that Derrida's criticisms of this "metaphysics of presence"—like Adorno's—deprives him of the possibility of more discursive modes of argument (Derrida, understandably, disputes this claim).

Habermas's criticism has two roots: First, he discerns in Derrida's claims about "iterability," or différance or arché-writing as an (impossible) "condition of possibility" for communication, a form of transcendental argument that is immune to criticism (see Derrida 1996, 82). Habermas thus reads Derrida as advocating a conception of philosophy as a privileged form of discourse—or perhaps novel form of "literary criticism" (PDM, 188). Second, Derrida undertakes a critique of Austin's analysis of speech acts whose aim is to show that Austin had completely failed to show how performatives such as making a promise could ever succeed. Very briefly, Derrida's claim was that in setting aside cases of non-literal or "non-serious" speech acts—such as making a wedding vow in a play—Austin left himself unable to explain the notion of iterability (or repetition of the "same" performative in different contexts) on which, according to Derrida, any plausible account of speech acts depends (Derrida 1988, 15). Since Habermas's own account of speech acts is greatly indebted to Austin, Derrida's criticism (if correct) would also threaten Habermas's own "communication-theoretic" alternative to the philosophy of the subject.

As Derrida understandably objected, it would have been preferable had Habermas then proceeded to engage Derrida's own essay directly rather than refer only to some secondary literature.[5] But, as anyone who has worked through Derrida's critique of Austin will attest, it is extremely difficult to reconstruct the argument.[6] It moves very quickly and culminates in an extremely obscure claim that "iterability" is (like the related notions of *différance* and *arché*-writing) a condition of possibility for a successful performative that necessarily eludes explication. "Iterability" seems not to be contained—as for Searle and Habermas—in the tacit know-how of a speaker who has mastered the rules governing a practice, but in an absent presence (or present absence) that cannot be further described (Derrida 1988, 17). While it would be hard to defend as a charitable reading, it is also not difficult to see how Habermas saw in Derrida's move something like Heidegger's attempt to replace an argument about transcendental conditions with a claim that the possibility of intelligible communication or meaningful discourse depends on a gift or dispensation of Being that eludes all attempts at rational reconstruction. In other contexts, in fact, Derrida makes just such a gesture toward Heidegger (Derrida 1971, 9). For Habermas it thus represented another example of a totalizing critique of reason (or attempt to explain the conditions of rational discourse) that failed to go beyond metaphysics.

(4) Habermas's largely critical treatment of Michel Foucault is perhaps most surprising of all (PDM, c. 9, 10). Both have had a long engagement with the social sciences—much more so than Derrida or Heidegger. Both have also been importantly influenced by Kant and the tradition of Weber and western Marxism which views the occident as the outcome of a long process of societal rationalization—compare, for example, Weber's "iron cage" and the *Dialectic of Enlightenment* to Foucault's discussion of the Panopticon. And, perhaps most importantly, both thinkers understand themselves to be engaged in a project of "detranscendentalizing" Kant or, to use Foucault's terminology, a project of replacing Kant's constitutive subject with a notion of a plural and historical *a priori* (Foucault 1972, 127f.; Han 1998).

However, despite these similarities their respective projects assume quite different shapes and there is ongoing debate about whether they can be brought into a fruitful engagement. Foucault, and more especially some of his followers, have maintained that Habermas's detranscendentalization of Kant—especially in connection with the identification of the idealizing suppositions contained in communicative action—remains far too Kantian and wedded to a notion of reason untainted by power. Habermas, and some of his followers, on the other hand, have argued that Foucault's treatment of power—which, at one level, assumes the constitutive role of Kant's transcendental subject—makes it difficult if not impossible to distinguish between objectionable and unobjectionable exercises of power (e.g. relativism). In PDM Habermas also accused Foucault of a "cryptonormativism" (PDM, 282): Foucault presumably advocates resistance to the disciplinary powers that are at work in constituting the modern subject, but in his call to "get rid of the subject" it is not clear where the normative resources for such resistance are to be found (Foucault 1980, 117). As for Adorno and Horkheimer modern rationality—along with its related ideals of knowledge and individual freedom—is complicit in the vast network of disciplinary power such that reason cannot obviously offer any guidance for its overcoming. It is not reason but rather its radical "other"—now in notion of the body or perhaps an aesthetics of the self—that is cited as a source of resistance and critique (PDM, 285, 291).

In response to this criticism, others have pointed out that Habermas has (again) failed to read Foucault carefully. Foucault's call to "get rid of the subject" is not offered as a rejection of all forms of subjectivity (and agency), but (like Habermas) an indication of an attempt to get beyond Kant's transcendental subject and its (supposed) world-constituting powers (Allen 2008, 37; Koopman 2013). Others sympathetic to Foucault's analysis of power suggest that he does not reject all notions of freedom but only those notions that describe freedom (or autonomy) in exclusive opposition to power or as radical freedom from constraint (Koopman 2013, 169f.). As Foucault later claimed, "Power is exercised only over free subjects, and only insofar as they are free" (Foucault 2001, 342). In developing this point Allen states that "autonomy is ... necessarily linked to power relations" (Allen 2008, 67; 2014). Moreover, according to Foucault, power (necessarily) presupposes freedom as well:

> Relations of power are then changeable, reversible and unstable. One must observe also that there cannot be relations of power unless the subjects are free. If one or the other were completely at the disposition of the other and became his thing, an object on which he can exercise an infinite and unlimited violence, there would not be relations of power. In order to exercise a relation of power, there must be on both sides at least a certain form of liberty.
>
> (Foucault 1997, 291–292)

But interpreting Foucault's somewhat limited remarks about the (necessary) inseparability of power and freedom is difficult. If the claim is that with reference to any individual life—or relatedly in reference to any claim to knowledge—power relations are at work, it seems important to ask whether these are objectionable or unobjectionable exercises of power or, if both, how any distinction between the two forms is to be made. The claim that "autonomy is necessarily linked to power relations" would be relatively uncontroversial if (1) we are making an empirical claim about a specific case or individual life-history or (2) if the type of power involved is itself unobjectionable (if the claim is, for example, that "individualization requires socialization"). Neither of these are claims that Habermas would deny. But, if the point is that, as a conceptual or normative matter, we cannot conceive of freedom (or autonomy) without it being necessarily linked to *objectionable* power relations it becomes more difficult to assess. As social actors and critics it would seem that we need some way to distinguish between objectionable and unobjectionable power relations. Habermas's charge concerning Foucault's "cryptonormativism" was not meant to show that we need an ultimate grounding to secure human freedom. It was meant to show that we need a relatively clear indication as to how the distinction might be drawn and how, when power relations are contested, such disagreements might be handled. Foucault's analysis of power does not seem to be able to do that.

But, those sympathetic with Foucault's analysis might raise another objection and here matters become more difficult. Habermas's own solution, as we have seen, is to point to the idealizing suppositions contained in our more mundane social practices. But what if those practices have themselves become so distorted by disciplinary power that the idealization are themselves manifestations of power. What if practical reason is not a resource for critique, but implicated in the (objectionable) relations of power? (Allen 2014, 77). This is a clear statement of the problem that confronts all ideology critique once it is framed as a "totalizing critique of reason." It is also difficult to see how Habermas could reply given that he has rejected "transcendent" critique in favor of some version of immanent critique. However, raising this objection does not seem to offer any advantage to his critics for there is little reason to suppose that a stronger contextualism is in any better position to respond. Rather, it seems preferable to admit that this presents a limit case for any practice-based approach like Habermas's. Moreover, critics of Habermas's attempt to locate the resources for critique in the idealizing suppositions of communicative reason still need to address the question of how they would propose distinguishing between objectionable and unobjectionable (or at least less objectionable) relations of power.

Even though Habermas does not offer the most charitable reading of these thinkers, it is fairly easy to identify his deeper worry. In what he calls the "totalizing critique of reason" (and modernity) he discerns a return to a conception of philosophy that he finds problematic. It is a conception that rests on a sharp contrast between a "world-disclosing" dimension, on the one side, and inner-worldly learning on the other (PT, 42; TJ, 25). This is for him clearest in Heidegger's distinction between the history of Being (as world-disclosing) and the realm of empirical (or ontic) entities. For Heidegger, the philosopher's special task is to be attuned to this history and to the revelations of Being. As students of Heidegger, Habermas fears that Derrida and Foucault, each in their own way, reinstate this sharp dichotomy. For Habermas, by contrast, philosophy is not able to fulfill such a role. It stands in a much closer relation to the empirical sciences and must also retain its connection with a human "common sense" found in the more mundane practices of the lifeworld (PDM, 208; PT, 18).

II. Postmetaphysical thinking

Habermas's defense of what he calls postmetaphysical thinking can easily be misleading. It is not (for the most part) intended as a rejection of the sort of inquiry pursued, for example, in the more recent revival of analytic metaphysics associated primarily with David Lewis and the Australian metaphysicians. Rather, at least in the first instance, it is directed against both the tradition of metaphysical thought that reached a culmination in the philosophy of Hegel and German idealism and in the various—and, ultimately, for Habermas, still metaphysical—attempts to escape that tradition in the writings of Nietzsche, Heidegger, and Derrida. The charge that these latter thinkers remain metaphysical is of course controversial. However, it should be recalled that Heidegger read Nietzsche as the last of the great metaphysicians and that Derrida also claimed that Heidegger had not sufficiently broken with the "metaphysics of presence." As a rejection of these forms of philosophical reflection, the call for postmetaphysical thinking is another way of expressing Habermas's attempt to move beyond the philosophy of the subject in a manner that would be more decisive than what he considers to be the failed attempts of much recent continental philosophy. It is thus also consistent with his arguments in *The Philosophical Discourse of Modernity* that Nietzsche and his "postmodern" successors remained ensnared in the philosophy of the subject despite their own intention: In their efforts to overcome the deficits of the philosophy of the subject, these thinkers either relinquished too much (sacrificing, for example, the achievements of modern reason) or continued to regard philosophy as a special or even privileged form of inquiry that yielded insight quite distinct from the empirical sciences). Or they did both (roughly, Habermas's controversial interpretation of Heidegger). In each case they draw an overly sharp distinction between forms of world-disclosure and inner-worldly knowledge (*Weltwissen*) and see the former as immune to any corrective testing or confirmation by the latter.

In *Postmetaphysical Thinking*, Habermas also takes issue with another influential return of metaphysics found in the post-Kantian philosophy of Dieter Henrich. In fact, the career-long engagement of these thinkers with each other's positions presents a concise and fascinating way of formulating Habermas's reservations about the continuation of metaphysical thinking. In a series of works, Henrich has repeatedly sought to show the indispensible need for a philosophical clarification of the structure and role of self-consciousness. As he argued in an influential essay on Fichte, if an unending regress is to be avoided, there must be a (non-objectivating) self-relation and self-knowledge that is prior to any (epistemic) relation between self and object (Henrich 1982). For Habermas, by contrast, Henrich's attempt to provide a central, even foundational, role for the philosophy of the subject fails to appreciate the significant achievements in philosophy, pragmatics and action theory that support his own call for a paradigm shift. Whatever insights such philosophical inquiry might offer a phenomenological clarification of self-consciousness, it is neither likely nor desirable that it will be able to fulfill the ambitious claims Henrich sets for it (PT, 11f.). In response, Henrich has charged that Habermas's "paradigm shift" from self-consciousness to communicative action is less radical than it appears and only gains its initial plausibility by sweeping unavoidable traditional metaphysical issues under the rug (Henrich 1999). Indeed, the exchange between these two theorists touches upon many pressing philosophical questions, such as the relationship between philosophy and naturalism, the place of philosophy in a modern and pluralist world, and the relationship between philosophy and the other sciences (including the social sciences). It is fair to conclude, however, that Habermas advocates a much less ambitious or more "sobered" role for philosophy than that held by many other philosophers (TJ, 277).

Given the wide range of thinkers Habermas identifies as metaphysical, it is appropriate to ask what it is that Habermas finds so objectionable in "metaphysical thinking" and what prospects there are for making a radical break with it. Further, at least the suspicion must be addressed that Habermas's characterization of metaphysics (now in the pejorative sense) is so broad that it would include almost all philosophical inquiry. How, in other words, does he propose to shun metaphysics (as he understands it) without dismissing philosophical reflection altogether? By metaphysical thinking Habermas means, most generally, the tradition of classical metaphysics from Plato, on through the medieval period, and up to the modern "philosophy of the subject" that arose in response to the emergence of science as a competing form of knowledge. However, as just indicated, he also includes under metaphysics the critique of these earlier forms of metaphysics in twentieth-century continental thought as well as some more recent attempts to continue the philosophy of the subject (again, as represented by Dieter Henrich). What these forms of thinking share in common, beginning especially with the philosophy of the subject in Descartes, is the view that there is a form of inquiry and knowledge proper to philosophy that is, on the one hand, quite distinct from that found in the natural and social sciences and, on the other, one that can nonetheless yield a special and authoritative insight into questions concerning both the meaning of life and how the world, in the broadest sense, "hangs together." What Habermas denies in his call for postmetaphysical thinking is that this remains a plausible and coherent task for philosophy today. However, if this description is not to be so broad so as to include potentially all philosophical inquiry, it must be made more precise. Habermas does not claim that there are no tasks left for philosophy—indeed, this would preclude the roles he assigns to philosophy as the "guardian of reason" and as cultural interpretation (MCCA, chap. 1). Rather, what he questions more specifically is whether there is a special form of knowledge—either in the sense of (strong) transcendental inquiry, or in a new form of thinking, such as Heidegger's *Andenken*— that yields a special and authoritative insight into the world or the meaning of life. For Habermas, by contrast, in a world distinguished by the "fact of reasonable pluralism" (Rawls) and a rationality that has turned increasingly procedural and non-substantive, philosophy must relinquish this larger ambition which it once competed for with religion. In this regard, two forms of metaphysical thinking are for him especially paradigmatic: again, first, the tradition of the philosophy of the subject or "philosophy of reflection" in which the knowing subject, through a special reflective turn or gaze, acquires knowledge that is more basic than, and indeed even foundational for, the warrant or justification of other forms of knowledge and, second, the form of "fundamental ontology" advocated by Heidegger and his successors that, in contrast to the knowledge of beings reserved for the empirical sciences, would yield a special kind of knowledge into the question of the meaning of Being. What Habermas objects to in particular is the way in which both of these forms of inquiry isolate themselves from any sort of challenge from the empirical sciences broadly understood.

This interpretation of what Habermas means by metaphysical thinking is supported by his own alternative sketch of the task of philosophy which he aligns either with the so-called "reconstructive sciences" that attempt to make explicit the practical knowledge of competent speakers and actors, on the one hand, and the more broadly interpretive or hermeneutic role of philosophy as an interpreter of culture, on the other (MCCA, chap. 1). In each of these roles, the knowledge yielded by philosophical inquiry is fallible, open to criticism from the sciences, and always dependent on prior social practices. First, as a "guardian of rationality," philosophy picks up and elaborates aspects of a (now largely procedural) conception of rationality as it emerges in various domains of inquiry (including the philosophy of language and pragmatics, action theory and moral psychology, and legal and political theory). However, in contrast to earlier models, philosophy is not an exclusively *a priori* discipline; though it still attempts to identify "conditions of possibility" that are constitutive for various human competences and social practices, it does not cut itself off from the insights of other empirical sciences and looks to them for confirmation of its fallible claims. Second, in its role as an interpreter, it attempts to mediate between various forms of expert knowledge, on the one hand, and the more mundane self-understandings and social practices that constitute the everyday lifeworld. In neither case, however, does philosophy possess a unique methodology or claim a special source of authority distinct from other disciplines or even from that of a self-reflective citizen (TJ, chap. 7). As others have pointed out, the dual tasks that Habermas assigns to philosophy are not without problems (Dews 1999a, 13f.). On the one hand, in connection with its more limited task in connection with the reconstructive sciences, it is not clear how philosophy can avoid simply being absorbed by the respective science (consider, for example, Quine's naturalized epistemology or the more recent fascination with "neurophilosophy"). On the other hand, in its role as an interpreter, it is not clear how philosophy can avoid some of the more ambitious claims previously assigned to it. That is, if philosophy wants to make convincing claims about, for example, the ideal or "proper" integration or balance of the competing claims of scientific knowledge, aesthetic (or 'world-disclosive') insight, and justified moral and legal norms for a given social lifeworld, or help relate the insights raised in one of the expert disciplines to a lifeworld where these claims are often less differentiated, it would seem that it must offer more than cultural interpretations. In this sense, even for many sympathetic critics, it remains an open question whether philosophy, even as Habermas conceives it, can successfully relinquish the privileged position that metaphysics once claimed for itself, while simultaneously retaining an important if non-exclusive role in capturing and making explicit its own time in thought.

III. A post-secular society

Although he has described himself as "tone-deaf in the religious sphere," Habermas has never been hostile or dismissive in his treatment of religion. On the contrary, more than perhaps any other secular philosopher at various points in his career he has actively engaged religious thinkers. Still in his writings up through at least TCA he subscribed to a Weberian understanding of secularization that was widely shared (until recently) among many sociologists: with the rise of modernity, a process of secularization was initiated in which religion plays an increasingly smaller role in social integration and the legitimation of political rule. For many, this secularization hypothesis also implied that those who continued to identify strongly with a religious tradition and, in particular, continued to insist on the relevance of religion for politics should be regarded with suspicion or viewed as less than fully rational or "modern."[7]

Habermas had begun to have second thoughts about the tight connection between modernity and secularization in the early 1990s after the Velvet Revolution in Eastern Europe. However, it was especially the catastrophic event of 9/11 that motivated him to take up again the question of the relationship between "faith and knowledge"—a topic that has been debated at least since Kant's attempt to establish a stable (if strained) truce between them. In the fall of 2001, on the occasion of the German Book Trade "Peace

Prize" awarded to him, Habermas gave a lecture on "Faith and Knowledge" (FK). Its central theme, after opening with a reference to 9/11, was the need for secular societies to re-evaluate the understanding of their relationship to religious traditions. In particular, he challenged a prevalent view—expressed most clearly in the French idea of *laïcité*—that a secular society must embrace "secularism." This term, as he defined it, assumes a sharp division between the public life of a political community and the private lives of its citizens and insists that, to the extent possible, religious expression should be minimized in public life. Habermas argued, by contrast, that this understanding of secularism did not even describe well the practices of many modern societies. More importantly, he also argued that it established a misleading "zero-sum" game between secular societies and citizens with deep religious convictions. Finally, he suggested that a "post-secular society" demanded a more balanced understanding of the relation between religious faith and the "secular" or public reason exercised by the neutral state. This, however, still presupposed the existence of a "democratic common sense" that could be the basis for a public reason that could be shared by all citizens (FK, 109).

For Habermas the idea of a "post-secular society" is not an empirical claim about the resurgence of religion or religiosity; even less is it a normative thesis that the idea of a neutral state should be abandoned (BRN, chap. 4). Rather, it is a claim that "secular reason" should adopt a different attitude toward religious traditions. Such traditions should not be considered as essentially irrelevant or exhausted as resource for meaning and normative orientations. Rather, secularists should have a more tolerant attitude and treat religious believers on an equal footing when it comes to participation in the public square (BNR, 111). It is also a plea for greater humility on the part of Western liberal democracies in their confrontation with traditions that (at present) have different views about the role of religion in public life. While this is perhaps a more subtle shift in his position than some have seen, and certainly less than what others advocate, Habermas believes that it is nonetheless an important step for understanding revisions or new learning within the project of modernity itself.

Habermas mentions two related discussions that have been influential for this new understanding of a "secular reason" in contrast to "secularism." First, he points to the debates around multiculturalism and the charge that, at least in some of its forms, even a supposedly "neutral" liberalism might be objectionably biased toward some forms of life and harbor an objectionable form of "nation-building" (Kymlicka 2007, 33–35). This discussion began in the 1980s and is found in his engagement with Charles Taylor's work on multicultural recognition (Taylor 1992). Habermas continues to defend a form of state neutrality but agrees that more "assimilationist" versions can place unreasonable (and morally objectionable) demands on citizens (Taylor 1992; BNR, chap. 10). By contrast, a more militant understanding of toleration requires citizens to examine continuously whether their political community's conditions for inclusion are too narrow or biased.

The second set of discussions he mentions concerns (again) Rawls's views on public reason and debates about the appropriate place for religiously motivated contributions to debates in the public square. Habermas credits Rawls's contribution for broadening the notion of public reason beyond a strong "secularist" notion of reason that excludes the voice of religious believers. Both Rawls and Habermas (as we saw in previous chapters) stress the importance of a shared public reason that citizens can make use of in political discourse. Both insist that a duty of civility requires that at least in the more formal context of political deliberation (though arguably also when they vote) citizens make their claims on the basis of considerations others can be expected to recognize as reasonable— that is, they should not be sectarian (Rawls 1996, 219). In response to criticisms of their positions, both have also resisted the charge that their ideas of public reason are hostile to religious believers and reflect a bias toward secularism, but beyond that their responses differ slightly.

Rawls proposed a "wide" view of public reason with a "proviso" that permits religious believers to introduce claims into the public sphere so long as these claims can in due course be translated into "properly public reasons" (Rawls 1999, 584). Habermas, by contrast, has expressed some sympathy for the charge that, even with this wider understanding, Rawls's notion of public reason imposes an unfair burden on religious citizens. He has thus suggested that the burden for translation should not fall exclusively on religious citizens and that, at least in the informal public sphere, religious citizens should be able to express their viewpoints in language that draws freely from their religious convictions (BNR, chap. 5). Some critics have suggested that, with this proposal, Habermas has silently dropped his earlier demand that political discourse (at least about binding law) must draw upon a pool of public reasons that citizens can share and now "repudiates" the Rawlsian proviso (Baxter 2011, 208).

However, this interpretation of Habermas's own "institutional translation proviso" seems too hasty. It is true that Habermas argues that religious citizens should be allowed "to couch their contributions to public discussions in religious language" and that secular citizens have an obligation to assist in translation (BNR, 310). He also envisions a quite strong divide and "institutional filter" between the reasons given in the informal public sphere and the formal political institutions of decision-making (BNR, 130). But Habermas also speaks of the "quite demanding epistemic mind-set" that, though not legally imposed, must be assumed by all parties (Habermas 2011, 26). Though religious language is permissible within the informal public sphere, he still believes it is a duty of civility that (at least most) religious citizens sincerely believe their considerations could be formulated in public reasons and, perhaps even more strongly than Rawls, he insists that religious citizens must also adjust their religious commitments to secular or mundane reason (BNR, 4; FK, 104). According to Habermas, this means that religious believers must acknowledge the plurality of religious (and non-religious) worldviews, acknowledge the authority of science in its domain, and accept a universalistic and egalitarian morality of human rights (Habermas 2011, 26–27; BNR, 4, 137). The burden on secular citizens is that they too must acknowledge a fundamental equality of religious citizens and grant that religious discourse could still be a source of new moral learning. Both secular and non-secular citizens though must be committed not only to the neutrality of the state but also to its "cultural presuppositions," which includes a shared public reason that is secular in character (FK, 104). Thus, despite some of Habermas's remarks that seem to relieve religious citizens from any obligation to frame their reasoning in terms intelligible to all, this interpretation risks returning to a *modus vivendi* conception that he (and Rawls) rightly reject (BNR, 112; R5, 376). The expectation that religious citizens "embed the egalitarian individualism of modern natural law and universalistic morality in a convincing way in the context of their comprehensive doctrines" does not apply only to public officials or to citizens in their formal institutional roles (although Habermas does not think this must be done by every citizen uniformly) (BNR, 137). Still, if there is no expectation that most citizens will strive to find public reasons—at least when it concerns matters of constitutional essentials—the division between "official" public deliberations and the reasoning of citizens in the (informal) public sphere could itself become too great (see also Boettcher 2009).

Finally, like Rawls, Habermas also argues that, when it comes to formal institutions, viewpoints based on religious or sectarian views must be fully translated into "secular" or public reason. In response to the charge of an asymmetrical burden and the claim that the demand is too great for believers he suggests that the burden must indeed be more fairly distributed and that secular citizens have a responsibility to listen and help make discourse more accessible. Secular reason should not be "secularist" in the sense that it dismisses religious language as a source of new insights. Nonetheless, and in some ways perhaps more strongly than Rawls, he insists that believers recognize not only the neutral state but also the legitimate authority of science if their perspectives are to be considered "reasonable." Habermas also now accepts Rawls's idea of a political conception as a freestanding module that can and should be embedded within a citizen's (reasonable) wider comprehensive worldview as long as this does not disturb their commitment to argue with one another as citizens on the terrain of public reason (BNR, 112). Finally, like Rawls's own understanding of a "freestanding" political conception based on shared values in the political public culture, Habermas also refers to the "independence" of "democratic common sense" from all comprehensive doctrines (FK, 105). The difference (if there is one) is that Habermas thinks that this democratic common sense need not be individually secured by each citizen in his or her comprehensive view (though of course it can be). Rather, he seems to think that citizens should be able to appeal to public reason alone for settling matters of deeper political disagreement. Of course, the contours of public reason will differ with different political communities given their own unique histories. But, as mentioned above, there is also an obligation for each community continuously to examine its own practices of nation-building to insure that it is not violating its own commitments or behaving in an unacceptably exclusionary manner. This seems, in fact, to be what Habermas has in mind in his description of the constitution of a political community as a dynamic and "self-correcting learning process" (TT, 122; see also Habermas 2012, 100f.).

Further reading

Passerin D'Entreves and Benhabib (1997) is a good place to look at some of the issues in Habermas's polemic against the postmodernists. McCarthy (1991) also develops the debate in greater detail though, like my own discussion, largely from Habermas's perspective. Bernstein (1985) and Dews (1999) also contain many good essays on PDM. Thomassen (2006) contains essays on Derrida and Habermas and the (limited) exchange between them. Wellmer (1991) attempts a more sympathetic engagement with postmodernism.

Habermas (2002) contains many of Habermas's earlier essays on religion and BNR includes important recent statements. Boettcher (2009) contains several important essays. Calhoun et al. (2013) is a valuable collection of essays with a lengthy reply by Habermas. Butler et al. (2011) is a lively and accessible exchange between Charles Taylor, Judith Butler, Habermas, and others, mostly on the question of secularism

Notes

1 Of course, Derrida would also not be content with this division of labor, but I will not pursue that question here; see Derrida 1996.
2 Rorty (2000, 6); Habermas (2000, 45); for related criticisms of Rorty's view on the norm of truth, see Price (2003); Engel (2002); and Stout (2007).
3 See, for example, Daniel Bell's influential The Cultural Contradictions of Capitalism (1976) and Habermas's references to it (Habermas 1997, 42f.)
4 "Young conservative" is Habermas's term for those who belonged to a movement in Germany in the 1920s, including Ludwig Klages, Ernst Jünger, and Oswald Spengler, greatly influenced by Nietzsche. Habermas sees similarities between them and some postmodernists in their aestheticism and rejection of modernity; see Wolin's Intro to NC, xxx, n.35.

5 See Derrida's harsh response to Habermas's discussion in Derrida (1988, 156–157).
6 For various attempts see Culler (1982), to which Habermas refers, Glendinning (2001) and Cavell (1995) as well as the initial critique by Searle (1977).
7 It should be emphasized that Habermas has never expressed this latter conviction; on the contrary, see BNR, 112. Rorty, at least as found in "Religion as Conversation-Stopper," could be described as moving in this direction (Rorty 1999, 171–172).

Nine
Conclusion

It is, of course, too soon to speak of Habermas's legacy. At present his published work covers a period of more than sixty years, and there is no indication that it is coming to a close. Habermas continues to maintain an extremely active speaking and publishing schedule. Nor has the range of topics to which he contributes abated. He is currently at work on another major study that explores the implications of the "axial age" for an understanding of our current intellectual or spiritual (*geistige*) situation, he is still engaged in debates about the meaning of postsecularism, and he contributes regularly to current debates about the political future of Europe. It is thus premature to venture any sweeping assessment about his influence.

Nonetheless, as I perhaps rashly claimed in the Introduction, a case can be made that he is the most influential and widely recognized philosopher of the last half-century. It is, in fact, difficult to think of another academic figure—someone who has spent his entire career within the academy—whose ideas have been (and continue to be) as widely debated and discussed not only within the academy but outside it as well. By way of conclusion, I offer just a few indications in support of the claim:

Habermas presented *The Theory of Communicative Action* as an ambitious attempt to provide an alternative description to Max Weber's account of the process of societal rationalization known as "modernity." Though many of the claims made in that work are surely controversial its significance continues to be explored and heatedly debated in sociological theory more narrowly conceived and within the wider fields of social and cultural studies. To mention just two related examples: Ongoing efforts to understand "what it means to be modern" have sparked a renewed interest in Karl Jasper's notion of the "axial age," particularly among sociologists with interests in the sociology of religion (Robert Bellah, S. N. Eisenstadt). Robert Bellah's *Religion in Human Evolution* (2011) and the companion volume *The Axial Age and its Consequences* (Bellah and Joas 2012) make repeated reference to Habermas's work and, as just mentioned, Habermas is currently at work on a full-length study on this topic as well. Similarly, the current discussions concerning "postsecularism"—which of course also extend into debates about the relation between modernity and religion—have been deeply influenced by Habermas's reflections and, in many cases, are being pursued by those who have been shaped by his work (see, for example, Calhoun et al. 2011 and Warner et al. 2013). Implications for both of these discussions can also be found in the recent collection on *Habermas and Religion* (Calhoun et al. 2013).

Debates among political theorists and others about the future of democracy also continue to be importantly shaped by Habermas's work. This is true for the still rapidly growing literature on the topic of deliberative democracy both at the theoretical level and in attempts to "make deliberative democracy practical" (Fishkin 2009). Although the work of Rawls and especially his student, Joshua Cohen, are important theoretical resources for these discussions, it would be difficult to overestimate the importance of Habermas for them as well (Parkinson and Mansbridge 2012; Dryzek 2010; Ferrara 2014). The same holds for the even more rapidly expanding literature on global or transnational democracy where, again, the work of Habermas is often central (Held 2004; Bohman 2007; Eriksen 2009). Additionally, the reception of *Between Facts and Norms* within legal theory is an ongoing project (Alexy 1990; Günther 1998; Zurn 2007).

Somewhat ironically (if one considers Habermas primarily as a philosopher), Habermas's significance in academic philosophy is more difficult to assess. On the one hand, a number of his students and close collaborators have continued to produce significant work of their own—including Albrecht Wellmer, Axel Honneth, Klaus Günther, Lutz Wingert, and Rainer Forst in Germany, and Thomas McCarthy, Seyla Benhabib, Richard Bernstein, Nancy Fraser and

Cristina Lafont in the USA. On the other hand, the ongoing reception of his own work in philosophy is likely to be closely bound up with the fate of the contemporaries he primarily engaged—Rorty, Putnam, Brandom, and Davidson in the analytic tradition, and Gadamer, Henrich, Derrida, and Foucault in the continental tradition—and, to repeat, it seems too soon to make any sure predictions about what that will be. Philosophy occupies a relatively small place in the academy and seismic shifts can occur relatively quickly. At the moment interest in these figures seems (in this writer's opinion) to be in decline within the discipline (at least in the USA), though others have voiced concern about this general trend within the academy (Kitcher 2011a). Still, there are some indications that interest in the general sort of Kantian pragmatism Habermas represents will persist and some reason to think that his work on action theory—and the related ideas of communicative freedom and communicative reason—might find resonance in action theory, moral theory, and even in an epistemology that is more pragmatically informed (see Misak 2007; Green 2014; Brandom 2011; Darwall 2006).

Finally, in ways that it is much too early to assess, Habermas's more direct interventions in the political life of Germans and Europeans continue to be felt. Times are very uncertain in Europe, but his attempts to reinvigorate the idea of constitutional patriotism and call for a more tolerant and multicultural political identity remain important, even pressing topics for the future of Europe. It is impossible to know what the assessment will be several decades or even a half-century from now. But it is not unreasonable to imagine that Habermas will be recognized as having embodied the ideal of the public intellectual that he finds in Heinrich Heine and argues is still relevant for our own time—namely, the individual who does not refrain from speaking out on matters of public concern but who also does not claim for himself any privileged insight or the ability to translate theory directly into practice (NC, chap. 3).

Philosophy, Hegel remarks in the Preface to *The Philosophy of Right*, is the comprehension of one's own time in thought. The remark was offered not as a prescription of what philosophy might become but as a statement about what philosophy is. As such, it also reflects Hegel's basic conviction about the unity of thought and being found in his absolute idealism. Habermas has always resisted the more ambitious understanding behind that claim—that philosophy can comprehend the world as it is *an sich*. But, at another level, Habermas's own account of a more modest Kantian pragmatism does not seem like an inapt description of what philosophy might aspire to be. On the one hand, a rich (communicative) reason is already contained in everyday social practices. The attempt to understand or identify that reason in isolation from those practices leads to various types of false abstraction, some of which can be found in the totalizing critiques of reason discussed earlier in this chapter. On the other hand, the practices of justification found in the mundane lifeworld invoke idealizing suppositions that can provide a resource for ongoing critique and so can't be reduced to "mere" social practices. Habermas's earlier criticism of Rorty's dismissal of attempts "to see social practices of justification as more than just such practices" captures nicely the way in which his pragmatism differs from stronger forms of contextualism without overcompensating in the other direction (MCCA, 20). Such an understanding of philosophy makes it an ongoing "task" (*Aufgabe*) rather than a descriptive claim and so expresses another important Kantian theme. Perhaps that conception of philosophy will also become part of Habermas's future legacy.

absolute idealism Hegel's philosophical position that there is a basic identity between mind and reality insuring that it is possible for humans to know the world as it is *an sich* or "in-itself."

accountability (*Zurechnungsfähigkeit*) In Habermas this refers primarily to the basic notion of freedom and responsibility that belongs to the ordinary or "manifest image" of the person; he accounts for this more general notion by appeal to the basic obligation between speaker and hearer to provide reasons for the claims raised in their speech acts and so it is associated with his notions of communicative freedom and communicative action.

administrative power/communicative power Habermas's contrast (in BFN) between the formal power exercised by the state and the informal power that belongs to public opinion and the ability of individuals and groups within civil society to influence the issues and topics that make their way onto the political agenda. See also strong/weak publics.

autonomy A central term for Rousseau and Kant that, in Habermas, refers both to the liberty of individuals to pursue their aims ("private autonomy") and to their ability to participate politically in making the laws to which they are subject ("public autonomy"); for Habermas the idea of autonomy ultimately derives from and depends upon the more basic idea of communicative freedom.

cognitive interests Habermas's term in KHI for the more or less invariant or "anthropologically deep-seated" interests that (in a Kantian sense) structure our empirical or "inner-worldly" knowledge; in KHI Habermas identified three: an interest in technical control, an interest in communication and understanding, and an interest in emancipation.

colonization of the lifeworld Habermas's phrase to describe how the social subsystems of the market economy ("money") and the state ("power") can have a disruptive effect on the communicative processes through which institutions in the lifeworld (broadly, the family and associations in civil society) reproduce social meanings and motivations ("solidarity"); it is also Habermas's own gloss on Marx's notion of social reification.

communicative action A central concept in Habermas's work that refers broadly to social interaction and coordination based on a shared understanding of background norms and practices; at other times it refers, in a more narrow and technical sense, to interaction and coordination based on the shared presuppositions contained in (illocutionary) speech acts and their idealizing presuppositions. His general thesis is that, as societies modernize and become more rational, communicative action shifts from reliance on traditionally secured consensus to one that is more directly achieved through the rational potential contained in illocutionary speech acts.

communicative freedom In Habermas, this is the fundamental form of freedom on the basis of which other freedoms and liberties are developed; it refers to the basic freedom to accept or reject the claims raised in basic types of speech acts, a normative capacity that must be presupposed given the illocutionary meaning or force of those speech acts.

constitutional patriotism A form of patriotism based on constitutional principles and a shared (liberal) political culture rather than a "thicker" national, ethnic, or cultural (religious) identity.

constructivism, moral and political The view that moral and political norms are the outcome of a rational or reasonable procedure, rather than practice-independent truths that are discovered or intuited; Kant's categorical imperative is an example of moral constructivism (as is also Habermas's Principle U); John Rawls's Original Position represents an example of political constructivism.

decisionism The view that conflicts of value cannot be rationally adjudicated but are ultimately a matter of non-rational preference and choice; Max Weber is a paradigmatic example, but there are many others, including most positivists.

deliberative democracy A conception of democracy that emphasizes the processes of opinion-formation and deliberation in contrast to conceptions that emphasize processes of the aggregation of preferences; deliberative democrats often emphasize the importance of the idea of a public reasoning among free and equal citizens (Joshua Cohen).

hermeneutics The art or science of interpretation, especially the interpretation of texts, but the notion has been extended to action and social meaning generally; in Gadamer's philosophical hermeneutics, it becomes a model for philosophy itself (in contrast to stronger forms of transcendental inquiry and to more classical metaphysics).

historicism The term has a variety of meanings, but it is primarily the view that to properly understand something it must be understood in its own historical context; it sometimes also suggests a form of relativism—since things are only intelligible in their historical context no comparison among them is possible.

illocutionary force The set of commitments or obligations created through various types of basic speech acts such as assertions, promises, avowals, and the like. For example, when I assert something, I claim to believe it and acquire (perhaps quite weak) obligations to give reasons in support of that belief, or when I promise something, I commit myself to a course of behavior to which others can hold me accountable. In Habermas's formal pragmatics this illocutionary force—and, specifically, the normative status of speaker/hearer to offer and respond to reasons—is introduced to clarify his central concepts of communicative freedom and action.

institutional framework (in TRS) Habermas's more abstract term for what Marx called the social relations of production; it refers to the core set of social institutions responsible for its particular collective identity and legitimacy and so can include institutions that exercise power and those responsible for producing norms. Different social forms can be identified in connection with different institutional frameworks (much as Marx proposed criteria for identifying different modes of production). One of

Habermas's criticisms of Marx was that the institutional framework can have an independent developmental logic and is not determined solely by the level of the "productive forces."

Kantian pragmatism Habermas's philosophical position which holds that human knowledge of the world is structured by our cognitive faculties and rooted in (more or less stable) social practices.

labor and interaction Habermas's earlier terms (in his Hegel essay in TP) for the distinction between instrumental and communicative action; in his writings in the early 1970s, "interaction" is also closely associated with his idea of the "institutional framework" of a society.

lifeworld Habermas adapts this important concept from Husserl. On the one hand, it refers to the complex of (often only implicit) shared norms, expectations, and practices of social actors that enables them to communicate and coordinate their conduct. It also refers to the social institutions that arise on the basis of those practices (and thus is often another term for what he earlier called the "institutional framework" of society). Habermas's thesis in TCA is that the lifeworld is reproduced through the interpretative activity of social actors, even as they at the same time implicitly rely upon it as a "background." It is thus also importantly connected to his concept of communicative action.

mode of production See productive forces/social relations.

overlapping consensus (Rawls) The consensus among reasonable broader (or "comprehensive") moral and religious doctrines on a political conception of justice.

participant's perspective/observer's perspective Habermas's basic contrast between the perspective of social actors engaged in the interpretation of the meaning of social action (including social theorists who approach action interpretively) and a perspective which either disregards or brackets such interpretation (such as behaviorism or systems theory); sometimes he also describes this in terms of the contrast between a first- or second-person and third-person perspective.

philosophy of the subject/philosophy of consciousness These are Habermas's labels for the long tradition in modern philosophy that focused attention on the individual self and, in particular, its capacity for thought (so, at least, Descartes through Husserl, and including importantly Kant); in contrast to some philosophers who continue this tradition and postmodernists who attempt to expose its inconsistencies or deconstruct it, Habermas follows pragmatists in proposing an alternative to it—in his case, the theory of communicative action.

positivism The view that only the empirical sciences constitute knowledge or rational forms of inquiry; such a view generally implies a strong distinction between questions of fact and questions of value, aspires to "value-neutrality" in the sciences, and regards values as subjective or non-rational preferences. See also scientism.

Principle U This is Habermas's reformulation of Kant's categorical imperative and the basic moral principle of his discourse morality; it states that a norm is valid (or morally justified) if and only if "all affected can accept the consequences and the side effects its general observance can be anticipated to have for the satisfaction of everyone's interests (and these consequences are preferred to those of known alternative possibilities for regulation)" (MCCA, 65).

productive forces/productive relations Marx identified different societies according to their "mode of production"; in a given mode of production, a further distinction was made between "productive forces" (roughly labor power, science and technology) and its "social relations" (the manner in which the productive forces were organized—through slavery, feudal indenture, private ownership, etc.). In orthodox "deterministic" interpretations of Marx, growing productive forces "determine" social relations and together these "determine" the further ideological forms of society (such as political, religious, and moral worldviews). See also **institutional framework**.

Rechtsstaat This can be translated as "constitutional state" or "state regulated by the rule of law"; in the German discussion, such a state could take the form of a (minimal) liberal state, a liberal welfare state, or a more extensive "social-welfare" state (Sozialstaat).

reification In Marx, the process by which a society reproduces itself such that the social relations appear as fixed permanent things rather than as the product of those (alterable) social relations— workers experience their social relations as "natural" things rather than as the result of alterable social conditions. At another level, as a result of that process, relations are also "thing-like" since the capacity for a more humane social reproduction has been disrupted. See also colonization of the lifeworld.

scientism The view that the sciences alone—and perhaps even only the natural sciences—are rational forms of inquiry and/or provide genuine knowledge about the world (in contrast, say, to morality, religion, or literature and art).

Sittlichkeit (ethical life) Hegel's term (in *The Philosophy of Right*) for the set of basic social institutions—the family, civil society, and the state—that are conditions for realizing individual freedom; more generally, it can refer to the social and political ethos of a community.

social integration/system integration Habermas's terms for the two ways in which social action can be coordinated—social integration works primarily through and depends crucially upon the linguistic understandings or interpretations of social actors (and is closely aligned with the lifeworld); whereas system integration need not take those interpretations directly into account but rather relies upon the predictable outcomes of action. Modern complex societies require both forms but, more controversially, Habermas claims the subsystems of the economy and administrative state are primarily systemically integrated.

society as lifeworld and system Habermas defines society broadly as "the systemically-stabilized complexes of action of socially-integrated groups" and argues that this definition preserves the ability to view society from two perspectives: from an interpretive (and "participant") perspective that focuses on the "meanings" of social actors (lifeworld) and from an external or "observer" perspective that views society functionally (system).

systems theory (Luhmann) In sociology, the study of society as a system itself composed of other (sub-)systems. Each system communicates with itself in its own language or code and "learns" how to reproduce itself and respond to changes in its surrounding environment. Each subsystem also communicates internally only in its own language and responds to other subsystems as part of its particular environment. Habermas is highly critical of some aspects of systems theory but considers other aspects of it an important approach in the analysis of society.

transcendental idealism Kant's philosophical view that knowledge is structured by basic categories or forms of the mind and that humans cannot know reality in itself (*an sich*) apart from those categories.

universal (or formal) pragmatics See illocutionary force.

weak/strong publics Habermas's categories for the more informal associations of civil society that generate communicative power and "opinion-formation" (weak publics) and the formal institutions of the state (including formal political parties and parliamentary bodies) that exercise decision-making power and "will-formation" (strong publics).

world-disclosing linguistic structure/inner-worldly learning This is Habermas's version of the transcendental/empirical distinction (Kant) and ontological/ontic distinction (Heidegger); unlike Kant and (arguably) Heidegger, for Habermas this distinction is not static or absolute—that is, inner-worldly learning can modify or alter world-disclosing linguistic structures.

Bibliography

Aboulafia, M., M. Bookman and C. Kemp, eds. 2002. *Habermas and Pragmatism*. New York: Routledge.

Adorno, Theodor. 1973. *Negative Dialectics*. New York: Seabury.

Adorno, Theodor, H. Albert, R. Dahrendorf, J. Habermas, H. Pilot and K. Popper. 1976. *The Positivist Dispute in German Sociology*. New York: Harper and Row.

Alexy, Robert. 1990. "A Theory of Practical Discourse," in Seyla Benhabib and F. Dallmayr, eds. *The Communicative Ethics Controversy*. Cambridge, MA: MIT Press, pp. 151–190.

Allen, Amy. 2008. *The Politics of Ourselves*. New York: Columbia University Press.

Allen, Amy. 2014. "The Power of Justification," in Rainer Forst, *Justice, Democracy, and the Right to Justification: Forst in Dialogue*. New York: Bloomsbury, pp. 65–86.

Anderson, Joel. 2007. Special Issue on "Free Will as Part of Nature: Habermas and his Critics," *Philosophical Explorations* 10(1).

Barry, Brian. 1979. "Is Democracy Special?" in P. Laslett, ed. *Philosophy, Politics and Society*. New York: Oxford University Press, pp. 155–180.

Baxter, Hugh. 1987. "System and Lifeworld in Habermas's *Theory of Communicative Action*," *Theory and Society* 16: 39–86.

Baxter, Hugh. 2011. *Habermas: The Discourse Theory of Law and Democracy*. Stanford, CA: Stanford University Press.

Baynes, Kenneth. 1992. *The Normative Grounds of Social Criticism*. Albany: SUNY Press.

Baynes, Kenneth. 1992a. "Liberal Neutrality, Pluralism and Deliberative Politics," *Praxis International* 12: 50–69.

Baynes, Kenneth. 2002. "Deliberative Democracy and the Limits of Liberalism," in Rene von Schomberg and K. Baynes, eds. *Discourse and Democracy: Essays on 'Between Facts and Norms'.* Albany: SUNY Press.

Baynes, Kenneth. 2004. "The Transcendental Turn: Habermas's 'Kantian Pragmatism,' in Fred Rush, ed. *The Cambridge Companion to Critical Theory.* New York: Cambridge University Press, pp. 194–218.

Baynes, Kenneth. 2007. "Disagreement and the Legitimacy of Legal Interpretation," in Omid Payrow Shabani, ed. *Multiculturalism and Law.* Cardiff: University of Wales, pp. 101–114.

Baynes, Kenneth. 2010. "Self, Narrative and Self-constitution: Revisiting Taylor's 'Self-interpreting Animals'," *The Philosophical Forum* 41: 441–458.

Baynes, Kenneth. 2012. "Making Global Governance Public," in L. Beckman and E. Erman, eds. *Territories of Citizenship.* Edinburgh: University of Edinburgh Press, pp. 123–145.

Baynes, Kenneth. 2014. "Rawls and Critical Theory," in Jon Mandle and David Reidy, eds. *A Companion to Rawls.* New York: Blackwell, pp. 487–503.

Beiser, Fred. 1987. *The Fate of Reason.* Cambridge, MA: Harvard University Press.

Beiser, Fred, ed. 1993. *The Cambridge Companion to Hegel.* New York: Cambridge University Press.

Beiser, Fred. 2014. *After Hegel: German Philosophy, 1840–1900.* Princeton, NJ: Princeton University Press.

Beitz, Charles. 1989. *Political Equality.* Princeton, NJ: Princeton University Press.

Bell, Daniel. 1976. *The Cultural Consequences of Capitalism.* New York: Basic Books.

Bellah, Robert. 2011. *Religion in Human Evolution.* Cambridge, MA: Harvard University Press.

Bellah, Robert and H. Joas, eds. 2012. *The Axial Age and its Consequences.* Cambridge, MA: Harvard University Press.

Bellamy, Richard and M. Hollis. 1999. "Consensus, Neutrality and Compromise," in Richard Bellamy and M. Hollis, eds. *Pluralism and Liberal Neutrality.* London: Frank Cass, pp. 54–78.

Bellamy, Richard and M. Hollis, eds. 1999a. *Pluralism and Liberal Neutrality*. London: Frank Cass.

Benhabib, Seyla. 1986. *Critique, Norm and Utopia*. New York: Columbia University Press.

Benhabib, Seyla. 1990. "Afterword: Communicative Ethics and Contemporary Issues in Practical Philosophy," in S. Benhabib and F. Dallmayr, eds. *The Communicative Ethics Controversy*. Cambridge, MA: MIT Press, pp. 330–369.

Benhabib, Seyla. 2011. *Dignity in Adversity: Human Rights in Troubled Times*. Malden, MA: Polity Press.

Benhabib, Seyla and F. Dallmayr, eds. 1990. *The Communicative Ethics Controversy*. Cambridge, MA: MIT Press.

Bernstein, J. M. 1995. *Recovering Ethical Life*. New York: Routledge.

Bernstein, Richard. 1985. *Habermas and Modernity*. Cambridge, MA: MIT Press.

Bernstein, Richard. 2010. "Jürgen Habermas's Kantian Pragmatism," in *The Pragmatic Turn*. Malden, MA: Polity Press, pp. 168–199.

Besson, Samantha and J. Marti, eds. 2006. *Deliberative Democracy and Its Discontents*. Burlington, VT: Ashgate.

Boettcher, James. 2009. "Habermas, Religion and the Ethics of Citizenship," *Philosophy and Social Criticism* 35: 215–238.

Bohman, James. 1996. *Public Deliberation*. Cambridge: MIT Press.

Bohman, James. 2007. *Democracy Across Borders*. Cambridge, MA: MIT Press.

Bohman, James and W. Rehg, eds. 1997. *Deliberative Democracy*. Cambridge, MA: MIT Press.

Bohman, James and W. Rehg. 2002. "Discourse and Democracy," in Rene von Schomberg and K. Baynes, eds. *Discourse and Democracy: Essays on 'Between Facts and Norms'*. Albany: SUNY Press, pp. 31–60.

Brandom, Robert. 1979. "Freedom and Constraint by Norms," *American Philosophical Quarterly* 16: 187–196.

Brandom, Robert. 1994. *Making It Explicit*. Cambridge, MA: Harvard University Press.

Brandom, Robert, ed. 2000. *Rorty and his Critics*. Oxford: Blackwell.

Brandom, Robert. 2000a. "Vocabularies of Pragmatism," in *Rorty and his Critics*. Oxford: Blackwell, 156–182.

Brandom, Robert. 2000b. "Facts, Norms and Normative Facts: A Reply to Habermas," *European Journal of Philosophy* 8: 356–374.

Brandom, Robert. 2001. "Modality, Normativity, and Intentionality," *Philosophy and Phenomenological Research* 63: 587–609.

Brandom, Robert. 2011. *Perspectives on Pragmatism*. Cambridge, MA: Harvard University Press.

Bratman, Michael. 1999. "Identification, Decision, and Treating as a Reason," in *Faces of Intention*, pp. 185–206. New York: Cambridge University Press.

Brown, Wendy and R. Forst. 2014. *The Power of Tolerance: A Debate*. New York: Columbia University Press.

Buchwalter, Andrew. 2001. "Law, Culture, Constitutionalism: Remarks on Hegel and Habermas," in R. Williams, ed. *Beyond Liberalism and Communitarianism*. Albany, NY: SUNY Press, pp. 207–227.

Burge, Tyler. 1998. "Reason and the First Person," in C. Wright, ed. *Knowing Our Own Minds*. Oxford: Clarendon, pp. 243–270.

Butler, Judith, J. Habermas, C. Taylor and C. West, eds. 2011. *The Power of Religion in the Public Sphere*. New York: Columbia University Press.

Calhoun, Craig, ed. 1992. *Habermas and the Public Sphere*. Cambridge: MIT Press.

Calhoun, Craig, M. Juergensmeyer and J. Van Antwerpen, eds. 2011. *Rethinking Secularism*. New York: Oxford University Press.

Calhoun, Craig, E. Mendieta and J. Van Antwerpen, eds. 2013. *Habermas and Religion*. Cambridge: Polity Press.

Caney, Simon. 1999. "Liberal Legitimacy, Reasonable Disagreement, and Justice," in Richard Bellamy and M. Hollis, eds. *Pluralism and Liberal Neutrality*. London: Frank Cass, pp. 19–36.

Carus, A. W. 2007. *Carnap and Twentieth-Century Thought*. New York: Cambridge University Press.

Cavell, S. 1995. *Philosophical Passages*. New York: Blackwell.

Celikates, Robin. 2006. "From Critical Social Theory to a Social Theory of Critique," *Constellations* 13: 21–40.

Chambers, Simone. 1996. *Reasonable Democracy: Habermas and the Politics of Discourse*. Ithaca, NY: Cornell University Press.

Child, William. 1994. *Causality, Interpretation and the Mind*. Oxford: Clarendon.

Cohen, G. A. 1978. *Karl Marx's Theory of History*. Princeton, NJ: Princeton University Press.

Cohen, Jean and A. Arato. 1992. *Civil Society and Social Theory.* Cambridge, MA: MIT Press.

Cohen, Joshua. 1989. "Deliberation and Democratic Legitimacy," in A. Hamlin and P. Pettit, eds. *The Good Polity.* Oxford: Blackwell Press, pp. 17–34.

Cohen, Joshua. 1994. "Pluralism and Proceduralism," *Chicago-Kent Law Review* 69: 589–618.

Cohen, Joshua. 1996. "Freedom, Equality and Pornography," in A. Sarat and T. Kearns, eds. *Justice and Injustice in Law and Legal Theory,* Ann Arbor: University of Michigan Press, pp. 99–137.

Cohen, Joshua. 1998. "Democracy and Liberty," in J. Elster, ed. *Deliberative Democracy.* New York: Cambridge University Press, pp. 185–231.

Cohen, Joshua. 1999. "Reflections on Habermas on Democracy," *Ratio Juris* 12: 385–416.

Cohen, Joshua. 2002. "For a Democratic Society," in S. Freeman, ed. *The Cambridge Companion to Rawls.* New York: Cambridge University Press, pp. 86–138.

Cohen, Joshua and J. Rogers, eds. 1995. *Associations and Democracy.* New York: Verso.

Cooke, Maeve. 1994. *Language and Reason.* Cambridge, MA: MIT Press.

Cronin, Ciaran. 2011. "Cosmopolitan Democracy," in Barbara Fultner, ed. *Jürgen Habermas: Key Concepts.* Durham, UK: Acumen, pp. 196–221.

Crowell, Steven and J. Malpas, eds. 2007. *Transcendental Heidegger.* Stanford, CA: Stanford University Press.

Culler, Jonathan. 1982. *On Deconstruction.* Ithaca, NY: Cornell University Press.

Dahl, Robert. 1989. *Democracy and Its Critics.* New Haven, CT: Yale University Press.

Darwall, Stephen. 2006. *The Second Personal Standpoint.* Cambridge, MA: Harvard University Press.

Darwall, Stephen, A. Gibbard and P. Railton, eds. 1997. *Moral Discourse and Practice.* New York: Oxford University Press.

Davidson, David. 1984. *Inquiries into Truth and Interpretation.* New York: Oxford University Press.

Davidson, Donald. 1980. "Actions, Reasons, and Causes," in *Essays on Actions and Events.* New York: Oxford University Press, pp. 3–19.

Davidson, Donald. 2004. *Problems of Rationality*. New York: Oxford University Press.

Dennett, Daniel. 1981. *The Intentional Stance*. Cambridge, MA: MIT Press.

Derrida, Jacques. 1971. *Positions*. Chicago: University of Chicago Press.

Derrida, Jacques. 1988. *Limited Inc*. Evanston: Northwestern University Press.

Derrida, Jacques. 1996. "Remarks on Deconstruction and Pragmatism," in C. Mouffe, ed. *Deconstruction and Pragmatism*. New York: Routledge, pp. 77–88.

Dews, Peter, ed. 1986. *Habermas: Autonomy and Solidarity. Interviews with Jürgen Habermas*. London: Verso.

Dews, Peter, ed. 1999. *Habermas: A Critical Reader*. Malden, MA: Blackwell.

Dews, Peter. 1999a. "Introduction," in P. Dews, ed. *Habermas: A Critical Reader*. Malden, MA: Blackwell, pp. 1–25.

Dryzek, John. 2006. *Deliberative Global Politics*. New York: Cambridge University Press.

Dryzek, John. 2010. *Foundations and Frontiers of Deliberative Governance*. New York: Oxford University Press.

Dworkin, Ronald. 1990. "Equality, Democracy and Constitution: We the People in Court," *Alberta Law Review* 28: 324–346.

Eder, Klaus. 1999. "Societies Learn and Yet the World is Hard to Change," *European Journal of Social Theory* 2: 195–215.

Ellis, Jonathan. 2011. "The Relevance of Radical Interpretation," in Jeff Malpas, ed. *Dialogues with Davidson*. Cambridge: MIT Press, pp. 191–218.

Elster, Jon, ed. 1998. *Deliberative Democracy*. New York: Cambridge University Press.

Ely, John. 1980. *Democracy and Distrust*. Cambridge, MA: Harvard University Press.

Engel, Pascal. 2002. *Truth*. Durham, UK: Acumen.

Eriksen, Erik. 2009. *The Unfinished Democratization of Europe*. New York: Oxford University Press.

Erman, Eva and R. Higgott. 2010. "Deliberative Global Governance and the Question of Legitimacy: What can we learn from the WTO?" *Review of International Studies* 36: 449–470.

Estlund, David. 1993. "Who's Afraid of Deliberative Democracy?" *Texas Law Review* 71: 1437–1477.

Estlund, David. 2008. *Democratic Authority*. Princeton, NJ: Princeton University Press.

Ferrara, Alessandro. 2014. *The Democratic Horizon*. New York: Cambridge University Press.

Finlayson, J. G. 2000. "Modernity and Morality in Habermas's Discourse Ethics," *Inquiry* 43: 319–340.

Finlayson, J. G. 2005. "Habermas's Moral Cognitivism and the Frege-Geach Challenge," *European Journal of Philosophy* 13: 319–344.

Finlayson, J. G. 2009. "Morality and Critical Theory: On the Normative Problem of Frankfurt School Social Criticism," *Telos* 146: 7–41.

Finlayson, J. G. 2013. "The Persistence of Normative Questions in Habermas's *The Theory of Communicative Action*," *Constellations* 20: 518–532.

Finlayson, J. G. and F. Freyenhagen. 2011. *Habermas and Rawls*. New York: Routledge.

Fishkin, James. 1990. *Democracy and Deliberation*. New Haven, CT: Yale University Press.

Fishkin, James. 2009. *When the People Speak: Deliberative Democracy and Public Consultation*. New York: Oxford University Press.

Flynn, Jeffrey. 2014. "Truth, Objectivity and Experience after the Pragmatic Turn: Bernstein on Habermas's 'Kantian Pragmatism'," in Judith Green, ed. *Richard J. Bernstein and the Pragmatist Turn*. New York: Palgrave, pp. 230–260.

Forst, Rainer. 2002. *Contexts of Justice*. Berkeley, CA: University of California Press.

Forst, Rainer. 2011. *Justification and Critique*. Cambridge: Polity Press.

Forst, Rainer. 2011a. "To Tolerate Means to Disrespect" in *Justification and Critique*. Cambridge: Polity Press, pp. 126–148.

Forst, Rainer. 2012. *The Right to Justification*. New York: Columbia University Press.

Forst, Rainer. 2014. *Justice, Democracy, and the Right to Justification: Forst in Dialogue*. New York: Bloomsbury.

Förster, Eckart. 2012. *The Twenty-Five Years of Philosophy: A Systematic Reconstruction*. Cambridge, MA: Harvard University Press.

Foucault, Michel. 1972. *The Archaeology of Knowledge*. New York: Harper and Row.

Foucault, Michel. 1980. *Power/Knowledge: Selected Interviews*. Ed. by Colin Gordon. New York: Pantheon.

Foucault, Michel. 1997. "The ethics of concern for self as a practice of freedom," in *Essential Works*, v. 1. New York: The New Press, pp. 281–302.

Foucault, Michel. 2001. "The Subject and Power," in *Essential Works*, vol. 3. New York: The New Press, p. 342.

Fraser, Nancy. 1989. *Unruly Practices*. Minneapolis, MN: University of Minnesota Press.

Fraser, Nancy. 1992. "Rethinking the Public Sphere," in Craig Calhoun, ed. 1992. *Habermas and the Public Sphere*. Cambridge: MIT Press, pp. 109–142.

Fraser, Nancy et al. 2008. *Transnationalizing the Public Sphere*. Malden, MA: Polity.

Freeman, Samuel. 1992. "Original Meaning, Democratic Interpretation and the Constitution," *Philosophy and Public Affairs* 21: 3–42.

Freeman, Samuel. 2000. "Deliberative Democracy: A Sympathetic Comment," *Philosophy and Public Affairs* 29: 371–418.

Freeman, Samuel. 2006. "Moral Contractarianism as a Foundation for Interpersonal Morality," in J. Dreier, ed. *Contemporary Debates in Moral Theory*. New York: Blackwell, pp. 57–76.

Freeman, Samuel. 2007. "The Burdens of Public Justification," *Politics, Philosophy, and Economics*. 6: 5–43.

Friedman, Michael. 2001. *Dynamics of Reason*. Stanford, CA: CSLI Publications.

Fulda, H.-F. 2011. "Science of the Phenomenology of Spirit," in Dean Moyar and M. Quante, eds. *Hegel's Phenomenology of Spirit*. New York: Cambridge University Press, pp. 21–42.

Fultner, Barbara, ed. 2011. *Jürgen Habermas: Key Concepts*. Durham, UK: Acumen.

Gadamer, Hans-Georg. 1960 [1989]. *Truth and Method*. New York: Continuum Books.

Gardner, Sebastian. 2007. "The Limits of Naturalism and the Metaphysics of German Idealism," in E. Hammer, *German Idealism: Contemporary Perspectives*. New York: Routledge, pp. 19–49.

Gaus, Daniel. 2013. "Rational Reconstruction as a Method of Political Theory between Social Critique and Empirical Political Science," *Constellations* 20: 518–533.

Gauthier, David. 1987. *Morals by Agreement*. New York: Oxford University Press.

Geuss, Raymond. 1981. *The Idea of a Critical Theory*. New York: Cambridge University Press.

Gibbard, Alan. 1990. *Wise Choices, Apt Feelings*. Cambridge, MA: Harvard University Press.

Giddens, Anthony. 1976. *New Rules for Sociological Method*. New York: Basic.

Gilabert, Pablo. 2005. "A Substantivist Construal of Discourse Ethics," *International Journal of Philosophical Studies* 13: 405–437.

Gledhill, James. 2011. "Procedure in Substance and Substance in Procedure: The Rawls/Habermas Debate," in J. G. Finlayson and F. Freyenhagen. *Habermas and Rawls*. New York: Routledge, pp. 181–199.

Glendinning, S., ed. 2001. *Arguing with Derrida*. New York: Blackwell.

Goodin, Robert. 1985. "Laundering Preferences," in J. Elster, ed. *Foundations of Social Choice Theory*. New York: Cambridge University Press, pp. 75–101.

Grannoveter, Mark. 1985. "Economic Action and Social Structure: The Problem of Embeddedness," *American Journal of Sociology* 91: 481–510.

Green, Judith, ed. 2014. *Richard J. Bernstein and the Pragmatist Turn in Contemporary Philosophy*. London: Palgrave.

Gunnarsson, Logi. 2000. *Making Moral Sense: Beyond Habermas and Gauthier*. New York: Cambridge University Press.

Günther, Klaus. 1993. *The Sense of Appropriateness*. Albany, NY: SUNY Press.

Günther, Klaus. 1998. "Communicative Freedom, Communicative Power and Jurisgenesis," in Michel Rosenfeld and Andrew Arato, eds. *Habermas on Law and Democracy*. Berkeley: University of California Press, pp. 234–256.

Gutmann, Amy and D. Thompson. 1996. *Democracy and Disagreement*. Cambridge, MA: Harvard University Press.

Guyer, Paul. 2014. *Kant*. New York: Routledge.

Habermas, J. 1954. "Dialektik der Rationalisierung," *Merkur* 28: 201–224.

Habermas, J. 1962/1989. *The Structural Transformation of the Public Sphere*. Cambridge: MIT Press.

Habermas, J. 1968. *Knowledge and Human Interests*. Boston: Beacon Press.

Habermas, J. 1969. *Protestbewegung und Hochschulreform*. Frankfurt: Suhrkamp.

Habermas, J. 1970. *Toward a Rational Society*. Trans. by J. Shapiro. Boston: Beacon Press.

Habermas, J. 1970a. "On Systematically Distorted Communication," *Inquiry* 13: 205–218.

Habermas, J. 1973. *Theory and Practice*. Boston: Beacon Press.

Habermas, J. 1973a. "A Postscript to Knowledge and Human Interests," *Philosophy of Social Science* 3: 157–189.

Habermas, J. 1973b. *Legitimation Crisis*. Boston: Beacon Press.

Habermas, J. 1974. "Social Identity," *Telos* 7: 91–102.

Habermas, J. 1975. "The Place of Philosophy in Marxism," *The Insurgent Socialist* 5: 41–48.

Habermas, J. 1979. *Communication and the Evolution of Society*. Boston: Beacon Press.

Habermas, J. 1979a. "History and Evolution," *Telos* 39: 5–44.

Habermas, J. 1983. *Philosophical-Political Profiles*. Cambridge, MA: MIT Press.

Habermas, J. 1984/1987. *The Theory of Communicative Action*. Boston: Beacon Press.

Habermas, J. 1985. "Remarks on the Concept of Communicative Action," in *Social Action*. Edited by G. Seebass and R. Tuomela. Boston: Reidel.

Habermas, J. 1985a. "Reply to Skjei," *Inquiry* 28: 105–113.

Habermas, J. 1967 [1988]. *On the Logic of the Social Sciences*. Cambridge: MIT Press.

Habermas, J. 1985 [1987]. *The Philosophical Discourse of Modernity*. Cambridge, MA: MIT Press.

Habermas, J. 1989. *The Structural Transformation of the Public Sphere*. Cambridge, MA: MIT Press.

Habermas, J. 1989a. *The New Conservatism: Cultural Criticism and the Historians' Debate*. Cambridge, MA: MIT Press.

Habermas, J. 1989b. "The New Obscurity," in J. Habermas, *The New Conservatism: Cultural Criticism and the Historians' Debate*. Cambridge, MA: MIT Press, pp. 48–70.

Habermas, J. 1990. *Moral Consciousness and Communicative Action*. Cambridge, MA: MIT Press.

Habermas, J. 1990a. "What Does Socialism Mean Today?" *New Left Review* 183: 3–21.

Habermas, J. 1991. "Martin Heidegger: On the Publication of the Lectures of 1935," in Richard Wolin, ed. *The Heidegger Controversy*. New York: Columbia University Press, pp. 186–197.

Habermas, J. 1992. *Postmetaphysical Thinking*. Cambridge, MA: MIT Press.

Habermas, J. 1994. *Justification and Application*. Cambridge, MA: MIT Press.

Habermas, J. 1996. *Between Facts and Norms: Contributions to a Discourse Theory of Law and Democracy*. Trans. by W. Rehg. Cambridge, MA: MIT Press.

Habermas, J. 1997 [1980]. "Modernity: An Unfinished Project," in Maurizio Passerin D'Entreves and S. Benhabib, eds. *Habermas and the Unfinished Project of Modernity*. Cambridge, MA: MIT Press, pp. 38–55.

Habermas, J. 1998. *The Inclusion of the Other*. Trans. by C. Cronin and P. de Greiff. Cambridge, MA: MIT Press.

Habermas, J. 1998a. *On the Pragmatics of Communicative Action*. Edited by Maeve Cooke. Cambridge, MA: MIT Press.

Habermas, J. 2000. "Rorty's Pragmatic Turn," in Robert Brandom, ed. *Rorty and his Critics*. Oxford: Blackwell, pp. 31–55.

Habermas, J. 2000a. "Nach dreissig jahren: Bemerkungen zu 'Erkenntnis und Interesse'," in S. Müller-Doohm, ed. *Das Interesse der Vernunft*. Frankfurt: Suhrkamp, pp. 12–20.

Habermas, J. 2001. *The Postnational Constellation*. Trans. by Max Pensky. Cambridge, MA: MIT Press.

Habermas, J. 2001a. *The Liberating Power of Symbols: Philosophical Essays*. Cambridge, MA: MIT Press.

Habermas, J. 2002. *Religion and Rationality*. Edited by E. Mendieta. Cambridge, MA: MIT Press.

Habermas, J. 2003. *Truth and Justification*. Trans. by Barbara Fultner. Cambridge, MA: MIT Press.

Habermas, J. 2003a. *The Future of Human Nature*. Trans. by W. Rehg. Cambridge: Polity Press.

Habermas, J. 2003b. "On Law and Disagreement," *Ratio Juris* 16: 187–194.

Habermas, J. 2006. "Political Communication in Media Society: Does Democracy Still Enjoy an Epistemic Dimension?," *Communication Theory* 16: 411–426.

Habermas, J. 2008. *Between Naturalism and Religion*. Cambridge: Polity Press.

Habermas, J. 2009. *Europe: The Faltering Project*. Trans. by C. Cronin. Cambridge: Polity Press.

Habermas, J. 2011. "'The Political': The Rational Meaning of a Questionable Inheritance of Political Theology," in J. Butler, J. Habermas, C. Taylor and C. West, eds. *The Power of Religion in the Public Sphere*. New York: Columbia University Press, pp. 15–33.

Habermas, J. 2012. *The Crisis of the European Union: A Response*. Trans. by C. Cronin. Cambridge: Polity Press.

Habermas, J. 2012a. "Von den Weltbildern zur Lebenswelt," in *Nachmetaphysisches Denken II*. Frankfurt: Suhrkamp, pp. 19–53.

Habermas, J. 2015. *The Lure of Technocracy*. Cambridge: Polity Press.

Habermas, J, and L. F Von Friedeburg, C. Oehler, and F. Weltz, eds. 1961. *Student und Politik*. Darmstadt: Luchterhand.

Hammer, Epsen. 2007. "Habermas and the Kant/Hegel Contrast," in *German Idealism: Contemporary Perspectives*. New York: Routledge, pp. 113–135.

Hampe, Michael. 2007. "Husserl's Concept of the Lifeworld and Sellar's Idea of a Synoptic Vision of a Manifest and a Scientific Image," in D. Hyder, *Science and the Life-world*. Stanford, CA: Stanford University Press.

Han, Beatrice. 1998. *Foucault's Critical Project*. Stanford, CA: Stanford University Press.

Heath, Joseph. 2001. *Communicative Action and Rational Choice*. Cambridge, MA: MIT Press.

Heath, Joseph. 2009. "Habermas and Analytic Marxism," *Philosophy and Social Criticism*, 891–920.

Heath, Joseph. 2011. "System and Lifeworld" in Barbara Fultner, ed. *Jürgen Habermas: Key Concepts*. Durham, UK: Acumen, pp. 74–90.

Heath, Joseph. 2014. "Rebooting discourse ethics," *Philosophy and Social Criticism* 40: 1–38.

Hedrick, Todd. 2010. *Rawls and Habermas*. Stanford: Stanford University Press.

Held, David. 2004. *Global Covenant*. London: Polity Press.

Henrich, Dieter. 1982. "Fichte's Original Insight," in D. Christensen, *Contemporary German Philosophy*. State College: Penn State University Press, pp. 15–53.

Henrich, Dieter. 1999. "What is Metaphysics? What is Modernity?" in Peter Dews, ed. *Habermas: A Critical Reader*, pp. 291–319.

Hesse, Mary. 1982. "Science and Objectivity," in John Thompson and D. Held, eds. *Habermas: Critical Debates*. Cambridge: MIT Press, pp. 98–115.

Heyd, David, ed. 1996. *Toleration: An Elusive Virtue*. Princeton, NJ: Princeton University Press.

Hiley, David, J. Bohman and R. Shusterman, eds. 1991. *The Interpretive Turn*. Ithaca, NY: Cornell University Press.

Holub, Robert. 1991. *Jürgen Habermas: Critic in the Public Sphere*. New York: Routledge.

Honneth, Axel. 1991. *The Critique of Power*. Trans. by Kenneth Baynes. Cambridge, MA: MIT Press.

Honneth, Axel. 1995. *The Fragmented World of the Social.* Albany: SUNY Press.

Honneth, Axel. 2008. *Reification.* New York: Oxford University Press.

Honneth, Axel. 2009. *Pathologies of Reason.* New York: Columbia University Press.

Honneth, Axel. 2014. *Freedom's Right.* Cambridge: Polity Press.

Honneth, Axel and Jans Joas, eds. 1991. *Communicative Action: Essays on Jürgen Habermas's* The Theory of Communicative Action. Trans. by J. Gaines and D. Jones. Cambridge: Polity Press.

Honneth, Axel and M. Hartman. 2014. "Paradoxes of Capitalist Modernization," in *The I in the We.* Cambridge: Polity Press, pp. 169–190.

Horkheimer, Max. 1972. *Critical Theory.* New York: Seabury Press.

Horkheimer, Max and Theodor Adorno. 1987. *Dialectic of Enlightenment.* Edited by G. Schmid Noerr. Stanford, CA: Stanford University Press.

Hoy, David and T. McCarthy. 1994. *Critical Theory.* New York: Blackwell.

Ingram, David. 2010. *Habermas: Introduction and Analysis.* Ithaca, NY: Cornell University Press.

Iser, Mattias. 2008. *Empörung und Fortschritt.* Frankfurt: Campus.

Iser, Mattias and D. Strecker. 2010. *Jürgen Habermas: zur Einführung.* Hamburg: Junius.

James, Aron. 2005. "Constructing Justice for Existing Practice: Rawls and the Status Quo," *Philosophy and Public Affairs* 33: 1–36.

James, Aaron. 2007. "Constructivism about Practical Reasons," *Philosophy and Phenomenological Research* 74: 302–325.

Jay, Martin. 1984. *Marxism and Totality.* Berkeley, CA: University of California Press.

Joas, Hans. 1991. "The Unhappy Marriage of Hermeneutics and Functionalism," in Axel Honneth and Jans Joas, eds. *Communicative Action: Essays on Jürgen Habermas's* The Theory of Communicative Action. Trans. by J. Gaines and D. Jones. Cambridge: Polity Press, pp. 97–118.

Jütten, Timo. 2013. "Habermas and Markets," *Constellations* 20: 587–603.

Kaldor, M. 2004. *Global Civil Society?* New York: Cambridge University Press.

Kant, Immanuel. 1956. *Critique of Practical Reason.* New York: Macmillan Publishing.

Kant, Immanuel. 1970. *Kant's Political Writings*. Edited by H. Reiss. New York: Cambridge University Press.

Kant, Immanuel. 1991. *The Metaphysics of Morals*. Edited by Mary Gregor. New York: Cambridge University Press.

Kant, Immanuel. 1998. *Critique of Pure Reason*. New York: Cambridge University Press.

Keane, John. 2003. *Global Civil Society?* New York: Cambridge University Press.

Kelly, Erin. 2000. "Habermas and Moral Justification," *Social Theory and Practice* 26: 223–249.

Kelly, Michael, ed. 1994. *Critique and Power: Recasting the Foucault/ Habermas Debate*. Cambridge, MA: MIT Press.

Kitcher, Philip. 2011. *The Ethical Project*. Cambridge, MA: Harvard University Press.

Kitcher, Philip. 2011a. "Philosophy Inside Out," *Metaphilosophy* 42: 248–260.

Knight, Jack and J. Johnson. 1994. "Aggregation and Deliberation: On the Possibility of Democratic Legitimacy," *Political Theory* 22: 277–296.

Kompridis, Nikolas. 2006. *Critique and Disclosure*. Cambridge, MA: MIT Press.

Koopman, Colin. 2013. *Genealogy as Critique: Foucault and the Problems of Modernity*. Bloomington, IN: Indiana University Press.

Korner, Stephen. 1967. "The Impossibility of Transcendental Deductions," *The Monist* 51: 317–331.

Korsgaard, Christine. 1996. *The Sources of Normativity*. New York: Cambridge University Press.

Kukla, Rebecca and M. Lance. 2009. *'Yo!' and 'Lo!': The Pragmatic Topography of the Space of Reasons*. Cambridge, MA: Harvard University Press.

Kymlicka, Will. 2007. "The New Debate on Minority Rights," in A. Laden and D. Owen, eds. *Multiculturalism and Political Theory*. New York: Cambridge University Press, pp. 25–59.

Lafont, Cristina. 2000. *Heidegger, Language and World-Disclosure*. New York: Cambridge University Press.

Lafont, Cristina. 2003. "Procedural Justice? Implications of the Rawls-Habermas Debate for Discourse Ethics," *Philosophy and Social Criticism* 29: 167–185.

Lafont, Cristina. 2004. "Moral Objectivity and Reasonable Agreement: Can Realism be Reconciled with Kantian Constructivism?," *Ratio Juris* 17: 27–51.

Lafont, Cristina. 2012. Agreement and Consent in Kant and Habermas. *The Philosophical Forum* 43: 277–295.

Lakatos, Imre. 1981. "History of Science and Its Rational Reconstruction," in I. Hacking, ed. *Scientific Revolutions*. New York: Oxford University Press, pp. 107–127.

Larmore, Charles. 1996. *The Morals of Modernity*. New York: Cambridge University Press.

Larmore, Charles. 2008. *The Autonomy of Morality*. New York: Cambridge University Press.

Lear, Jonathan. 1998. "Transcendental Anthropology," in *Open Minded*. Cambridge: Harvard University Press, pp. 247–281.

Levine, Steven. 2010. "Habermas, Kantian Pragmatism and Truth," *Philosophy and Social Criticism* 36: 677–695.

List, Christian. 2002. "Two Concepts of Agreement," *The Good Society* 11: 72–79.

List, Christian and J. Dryzek. 2003. "Social Choice Theory and Deliberative Democracy: A Reconciliation," British Journal of Political Science 33: 1–28.

Littleton, Christine. 1993. "Reconstructing Sexual Equality," in Patricia Smith, ed. *Feminist Jurisprudence*. New York: Oxford University Press, pp. 110–135.

Lockwood, David. 1992. "Social Integration and System Integration," in *Solidarity and Schism*. New York: Oxford University Press, pp. 399–412.

Luhmann, Niklas. 1995. *Social Systems*. Stanford, CA: Stanford University Press.

Lukács, Georg. 1971 [1932]. *History and Class Consciousness*. Cambridge, MA: MIT Press.

Lukes, Steven. 1982. "Relativism in its Place," in Martin Hollis and S. Lukes, eds. *Rationality and Relativism*. Cambridge, MA: MIT Press, pp. 261–305.

Lukes, Steven. 1983. "Can the Base be distinguished from the Superstructure?" in D. Miller and L. Seidentop, eds. *The Nature of Political Theory*. Oxford: Clarendon, pp. 103–119.

McCarthy, Thomas. 1978. *The Critical Theory of Jürgen Habermas*. Cambridge, MA: MIT Press.

McCarthy, Thomas. 1991. "Complexity and Democracy" in Axel Honneth and Jans Joas, eds. *Communicative Action: Essays on Jürgen Habermas's* The Theory of Communicative Action. Trans. by J. Gaines and D. Jones. Cambridge: Polity Press, pp. 119–139.

McCarthy, Thomas. 1991a. *Ideals and Illusions.* Cambridge, MA: MIT Press.

McCarthy, Thomas. 1998. "Legitimacy and Diversity" in Michel Rosenfeld and Andrew Arato, eds. *Habermas on Law and Democracy.* Berkeley: University of California Press, pp. 115–153.

McClure, Kirstie. 1996. *Judging Rights.* Ithaca, NY: Cornell University Press.

McDowell, John. 2002. "Gadamer and Davidson on Understanding and Relativism," in Jeff Malpas, U. Arnswald and J. Kertscher, eds. *Gadamer's Century: Essays in Honor of Hans-Georg Gadamer.* Cambridge, MA: MIT Press, pp. 173–193.

MacIntyre, Alasdair. 1986. "The Intelligibility of Action," in M. Krausz and R. Buridean, eds. *Rationality, Relativism, and the Human Sciences.* Dordrecht: Nijhoff, pp. 63–84.

MacKinnon, Catherine. 1987. *Feminism Unmodified.* Cambridge, MA: Harvard University Press.

McMahon, Christopher. 2000. "Discourse and Morality," *Ethics* 110: 514–536.

McMahon, Christopher. 2002. "Why There Is No Issue Between Habermas and Rawls," *Journal of Philosophy* 99: 111–129.

McMahon, Christopher. 2011. "Habermas, Rawls and Moral Impartiality," in J. G. Finlayson and F. Freyenhagen. *Habermas and Rawls.* New York: Routledge, pp. 200–223.

Mackie, John. 1977. *Ethics: Inventing Right and Wrong.* New York: Penguin.

Malpas, Jeff, ed. 2011. *Dialogues with Davidson.* Cambridge: MIT Press.

Malpas, Jeff, U. Arnswald and J. Kertscher, eds. 2002. *Gadamer's Century: Essays in Honor of Hans-Georg Gadamer.* Cambridge, MA: MIT Press.

Manin, Bernard. 1987. "On Legitimacy and Political Deliberation," *Political Theory* 15: 338–368.

Margalit, Avashi. 1996. *The Decent Society.* Cambridge, MA: Harvard University Press.

Marx, Karl. 1994. *Selected Writings.* Edited by L. Simon. Indianapolis, IN: Hackett Publishing.

Matustik, Martin. 2001. *Jürgen Habermas: A Philosophical-Political Profile*. Lanham, MD: Rowman and Littlefield.

Maus, Ingeborg. 2002. "Liberties and Popular Sovereignty," in Rene von Schomberg and K. Baynes, eds. *Discourse and Democracy: Essays on 'Between Facts and Norms'*. Albany: SUNY Press, pp. 89–127.

Meerbote, Ralph. 1984. "Kant on the Nondeterminate Character of Human Action," in W. Harper and R. Meerbote, eds. *Kant on Causality, Freedom and Objectivity*. Minneapolis, MN: Minnesota University Press, pp. 138–164.

Menke, Christoph. 2001. *Reflections on Equality*. Stanford, CA: Stanford University Press.

Michelman, Frank. 1988. "Law's Republic," *The Yale Law Journal* 97: 1493–1537.

Miller, Richard. 1984. *Analyzing Marx*. Princeton, NJ: Princeton University Press.

Minow, Martha. 1990. *Making All the Difference*. Ithaca, NY: Cornell University Press.

Minow, Martha. 1993. "Justice Engendered" in Patricia Smith, ed. *Feminist Jurisprudence*. New York: Oxford University Press, pp. 217–243.

Misak, Cheryl, ed. 2007. *New Pragmatists*. New York: Oxford University Press.

Moeller, Hans-Georg. 2006. *Luhmann Explained*. Chicago: Open Court.

Moody-Adams, Michelle. 1997. *Fieldwork in Familiar Places*. Cambridge, MA: Harvard University Press.

Moon, J. Donald. 1991. "Constrained Discourse and Public Life," *Political Theory* 19: 202–229.

Moran, Dermot. 2012. *Husserl's Crisis of the European Sciences and Transcendental Phenomenology: An Introduction*. New York: Cambridge University Press.

Moses, A. Dirk. 2007. *German Intellectuals and the Nazi Past*. New York: Cambridge University Press.

Mouzelis, Nicos. 1991. *Back to Sociological Theory*. London: Macmillan.

Moyar, Dean and M. Quante, eds. 2011. *Hegel's Phenomenology of Spirit*. New York: Cambridge University Press.

Müller, Jan-Werner. 2000. *Another Country: German Intellectuals, Unification and National Identity*. New Haven, CT: Yale University Press.

Müller, Jan-Werner. 2007. *Constitutional Patriotism*. Princeton, NJ: Princeton University Press.

Müller-Doohm, S., ed. 2000. *Das Interesse der Vernunft.* Frankfurt: Suhrkamp.

Müller-Doohm, Stefan. 2014. *Jürgen Habermas: Eine Biographie.* Frankfurt: Suhrkamp.

Müller-Vollmer, Kurt, ed. 1985. *The Hermeneutic Reader.* New York: Continuum.

Münch, Richard. 1987. *Theory of Action: Towards a New Synthesis Going Beyond Parsons.* Boston, MA: Routledge.

Nanz, Patricia and J. Steffek. 2004. "Global Governance, Participation and the Public Sphere," *Government and Opposition* 39: 314–335.

Nanz, Patricia and J. Steffek. 2005. "Assessing the Democratic Quality of Deliberation in International Governance," *Acta Politca* 40: 368–383.

Nanz, P. and J. Steffek. 2007. "Zivilgsellschaftliche Participation und die Demokratisierung internationalen Regierens," in P. Niesen and B. Herborth, eds. *Anarchie der kommunikativen Freiheit.* Frankfurt: Suhrkamp.

Neiman, Susan. 1994. *Unity of Reason: Rereading Kant.* New York: Oxford University Press.

Nell, Onora. 1975. *Acting on Principle.* New York: Columbia University Press.

Neuhouser, Fred. 1990. *Fichte's Theory of Subjectivity.* New York: Cambridge University Press.

Neuhouser, Fred. 1993. "Freedom, Dependence and the General Will," *The Philosophical Review* 102: 363–395.

Nielsen, Kai. 1994. "How to Proceed in Philosophy," *Thesis Eleven* 37: 10–28.

Niesen, Peter. 2008. "Deliberation ohne Demokratie?" in R. Kriede and A. Niederberger, eds. *Transnationale Verrechtlichung.* Frankfurt: Campus Verlag.

Niesen, Peter and B. Herborth, eds. 2007. *Anarchie der kommunikativen Freiheit.* Frankfurt: Suhrkamp.

Offe, Klaus. 1992. "Binding, Shackles, Brakes: On Self-Limitation Strategies," in A. Honneth, T. McCarthy, C. Offe and A. Wellmer, eds. *Cultural-Political Interventions in the Unfinished Project of Enlightenment.* Cambridge, MA: MIT Press.

Okrent, Mark. 1984. "Hermeneutics, Transcendental Philosophy, and Social Science," *Inquiry* 27: 23–49.

O'Neill, Onora. 1989. "The Public Use of Reason," in Constructions of Reason. New York: Cambridge University Press, pp. 28–50.

O'Neill, Onora. 1992. "Vindicating Reason," in Paul Guyer, ed. The Cambridge Companion to Kant. New York: Cambridge University Press, pp. 280–308.

Ottmann, Henning. 1982. "Cognitive Interests and Self-Reflection," in John Thompson and D. Held, eds. Habermas: Critical Debates. Cambridge, MA: MIT Press, pp. 79–97.

Outhwaite, William. 2009. Habermas: A Critical Introduction (2nd ed.). Stanford, CA: Stanford University Press.

Owen, David. 2002. Between Reason and History: Habermas and the Idea of Progress. Albany: SUNY Press.

Pallikkathayil, Japa. 2010. "Deriving Morality from Politics: Rethinking the Formula of Humanity," Ethics 121: 116–147.

Parkinson, John and Jane Mansbridge, eds. 2012. Deliberative Systems. New York: Cambridge University Press.

Parsons, Talcott. 1970. The System of Modern Societies. Englewood Cliffs, NJ: Prentice Hall.

Passerin D'Entreves, Maurizio and S. Benhabib, eds. 1997. Habermas and the Unfinished Project of Modernity. Cambridge, MA: MIT Press.

Patten, Alan. 2014. Equal Recognition: The Moral Foundations of Minority Rights. Princeton, NJ: Princeton University Press.

Pensky, Max. 1989. "On the Use and Abuse of History: Habermas, Anamestic Solidarity, and the Historikerstreit," Philosophy and Social Criticism 15: 351–381.

Pensky, Max. 1995. "Universalism and the Situated Critic," in Stephen White, ed. The Cambridge Companion to Habermas. New York: Cambridge University Press, pp. 67–96.

Pensky, Max. 2008. The Ends of Solidarity: Discourse Ethics in Ethics and Politics. Albany, NY: SUNY Press.

Peter, Fabienne. 2008. "Democratic legitimacy and proceduralist social epistemology," Politics, Philosophy and Economics 6: 329–353.

Peters, Bernard. 1993. Die Integration moderner Gesellschaften. Frankfurt: Suhrkamp.

Peters, Bernhard. 1993a. "On Reconstructive Legal and Political Theory," Philosophy and Social Criticism 20: 101–134.

Pettit, Philip. 1997. Republicanism. Oxford: Clarendon.

Pettit, Philip. 2000. "Two Construals of Scanlon's Contractualism," Journal of Philosophy 97: 148–164.

Pettit, Philip. 2006. "Can Contract Theory Ground Morality," in James Dreier, ed. *Contemporary Debates in Moral Theory*. New York: Blackwell, pp. 77–96.

Pettit, Philip and M. Smith. 1996. "Freedo in Belief and Desire," Journal of Philosophy 93: 429–49.

Philipse, Herman. 1999. *Heidegger's Philosophy of Being*. Princeton, NJ: Princeton University Press.

Pinkard, Terry. 1994. *Hegel's Phenomenology: The Sociality of Reason*. New York: Cambridge University Press.

Pippin, Robert. 1989. *Hegel's Idealism*. New York: Cambridge University Press.

Pippin, Robert. 1993. "You Can't Get from Here to There: Transition Problems in the *Phenomenology*," in Fred Beiser, ed. *The Cambridge Companion to Hegel*. New York: Cambridge University Press, pp. 52–85.

Pollner, Melvin. 1987. *Mundane Reason*. New York: Cambridge University Press.

Postone, Moishe. 1993. *Time, Labor and Social Domination*. New York: Cambridge University Press.

Power, Michael. 1993. "Habermas and Transcendental Arguments," *Philosophy of the Social Sciences* 23: 26–49.

Prado, C., ed. 2003. *A House Divided*. New York: Prometheus Books.

Price, Huw. 2003. "Truth as Convenient Friction," *Journal of Philosophy* 100: 167–190.

Ramberg, Bjorn. 1989. *Donald Davidson's Philosophy of Language*. Oxford: Basil Blackwell.

Ramberg, Bjorn. 2003. "Illuminating Language: Interpretation and Understanding" in C. Prado, ed. *A House Divided*. New York: Prometheus Books, pp. 213–234.

Rasmussen, David. 1990. *Reading Habermas*. Malden, MA: Blackwell.

Rawls, John. 1996. *Political Liberalism* (2nd edition). New York: Columbia University Press.

Rawls, John. 1999. *Collected Papers*. Edited by Samuel Freeman. Cambridge, MA: Harvard University Press.

Rawls, John. 1999a. "Kant's Transcendental Deductions," in John Rawls, *Collected Papers*. Edited by Samuel Freeman. Cambridge, MA: Harvard University Press, pp. 497–528.

Raz, Joseph. 1990. "Facing Diversity: The Case for Epistemic Abstinence," *Philosophy and Public Affairs* 19: 3–46.

Rehg, William. 1994. *Insight and Solidarity: A Study in the Discourse Ethics of Jürgen Habermas.* Berkeley, CA: University of California.

Rehg, William. 2011. "Discourse Ethics," in Barbara Fultner, ed. *Jürgen Habermas: Key Concepts.* Durham, UK: Acumen, pp. 115–139.

Rhode, Debra. 1989. *Justice and Gender.* Cambridge, MA: Harvard University Press.

Ridge, Michael. 2001. "Saving Scanlon," *The Journal of Political Philosophy* 9: 472–481.

Riley, Patrick. 1983. *Kant's Political Philosophy.* Totowa, NJ: Rowman and Littlefield.

Risjord, Mark. 2013. *Philosophy of Social Science.* New York: Routledge.

Root, Michael. 1986. "Davidson and Social Science," in Esrnest Lepore, ed. *Truth and Interpretation.* New York: Basil Blackwell, pp. 272–304.

Rorty, Richard. 1988. *Contingency, Irony and Solidarity.* New York: Cambridge University Press.

Rorty, Richard. 1998. "Habermas, Derrida and the Functions of Philosophy," *Truth and Progress* (Philosophical Papers, vol. 3). New York: Cambridge University Press, pp. 307–326.

Rorty, Richard. 1999. *Philosophy and Social Hope.* New York: Penguin.

Rorty, Richard. 2000. "Universality and Truth," in Robert Brandom, ed. *Rorty and his Critics.* Oxford: Blackwell, pp. 1–30.

Rosenfeld, Michel and Andrew Arato, eds. 1998. *Habermas on Law and Democracy.* Berkeley, CA: University of California Press.

Rouse, Joseph. 1991. "Interpretation in Natural and Human Science" in D. Hiley, J. Bohman and R. Shusterman, eds. *The Interpretive Turn.* Ithaca, NY: Cornell University Press, pp. 42–57.

Rouse, Joseph. 2007. "Practice Theory," in S. Turner and M. Risjord, eds. *Philosophy of Anthropology and Sociology.* Boston: North Holland, pp. 639–680.

Rummens, S. 2006. "The Co-originality of Private and Public Autonomy," *Journal of Political Philosophy* 14: 469–481.

Rush, Fred, ed. 2004. *The Cambridge Companion to Critical Theory.* New York: Cambridge University Press.

Sacks, Mark. 2000. *Objectivity and Insight.* New York: Oxford University Press.

Scanlon, T. M. 1996. "The Difficulty of Tolerance," in David Heyd, ed. *Toleration: An Elusive Virtue.* Princeton, NJ: Princeton University Press, pp. 226–240.

Scanlon, T. M. 1998. *What We Owe to One Other*. Cambridge, MA: Harvard University Press.

Scanlon, T. M. 2003. "Reply to Gauthier and Gibbard," *Philosophy and Phenomenological Research* 70: 176–189.

Scanlon, T. M. 2004. "Reply" in P. Stratton-Lake, ed. *On What We Owe to One Another*. London: Blackwell, pp. 123–138.

Scheuerman, William. 2002. "Between Radicalism and Resignation," in Rene von Schomberg and K. Baynes, eds. *Discourse and Democracy: Essays on 'Between Facts and Norms'*. Albany: SUNY Press, pp. 61–85.

Scheuerman, William. 2008. "Global Governance without Global Government?," *Political Theory* 36: 133–151.

Scheuerman, William. 2013. "Capitalism, Law and Social Criticism," *Constellations* 20: 571–586.

Schmalz-Bruns, R. 2007. "An den Grenzen der Entstaatlichung," in Peter Niesen and B. Herborth, eds. *Anarchie der kommunikativen Freiheit*. Frankfurt: Suhrkamp.

Schnädelbach, Herbert. 1991. "The Transformation of Critical Theory," in Axel Honneth and Jans Joas, eds. *Communicative Action: Essays on Jürgen Habermas's* The Theory of Communicative Action. Trans. by J. Gaines and D. Jones. Cambridge: Polity Press, pp. 7–22.

Scholte, J. 2004. "Civil Society and Democratically Accountable Global Governance," *Government and Opposition* 39: 211–233.

Scholte, J., ed. 2011. *Building Global Democracy? Civil Society and Accountable Global Governance*. New York: Cambridge University Press.

Schomberg, Rene von and K. Baynes, eds. 2002. *Discourse and Democracy: Essays on 'Between Facts and Norms'*. Albany: SUNY Press.

Schutz, Alfred. 1962. "Concept and Theory Formation in the Social Sciences," in M. Natanson, ed. *Collected Papers*, vol. I. The Hague: Martin Nijhoff.

Schutz, Alfred and Thomas Luckmann. 1973. *The Structures of the Lifeworld*. Trans. by R. Zaner and H. T. Engelhardt, Jr. Evanston: Northwestern University Press.

Searle, John. 1969. *Speech Acts*. New York: Cambridge University Press.

Searle, John. 1977. "Reiterating the Differences," *Glyph* 1: 198–208.

Sellars, Wilfrid. 1963. "Philosophy and the Scientific Image of Man," in *Science, Perception and Reality*. New York: Routledge and Kegan Paul, pp. 1–40.

Singer, Peter. 1974. *Democracy and Disobedience*. New York: Oxford University Press.

Smith, Patricia, ed. 1993. *Feminist Jurisprudence*. New York: Oxford University Press.

Smith, W. and J. Brassett. 2008. "Deliberation and Global Governance," *Ethics and International Affairs* 72: 67–90.

Southwood, Nicholas. 2010. *Contractualism and the Foundations of Morality*. New York: Cambridge University Press.

Specter, Matthew. 2010. *Habermas: An Intellectual Biography*. New York: Cambridge University Press.

Stahl, Titus. 2013. "Habermas and the Project of Immanent Critique," *Constellations* 20: 533–552.

Steffek, Jens. 2010. "Public Accountability and the Public Sphere of International Governance," *Ethics and International Affairs* 24: 45–67.

Stout, Jeffrey. 2007. "On Our Interest in Getting Things Right: Pragmatism without Narcissism," in Cheryl Misak, ed. *New Pragmatists*. New York: Oxford University Press, pp. 7–31.

Stoutland, Frederick. 1980. "Oblique Causation and Reasons for Action," *Synthese* 43: 35–67.

Stoutland, Frederick. 2011. "Interpreting Davidson on Intentional Action," in Jeff Malpas, ed. *Dialogues with Davidson*. Cambridge: MIT Press, pp. 297–324.

Stratton-Lake, P., ed. 2004. *On What We Owe to One Another*. London: Blackwell.

Strawson, P. F. 2003. "Freedom and Resentment," in G. Watson, ed. *Free Will*. New York: Oxford University Press, pp. 72–93.

Sunstein, Cass. 1988. "Beyond the Republican Revival," *Yale Law Journal* 97: 1539–1590.

Sunstein, Cass. 1991. "Preferences and Politics," *Philosophy and Public Affairs* 20: 4–23.

Talisse, Robert. 2009. *Democracy and Moral Conflict*. New York: Cambridge University Press.

Taylor, Charles. 1981. "Explanation and Understanding in the Geisteswissenschaften" in S. Holtzman and C. Leich, eds. *Wittgenstein: To Follow a Rule*. Boston: Routledge, pp. 192–210.

Taylor, Charles. 1985. "Interpretation and the Sciences of Man," in *Philosophical Papers*, vol. 2. New York: Cambridge University Press, pp. 15–57.

Taylor, Charles. 1985b. "What's Wrong with Negative Liberty," in *Philosophical Papers*, vol. 2. New York: Cambridge University Press, pp. 211–229.

Taylor, Charles. 1989. "Cross-Purposes: The Liberal-Communitarian Debate," in Nancy Rosenblum, ed. *Liberalism and the Moral Life*. Cambridge, MA: Harvard University Press.

Taylor, Charles. 1992. *Multiculturalism and the Politics of Recognition*. Princeton, NJ: Princeton University Press.

Taylor, Charles. 1993. "The Motivation behind a Procedural Ethics," in Ronald Beiner and W. Booth, eds. *Kant and Political Philosophy*. New Haven: Yale University Press, pp. 337–359.

Thomassen, Lasse, ed. 2006. *The Derrida-Habermas Reader*. Chicago: University of Chicago Press.

Thompson, John and D. Held, eds. 1982. *Habermas: Critical Debates*. Cambridge: MIT Press.

Tugendhat, Ernst. 1994. "Heidegger's Idea of Truth," in B. Wachterhauser, ed. *Hermeneutics and Truth*. Evanston: Northwestern University Press, pp. 83–97.

Vogel, Steven. 1996. *Against Nature: The Concept of Nature in Critical Theory*. Albany: SUNY Press.

Waldron, Jeremy. 1999. *Law and Disagreement*. Oxford: Clarendon Press.

Walzer, Michael. 1990. "The Communitarian Critique of Liberalism," *Political Theory* 18: 6–23.

Warner, Michael, J. Van Antwerpen and C. Calhoun, eds. 2010. *Varieties of Secularism in a Secular Age*. Cambridge, MA: Harvard University Press.

Weber, Max. 1968. *Economy and Society*. Edited by G. Roth and C. Wittich. Berkeley, CA: California University Press.

Weber, Max. 1981. *Roscher and Knies*. Trans. By G. Oakes. New York: Free Press.

Weinstock, Daniel. 2000. "Saving Democracy from Deliberation," in R. Beiner and R. Norman, eds. *Canadian Political Philosophy*. New York: Oxford University Press, pp. 78–91.

Wellmer, Albrecht. 1991. *The Persistence of Modernity*. Cambridge, MA: MIT Press. ["Ethics and Dialogue," pp. 113–233]

Wellmer, Albrecht. 1998. *Endgames*. Cambridge, MA: MIT Press.

Westlund, Andrea. 2009. "Rethinking Relational Autonomy," *Hypatia* 24: 26–49.

White, Stephen. 1989. *The Recent Work of Jürgen Habermas*. New York: Cambridge University Press.

White, Stephen, ed. 1995. *The Cambridge Companion to Habermas*. New York: Cambridge University Press.

Wiggershaus, Rolph. 1994. *The Frankfurt School*. Cambridge, MA: MIT Press.

Wiggershaus, Rolph. 2004. *Jürgen Habermas*. Hamburg: Rowohlt.

Williams, Marc. 2011. "Civil Society and the WTO," in J. Scholte, ed. *Building Global Democracy? Civil Society and Accountable Global Governance*. New York: Cambridge University Press.

Winch, Peter. 1958. *The Idea of a Social Science*. London: Routledge.

Wolin, Richard, ed. 1991. *The Heidegger Controversy*. New York: Columbia University Press.

Wolin, Sheldon. 1996. "The Liberal/Democratic Divide: On Rawls's *Political Liberalism*," *Political Theory* 24: 95–119.

Wrathall, Mark. 2010. *Heidegger and Unconcealment*. New York: Cambridge University Press.

Wren, Thomas. 1990. *The Moral Domain*. Cambridge, MA: MIT Press.

Young, Iris. 1990. *Justice and the Politics of Difference*. Princeton, NJ: Princeton University Press.

Young, Iris. 1997. "Communication and the Other: Beyond Deliberative Democracy," in *Intersecting Voices*. Princeton, NJ: Princeton University Press, pp. 60–74.

Zurn, Christopher. 2007. *Deliberative Democracy and the Institutions of Judicial Review*. New York: Cambridge University Press.

Zurn, Christopher. 2011. "Discourse Theory of Law," in Barbara Fultner, ed. *Jürgen Habermas: Key Concepts*. Durham, UK: Acumen, pp. 140–155.

Index

Please note that page numbers relating to Notes will contain the letter "n." followed by note number.